Changing Scenes

HBJ BOOKMARK READING PROGRAM

MARGARET EARLY

SARA KRENTZMAN SRYGLEY

EVELYN L. WENZEL

Changing Scenes

 HARCOURT BRACE JOVANOVICH

New York Chicago San Francisco Atlanta Dallas and *London*

PRINTED IN THE UNITED STATES OF AMERICA

ISBN 0-15-331789-2

ACKNOWLEDGMENTS: For permission to reprint copyrighted material, grateful acknowledgment is made to the following sources:

ATHENEUM PUBLISHERS: "Foghorns" and "Pigeons" from *I Thought I Heard the City* by Lilian Moore. Text copyright © by Lilian Moore. "Autumn Leaves" from *There Is No Rhyme for Silver* by Eve Merriam. Copyright © 1962 by Eve Merriam.

BRANDT & BRANDT: "Nancy Hanks" from *A Book of Americans* by Rosemary & Stephen Vincent Benét, Holt, Rinehart & Winston, Inc. Copyright 1933 by Stephen Vincent Benét. Copyright renewed by Rosemary Carr Benét.

BRIDGE MAGAZINE: "I am a Bridge . . ." by Carole Lin from *Bridge,* An Asian American Perspective, August 1975, Volume 3, No. 6.

CURTIS BROWN LTD., LONDON, ON BEHALF OF THE ESTATE OF A. A. MILNE: "Howard" from *The Sunny Side* by A. A. Milne.

JOSEPH BRUCHAC: "Birdfoot's Grampa" from *Entering Onondaga* by Joseph Bruchac, Cold Mountain Press, Austin, Texas. Copyright by Joseph Bruchac.

COWARD MCCANN & GEOGHEGAN, INC.: "The Temper of Tempe Wick" from *This Time, Tempe Wick?* by Patricia Lee Gauch. Copyright © 1974 by Patricia Lee Gauch. Excerpts from *The Little Riders* by Margaretha Shemin. Copyright © 1963 by Margaretha Shemin.

THE CROSSING PRESS, TRUMANSBURG, N.Y.: "The Coming of Legends" from *Turkey Brother and Other Tales: Iroquois Folk Stories* by Joseph Bruchac.

THOMAS Y. CROWELL AND CURTIS BROWN, LTD.: Adaptation of "The Seeing Stick." Copyright © 1976 by Jane Yolen. From *The Seeing Stick* by Jane Yolen, pictures by Remy Charlip and Demetra Maraslis. Text copyright © 1977 by Jane Yolen. First appeared in *Cricket* Magazine.

DODD, MEAD & COMPANY, INC.: An adapted excerpt from *Rafael and the Raiders* by Hilary Beckett. Copyright © 1972 by Hilary Beckett. "There Was an Old Man with a Beard" from *The Complete Nonsense Book* by Edward Lear.

DOUBLEDAY & COMPANY, INC.: "I Go Forth to Move About the Earth" by Alonzo Lopez from *The Whispering Wind* edited by Terry Allen. Copyright © 1972 by the Institute of American Indian Arts.

DOUBLEDAY & COMPANY, INC. AND INTERNATIONAL CREATIVE MANAGEMENT: "My Fingers" from *My Fingers Are Always Bringing Me News* by Mary O'Neill. Copyright © 1969 by Mary O'Neill.

E. P. DUTTON AND DAVID HIGHAM ASSOCIATES, LTD.: "The Sleeper" from *A Book of Sorcerers and Spells* by Ruth Manning-Sanders. Copyright © 1973 by Ruth Manning-Sanders. Published in Britain by Metheun.

FARRAR, STRAUS & GIROUX, INC.: "Thunder Appoints the Eagle Ruler of Earth" from *The Path to Snowbird Mountain* by Traveller Bird. Copyright © 1972 by Traveller Bird.

FOLLETT PUBLISHING COMPANY: Adapted from *The Great Minu* by Beth P. Wilson, based on "The Honourable Minu" originally published in *West African Folk Tales* by George Harrap & Company Ltd., London, England. Copyright © 1974 by Beth P. Wilson.

HARCOURT BRACE JOVANOVICH, INC.: Adapted from "The Woodsman's Daughter and the Lion" in *The Three Wishes: A Collection of Puerto Rican Folktales* by Ricardo E. Alegría. Copyright © 1962 by Ricardo E. Alegría. Short pronunciation key from *The HBJ School Dictionary*, copyright © 1977, 1972, 1968 by Harcourt Brace Jovanovich, Inc. Entries from (or adapted from) *The HBJ School Dictionary*. Copyright © 1977, 1972, 1968 by Harcourt Brace Jovanovich, Inc.

Contents

PART **2**

How They Told It

PART

The Little Riders

PART

The Poet's Way

PART **5**

You Can't Help Laughing

PART **6**

Robert McCloskey: An Artist with Words and Pictures

To the Reader

You are about to begin a very special journey. One nice thing about this journey is that there will always be someone with you. This is not someone you can see. It is someone whose voice you hear through stories, poems, and plays. Because people have been telling, singing, and writing stories for a very long time, you have a rich and adventurous journey ahead of you.

The best thing about this journey is that once it begins it never has to end. This is a journey into literature. All you need is some time and the willingness to go. You never know where you might find yourself. Some places you visit will be very far away, others will almost seem like home. Sometimes you will travel in the past, sometimes the present, sometimes the future. No matter where you go, your journey will show you many new scenes. Just as when you ride a train, the scene may change with each town you pass, in this book the scene will change with each story you read. That is why this book is called *Changing Scenes*.

PART 1

Then and Now

Then and Now

Realistic stories may be about people and events of today or of the past. *Historical* stories are those set in the past. The setting may be in pioneer times, in the time of the Revolutionary War, or even as far back as the days of knights and castles. Whatever the period, we get a picture of life as it was then. We learn how people traveled, how they talked, how they earned a living, and what they believed. *Modern* stories tell us these same things about people living in different parts of the world today.

Here are some realistic stories, both historical and modern. The people you will meet are different because they live in different times and places. But you will notice that they are alike, too. For people everywhere meet danger, learn to get along together, and bear up under disappointments and hardships.

Tempe Wick was a young woman who lived in a young country. The United States was only five years old when Tempe and her horse Bonny had this adventure.

For Rafael, Queens, New York, is a very long way from his home in Mexico City. With the help of his cousin Miguel and Aunt Teresa, he finds that getting used to a new home isn't always as hard as it seems.

Tempe Wick was glad to help feed and clothe the Revolutionary soldiers who spent the winters of 1780 and 1781 in Jockey Hollow, New Jersey. But then some soldiers mutinied, and things changed.

The Temper of Tempe Wick

by PATRICIA LEE GAUCH

It was the camp blacksmith who ran by and told Tempe the news.

"It's a mutiny, ma'am. Take cover," said the blacksmith.

"From our own soldiers, sir?" said she.

"Aye. They're agin their own captains. They're agin their own general. They may be agin you! You've food to fill their stomachs and a horse to get them away. That's reason enough!"

And off he ran.

He didn't even see Tempe get mad. But she did.

"Agin me!" she said to herself, pushing up the sleeves of her nightgown. "Agin me, indeed! I've shared the

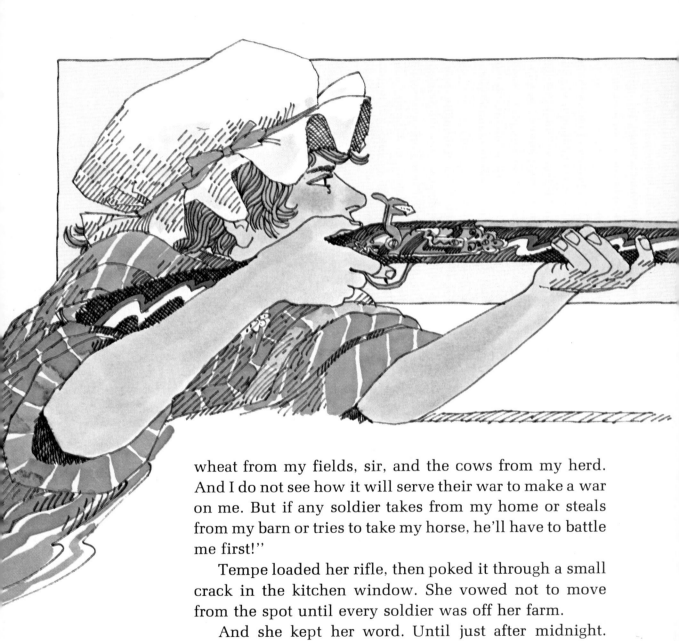

wheat from my fields, sir, and the cows from my herd. And I do not see how it will serve their war to make a war on me. But if any soldier takes from my home or steals from my barn or tries to take my horse, he'll have to battle me first!''

Tempe loaded her rifle, then poked it through a small crack in the kitchen window. She vowed not to move from the spot until every soldier was off her farm.

And she kept her word. Until just after midnight. Then a thousand soldiers, followed by one general, marched off to Philadelphia. They wanted to tell the leaders of all America how they were hungry and cold and poor. As they passed, the men shouted. The fifers fifed. The drummers drummed. But when the cannoneer

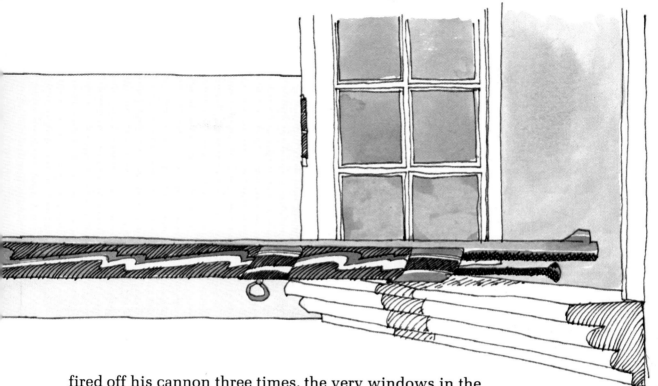

fired off his cannon three times, the very windows in the Wick house rattled. Mrs. Wick woke up and started to cough.

Nor was it an ordinary cough. Mrs. Wick coughed until her ears flushed pink. She coughed until the bed shook. She coughed and coughed and coughed.

And Tempe knew she wouldn't stay put. Her mother needed medicine, and only Dr. William had it. At daybreak, soldiers or no soldiers, she would have to leave the house. She would have to get to the barn. Then she would ride Bonny down the trail to the doctor's farm.

It was then she learned that all the soldiers had not gone to Philadelphia. Soldiers were everywhere. Some were still celebrating in the cornfield. Some were sleeping against the smoke-shed. Others were at the well.

But Tempe went anyway. She didn't go shouting, and she didn't go shooting. Not this time. After hiding her mother in the cellar, she bundled up in her Sunday coat and fine hat. She walked . . . slowly . . . to the barn, just as if she were alone in the world. She pretended not to see the soldier peeking through the fence at her. She pretended not to see the soldier duck up into the loft.

She whistled a little tune and went right to Bonny's stall. Coolly and calmly and casually she put on her bridle and saddle and rode, coolly and calmly and casually, right past them all. It was as if she were the white-horse lead in a military parade.

The soldiers just watched.

Not until she got to the road did she hurry. Then she touched her Bon with a stick and raced down the road to Dr. William's. It had all been so easy. Probably, she thought, those soldiers didn't want anything from the Wicks at all. Probably the blacksmith had been just the smallest bit nervous.

But when she left Dr. William's with a full bottle of medicine, she learned differently. Out of the thicket, right in front of the doctor's house, jumped two soldiers.

Even Tempe's stomach took a flip.

"Pretty young lady," said the one, "that's a fine horse you have."

"Thank you, sir." She smiled and started by.

But the other, a thin man with sideburns that curled like an S around his ears, stopped her.

"I imagine a fine mare like that could carry me and my friend, say, all the way to Philadelphia," he said.

"I imagine," Tempe said. She tried to get by again.

"Then we'll try her now!" he said. Quickly, he grabbed the reins from Tempe. "Get down!"

Tempe didn't even blink. Not this time. She turned her head, coyly, so sweetly, so perfectly, and said, "But, sir, 'tis my best horse Bon."

"Then she'll do her best for us. Get down I say." He was terribly gruff.

But Tempe was not. She said, still coyly and sweetly and perfectly, "Then perhaps you will help me down, sir."

And, frowning, he reached to help. But as he did, Tempe snatched the reins back. Then she put a stick to Bon's hide, and raced off down the lane toward the Wick farm.

"Come on, speeder," she whispered as she hung on Bon's neck.

Both of the soldiers started running after them. The one fired a shot. BAM! But it merely sent Bonny flying faster and faster down the road. Her nostrils steamed. Her hooves pounded so fast, they barely touched the ground. The clickety-clackety sounded more like a gentle rain on the frozen road.

All of the other soldiers were gone when Tempe rode up under the willow that guarded the back door. But she didn't try to squeeze Bonny in the smoke-shed. She'd quickly be found. Nor did Tempe even hide Bon in the woods. The soldiers knew the woods well.

No, Tempe did a most surprising thing. She led Bonny right in the back door and into the kitchen of the Wick house!

Of course, Tempe didn't tie her there. Everyone visited the kitchen first, particularly when the blizzards whipped around the Wick house in January. Tempe led Bon straight through the sitting room, too. Old Bon might not treat kindly her Grandmother Wick's fine desk from England or her mother's favorite fiddleback chair. And Tempe's mother's cough was not apt to improve with a horse sharing her bedroom!

So Tempe took the mare into her own room, the tiny dark room with the two tiny windows in the back of the house. She left her, happily nibbling at the flax-woven spread on Tempe's bed.

And just in time. Tempe had just brought her mother up from the cellar when there came a terrible thumping on the back door.

It was the man with the curled sideburns. He bellowed through the crack in the door, "I want that gray mare!"

But Tempe answered lazily, as if she had been spinning wool all afternoon, "A gray mare, sir? Have you lost one?"

Well, the man and his friend didn't even reply. They stalked off across the kitchen garden. Tempe scratched a peekhole in the frosted window. It was just big enough

for her to see them stomp into the barn. They sent the cow out mooing. They sent chickens out flying. And hay tumbled out of the loft like a dust storm in January when they searched there. Nor had they any better luck in the smoke-shed or the woods.

The soldiers by now were terribly red in the face. They returned to the Wick house just long enough to promise, "We know she's here . . . somewhere, pretty lady. And we intend to wait until we find her!"

Wait?

Even Tempe was surprised at that! How long could she hide a horse in her bedroom?

But Tempe didn't worry long. Not this time. For now, her house was her fort. For later, perhaps the general and his men would come back from Philadelphia and capture the runaway soldiers. Perhaps Dr. William would drop by to see how her mother was faring and run the soldiers off. Perhaps with a healthy dose of medicine her mother could help. Two against two were happier odds. Or perhaps the two soldiers would just go away by themselves.

Satisfied with all the possibilities, Tempe stayed at her window post until dark. Then she curled up on the kitchen settee (having a guest in her bedroom) and went to sleep.

But the next morning the general and his men were not back from Philadelphia. There was no sight of Dr. William. The medicine had stopped Mrs. Wick's cough, but it had also made her sleep and sleep and sleep. And the two soldiers were still there. They were pacing the barnyard.

To make things worse, Bonny was hungry.

First she just walked angry circles around Tempe's bed. Then she started thumping her hoof at the door.

Finally she let out a "Whiiiiiiinnnnnnnyyyyy" that Tempe was sure could be heard all the way to the barn.

Tempe knew Bonny had to be fed.

She bundled herself up and headed into the north wind toward the barn.

She quickly fed the other animals, then stacked both arms full of hay and was about to return when a voice boomed at her from the loft.

"Ah-ha!" It was the soldier with the curled sideburns. "Where are you going with the hay, miss?" he asked.

"To the house, sir," Tempe answered lightly. "My mother is ill, and last night the wind blew through the cracks in our roof like a gale of ice. The hay will stop up the cracks."

The soldier grumbled something quietly to himself. But he let her pass.

All day the two soldiers hovered around the barnyard. There was nothing for Tempe to do but wait. Yet little happened. Her mother slept on and on. The general did not come, nor did Dr. William. And while the hay promised to last another day, Tempe saw the little water she had for Bonny was quickly disappearing.

In the morning it was gone. Bonny grew so thirsty she licked the frost off the window. She licked Tempe's washbowl dry. Finally she whinnied, this time so loudly Tempe was sure, had the soldiers been anywhere in Jockey Hollow, they would have heard her!

Bonny had to be watered.

When Tempe had drawn three buckets at the well, both soldiers stepped up behind her.

"May we help, pretty lady," said the one.

"No thank you, sir," said she. "I go only to the house, and I am quite able." She balanced one bucket under her arm and gripped the two in her hands.

"You must be very thirsty," said the other. "Why, there is enough water there for a horse!"

Tempe smiled. "Perhaps," she said, "but these bucketfuls are to wash my floors. It is said a fierce winter is followed by an early spring, and I am but preparing for that. But I thank you."

She curtsied slightly and started toward the door.

Again the soldiers grumbled, but let her pass.

On the third day, Tempe had stopped looking for anyone to come to help. The soldiers had moved closer to the house, and she worried about Bonny.

Bon didn't circle the bed or thump the door, and she let loose only the tiniest whinny. Tempe barely heard it in the kitchen. But that is what worried Tempe.

"Bonny's spirits are low," Tempe said to her mother, who was still half asleep. "She must need oats."

That morning Tempe fed the hog and the cows and the sheep as usual. Then she began to gather her oats. She put some in her pockets. She stuffed more in her bag. She filled her bucket to the brimful, then started back. The soldiers were waiting by the gate when she passed.

"Surely," said the one, looking in the bucket, "you don't eat unground oats, my dear."

"Oh yes," said Tempe, walking on. "Boiled, they make a fine porridge."

"But," said the one, following her, "so many oats for two ladies, and one so ill?"

"It is barely enough," said Tempe. "Some days, after chores, I eat three bowls at one sitting."

Still he followed.

"Some days," Tempe went on, "I eat four!"

He was at the door in front of her.

"Next to applesauce with brown sugar, I like oats most!" she said, looking directly into his eyes. "These will last only a day."

"Just the same," said the soldier, "I begin to think there is a third lady in the house. A gray mare that can race like the wind. And I wish to see for myself."

With that, the one soldier pushed right past Tempe into the house. He stomped into the kitchen, knocking the pots off the table and the wood across the floor. He stomped into the pantry, shaking the jars from the shelf.

Then he heard the slightest whinny—or was it a cough? He stomped through the sitting room toward the bedroom, brushing the ink from Grandmother's desk and finally tipping over Mrs. Wick's favorite fiddleback chair.

But that was one push too many. And this time Tempe didn't get mad, she got storming, had-quite-enough mad. She began to look a good bit like the Wicks' bull Joshua.

"That," she said — neither coyly, nor sweetly, nor perfectly — "was my mother coughing. But if it were a herd of gray horses feeding on my bed, I would not let you through that door, smashing and breaking."

The soldier scoffed. He went for the cellar door.

Tempe was there first. "Not into the cellar, sir."

He darted for the attic door.

Tempe beat him there, too. "Not into the attic."

He eyed the bedroom door again.

"Not anywhere," she said.

And before the solider had time to doubt it, Tempe kicked open the door with one foot, kicked his musket out of his hand with the other — and pushed him right out the doorway.

For a moment — was it two? — the soldier lay sprawled on the path. He glared at Tempe, his face reddening around his curled sideburns. But Tempe stood firm in the doorway with *his* musket in *her* hand and glared back.

Finally, he picked up his hat and paced to his friend at the fence. They huddled, then started — on foot — down the road to Pennsylvania. At last they disappeared.

Rafael usually lives with his parents in Mexico City. But his parents are traveling to Europe on an important business trip. So now Rafael is spending a semester with his widowed Aunt Teresa and his cousins Miguel and Francisco in Queens, New York.

Rafael

by HILARY BECKETT

Aunt Teresa and Francisco and I sat at the table in the dinette. She offered to put bread in the toaster for me. I said, "No thanks, Aunt Teresa. I'm not hungry."

She laughed. It was a nice laugh, not a teasing one.

"Thinking about Monday, about a new school, and about meeting new people, Rafael?"

I shrugged. "I guess they'll laugh at my English."

I figured the English I'd learned as a kid growing up in Mexico was going to turn out to be about as much like the English kids spoke in Queens as apples are like oranges.

"Try speaking it more with us," she said. "You speak it already with Francisco."

It was true. He knew hardly any Spanish. I'd used English with him all the time. I guess I wasn't scared because he was so young. I didn't expect a *little* kid to laugh at me.

"I know how you feel about school, Rafael. I remember how I felt when we moved to a new city when I was a little girl. Nobody disliked school like I did, for a while. It was because I was afraid I'd be laughed at."

"How come, Aunt Teresa?"

"Would you believe it was because of a jar of preserves? Of jam? The lunch I took to the new school wasn't exactly like the other kids'." She laughed again. "It was —well, a little unusual. A little funny. All because *mamacita* used to put in a little jar of jam my grandmother made. As a treat. None of the children had ever heard of taking jam to school in their lunch in a jar. They thought it was funny. They all enjoyed something to laugh at. *Me.* For a while I was the saddest child in the new school."

"What could you do about it, Aunt Teresa?"

"I came home in tears to my mother. And she told me that of course if I didn't want to take the jam, I didn't have to. But if I wanted it, I would have to stand up to the other children."

"What did you decide?"

"I decided there was a day now and then when I liked the jam, and that I wouldn't be bullied into leaving it at home. I told the children to stop laughing."

"Did they?"

"Some did. Some didn't. But I didn't give anyone the satisfaction of seeing me cry any more. And after a while, the children respected me. Some of them even asked for a taste of the jam."

"It sounds scary."

"Oh, it was. But, you see, it was the only thing to do. Want some toast now, Rafael?"

"O.K."

Miguel was on the phone, his feet up over one end of the sofa. How was he dressed? I looked carefully to check.

It was O.K. to listen to a grown-up person like Aunt Teresa tell me how brave she'd been about a jar of jam, but I still didn't intend to make any more mistakes than I had to, to stand out any more than I had to, in Queens.

I especially didn't intend to *look* funny. Whatever Miguel had on, I'd wear it, too.

Jeans?

I checked out mine.

He had on sneakers.

Right. I had mine on, too.

"What do you want to eat tonight, Rafael? *Comida mexicana?*" Aunt Teresa asked. She was on her way to the shopping center.

"Something American. . . ." I kept looking at Miguel's clothes.

"All right. American food it will be. So long, kids!" She took Francisco with her, even though he wanted to stay with us, wanting to be in on any fun we might be having. "Have a good day!"

Miguel got off the phone. "What do you do in Mexico on a Saturday? Or on a vacation day? I forget. It's been such a long time."

"See friends. Play ball."

Miguel grinned. "Exactly the same as in Queens! Let's go."

To look at, Queens wasn't too different from the part of Mexico City I lived in. I lived in a taller apartment building (we had an elevator). And we had a balcony, not a small backyard. Also, the trees are different in Mexico City (more tropical). But the highways, the traffic, the parks reminded me of home. Except that signs were all in English, not in Spanish.

"Any other new kids going to start school Monday besides me?" I asked Miguel. "Will I be the only one?"

"There are always a lot of kids coming and going." Miguel sighed. "Hey, I wish you'd stay the whole year, Rafe, not just one semester. Any chance? It would really be great to have you around!"

Wow, he was planning my entire year, and I wasn't even eager for the first day of school.

"Thanks," I said, and meant it. Miguel was my favorite cousin.

Which made it all the harder meeting his friends.

Not only did I want him not to *have* friends—except for me—but I wanted to be cool. I wanted to be friendly, but I didn't want to open my mouth and sound foolish. Don't think it wasn't a strain.

Yet I really liked his friends, I decided, after we'd gone to visit some. We ended up in Josh's backyard. He was Miguel's closest friend. Josh, Karen (another friend), and Miguel and I sat in the sun on the edge of Josh's kid brother's sandbox. Like kids, we played in the sand while we talked.

"Hey, Rafe, are you hungry?" Miguel asked when the sun was directly over our heads.

"Let's go to Louie's for lunch," Josh suggested.

We called Aunt Teresa and told her we'd eat lunch out. Then we went to this special hamburger place.

Now, we have big, fancy hamburger stands in Mexico, but I'd never seen one as big as this one. It had an arch over it that made it look about a mile high. And the big glass front looked about a mile wide. A million people seemed to be inching in, then inching out, with their arms full of paper bags.

"They've got thirty-one kinds of hamburgers," Miguel boasted. "Anything you want!"

I looked at the giant menu over the counter while we waited in line. "Hey, what's a Luau Burger?" I spelled it out.

"Hawaiian. It's got pineapple," Karen said.

"And a True Blue Burger?"

"Blue cheese on top," Josh said.

To be polite, the other kids pushed me ahead of them in the line. I was the visitor, the guest. It was hard making my mind up. I finally settled on a Chili Burger.

That was great. But why, oh, why didn't I keep my mouth shut after that? The kids kept nudging me, asking me if I wanted potatoes, relish, catsup—

So I finally asked for "potato ships."

Or maybe I said "potato sheeps."

Whatever it was, the kids cracked up, laughing. I knew they didn't want to hurt my feelings, but they thought what I said was funny. And it really upset me. I hate being laughed at.

Which was why I spent the rest of the weekend dreaming of every possible way I could think of to make my parents come back and get me. Could I tell them I was dying of a mysterious disease, that they'd have to hurry back if they wanted to see me alive? No, they wouldn't really believe that. Nor would they believe the other phony excuses I thought up.

There really wasn't any reason, any way, I could get out of staying at Aunt Teresa's, and I knew it.

Sunday I was a miserable blob of homesickness. Only I didn't want Miguel to know that was the reason I was refusing to go out with him.

He knew, anyway. "Listen, Rafe, they laughed at my English too when I first came to Queens. There's no way to keep kids from laughing. But that doesn't mean they don't like you. Come on, let's go see Karen and Josh."

I let him drag me out of the house. But I didn't feel like talking much that day. I went to bed early, worrying about the next day.

"Are you sure school really starts today?" I asked Miguel in the morning.

"Sure. Come on and eat breakfast, Rafe."

Miguel sat there and calmly buttered his second piece of toast while elephants played soccer in my stomach. As much alike as we were, I remembered one of the main differences between Miguel and me.

When we were kids the relatives always called him "daring" and me "thoughtful." I think they meant I could think of all the scary sides to everything.

"Are you positive this isn't the wrong day?" I asked again.

"Today," Miguel insisted.

"Yeah, today." Francisco nodded vigorously. He stopped listening to his cereal crackle in the milk long enough to say, "It's the first day of kindergarten, too. Maybe I can be milk monitor, like I was in nursery school." His brown eyes widened at the happy thought.

"Maybe this year you'll be late. Hurry up, Francisco!" Aunt Teresa had to leave him at school before she went to the office where she worked. "*Andale,* Francisco!"

Miguel and I were the first ones out the door. Francisco and Aunt Teresa waved good-by.

"Smell the fall leaves, Rafe!" Miguel said, happily shuffling his way to school through them.

"I don't feel like it," I said. The nearer we got to school the slower my steps got. Like I was walking through warm tar instead of through crisp leaves.

"I keep telling you, Rafe, you won't be the only new kid." Miguel dragged me up the front steps of the school.

"You naturally like people!" I said. "I'm afraid of them."

"But people like *you,* Rafe."

Everyone said hello to Miguel. He tried to introduce me to kids but I was afraid to start talking. I stood alone. Everyone else but me had someone to talk over the good times of summer with. I deliberately stood alone. I felt like I was watching a foreign movie with fuzzy subtitles.

When the bell rang, we pushed in. Miguel pointed out a line to me, a line in the front hall where new kids waited for their homeroom assignments. I got on it automatically, like I was sleepwalking.

I began writing a letter (in my head) to my parents. "Dear Mother and Father, come to my rescue!" Then before I wrote much more, I found myself at the front of the line and I froze, remembering the "potato ships."

"Your name, please."

"Ortiz. Rafael Ortiz," I managed to say.

"Are you new?"

"Y-yes. My aunt t-telephoned about me." I took a deep breath and spoke slowly.

"Do you have a passport? Or other identification?"

Aunt Teresa had told me to bring my birth certificate. I handed it to the lady behind the desk.

She looked at it. Then she filled out a card with my name, a room number, the name of a teacher.

"Out that way." She pointed.

I found myself in the hall again. Every doorway looked exactly alike. There were miles of steel lockers. The number on the card was 243. Where was 243?

"You lost, kid?"

A huge guy with a tag saying STUDENT GUIDE stopped me.

I handed him my card without speaking.

"Down the hall, then go upstairs, but be sure you take the steps marked UP not DOWN."

My feet echoed on the steps.

I found 241, 242, 243. . . .

And I didn't want to go in.

Through the little window in the door I could see kids laughing and joking. No doubt, in *English*. No doubt, they already all knew each other. I went in.

The teacher was just inside, sitting at his desk. He took my white card. "Welcome," he said, and shook my hand. "My name is Schwartz. Let's see what yours is." He looked at the card.

"Nice to have you—" he started to say, when a familiar voice said, "Hey, Rafe! You in my homeroom? Hey, great!"

"Wow, Josh!"

"Well, I guess the two of you already know each other." The teacher grinned. Then he called the class to order. And he sat us next to each other.

It was one of the longest days in my life, but it turned out not to be quite the worst. Not only was Josh in my homeroom, but Miguel was in my social studies class. Twice I saw Karen in the hall. I felt—a little—like I belonged in the new school.

That night after dinner I decided to write a letter to my parents. I wanted them to know things were really going all right with me.

In the spring of 1886, the Kimballs' old cookstove was badly rusted in the damp climate along the Pacific Ocean in Washington Territory. Whit, the oldest of the seven Kimball children, decided that something must be done about replacing the old stove. But the Kimballs had little money, and there was a big bill at Mr. Willard's store, where Whit worked after school. Whit's sister Hester tells the story of what happened.

The Wonderful Wish Book

by PATRICIA BEATTY

That night Whit brought the new Montgomery Ward catalogue home with him. After supper, all of us crowded around the marble-topped table in the parlor. Mama turned the kerosene lamp up as high as it would go without smoking. What a wonderful wish book it was! I blessed Mr. Montgomery and Mr. Ward for it. Clarrie and Cameron gazed at bicycles for $17.45 — grand bicycles, fit to ride on in Portland or Astoria. Anna wanted a Texas saddle for $13.95. Tom and Sarah asked right out for shoofly rocking horses. Mama promised quickly that Pa would make them one this winter. We couldn't afford it just now.

Shoo Fly Rockers.
No. 29R43 Shoo Fly
18x36 inche   inted a
dappled;   i r
hardwood
rocker an
Price, each.
Shipping wgt., 1
No. 29R45 Sh
21x38, same as
but is up
tonne. Shipping weight, 12 poun
No. 29R47 Shoo Fly, 24x40 inches,
and dappled; has box in front to hold child
and is upholstered in cretonne; hair tail, bent r
Shipping weight, 13 pounds. Price.........

Whit and Pa didn't look at the catalogue at all. All evening my brother sat scowling in the ladder-back chair next to Mama's quilting frame. "Don't you want to see the wish book, Whit?" I asked.

"Nope," he replied. "I already looked at it."

Pa was out in the barn. He was doing something to Regent's hoof that might stop the chestnut from balking. I wasn't fooled much when he told us he didn't want to see the catalogue. Mr. Willard's turning him down on the stove had made Pa sad.

The Montgomery Ward catalogue went back to the general store the next morning. We talked about it for a long time and about all of the pretty things we'd looked at. But after a while we got onto other matters — like how fat our pig was getting, and how much bacon and ham we'd have for winter, and how many mice Willoughby, the big gray barn cat, was catching.

The kitchen stove seemed to be holding up. Pa put the bolts back in as fast as they fell out. Mama didn't talk about rust anymore. But we all knew that, once it got started, rust never stopped in the salt air at the beach.

Everything was just the same, except for one thing. Whitney acted funny. He moped. He didn't have much to say, and he glowered quite a bit. He wasn't doing well at school, either, these days. Miss Jenny Pitchford, who taught all the grades from Tom's first grade up to Whitney's eighth all in a one-room schoolhouse, looked upset when he couldn't recite the multiplication table. He used to be able to do it. There was something wrong, I knew. Something was on his mind.

It all came out one morning the first week in May, when we started for school. Cameron and Tom complained to me that Whitney had talked in his sleep all night. He had kept them awake. Whit looked pretty bad. He had dark circles under his eyes, and he was pale when he came to walk beside me. He didn't swing his lunch pail, either.

"I got to talk to you, Hester," he said, as we went by Pa's stacked wood. By now it was so high we couldn't look over it.

"Something's been bothering you, Whit," I told him. "What's it about?"

"The stove," he explained.

"It's holding up all right."

Whit shook his head. He needed to have Mama cut his hair. "I don't mean the old stove. I'm talking about the new one."

"What new one?" I stopped.

"The new one I ordered from the wish book."

I gasped at that like a gaffed salmon. I guess I must have turned as pale as my brother. Then Whit told me about it. One day Mr. Willard had made out a C.O.D. order to Montgomery Ward. He had told Whit to seal the envelope and put the stamp on the letter. Whit knew something about C.O.D., because he heard the summer people talking about it. He remembered a lady saying, "C.O.D. is really a blessing when you don't have the cash handy. It's the quickest way to get anything you need delivered right away." Whit looked at the stove part of the wish book, where there was a picture of a Sunshine Stove, the fanciest and most expensive stove in the whole catalogue. It was called the Nickel-Plated Beauty. He added it to Mr. Willard's order.

Mr. Willard's order had come through yesterday, and so had Whit's stove. Mr. Willard was surprised to find a cookstove with his order. He had put two and two together and thought of Whit. He got the truth out of him

33

right off. And when he found out what Whit had done, he fired him.

"Have you told anybody yet?" I asked.

"No. That's what I wanted to talk to you about, Hester. What am I going to tell Pa?"

"I don't know, Whit. He won't be mad because you tried to buy Mama a stove, but we need what Mr. Willard pays you pretty bad."

"I know we do. I sure wish I'd known what C.O.D. meant," Whit said. "But I guess I know now."

"What does it mean?" I asked him.

"Mr. Willard explained it to me without my even asking him. It means 'cash on delivery.' "

I gasped again. The information surprised me as much as it had Whit.

He went on. "The Sunshine Stove cost twenty-five dollars. Mr. Willard paid for it. He sure got mad, Hester!"

I guess I must have looked sick, because Clarrie came up to me and asked if I had a headache or something. "I don't feel sick. I'm thinking," I told her. "We're in real bad trouble."

"What about?"

Whit groaned. "Guess we might as well all know now." He called Cameron back from where he was walking on a rail. Tom, who followed Cameron everywhere, came with him. In a minute Anna was there, too. Whit told the story again while all of us, even Red the dog, listened.

He told it fast, because we could see Vestal and Virgil Johnson walking the ties behind us. We didn't want them to know about this, though. When we had trouble, we Kimballs kept it to ourselves if we could.

"What'll Whit do?" Clarrie asked.

"I don't know what Whit will do," Whit said sadly. Red whined, and he reached down to rub his ears.

34

"I know!" Anna piped up. "We'll ask Miss Jenny. She knows all about everything. She'll fix it for us."

So that was just what we did. We waited until morning recess. Instead of going out to play, we went up, all together, to Miss Jenny Pitchford's desk at the end of the schoolroom. She was grading papers, but she looked up right away.

"What's this, a delegation from the Kimballs?" she asked.

We didn't know what a delegation was, but we nodded. Miss Pitchford had smiled when she said it, and her dark blue eyes had been friendly.

Then Whit told her all about the stove, while she looked at her desk and played with her red pencil. She didn't say anything right off. She got up and picked up the old school bell. Miss Pitchford gave the recess bell a good long ring and then spoke to us. She was frowning. "I'm going to let school out a half hour early today, children. We'll all go visit Jacob Willard and see if we can't straighten this out."

We went, too, right after school, the seven of us. Miss Pitchford lead the way, the strings of her white sunbonnet flapping. She was fighting mad. I thought that was peculiar, because everybody knew she and Mr. Willard were courting.

The general store was empty this late in the day. Miss Pitchford, with us trailing behind her like a flock of wet chickens, went right up to Mr. Willard. He saw the look in her eye and us at her heels. I think he wanted to duck behind his counter, but she saw him first.

"I'd like a word with you, Jacob," she said.

$25.⁰⁰

"Nothing could be more pleasant." He grinned at her. He was trying to buy her off, I guess, but she wasn't having any of his sweet talk.

"Whitney Kimball has told me that he ordered a stove for his mother C.O.D., and that you fired him."

"That's right, Jenny."

She pointed to us. "The Kimballs need the money Whitney earns. Have you thought of that?"

"The boy did a dishonest thing." Mr. Willard stood right up to her, even if she did have blood in her eye.

"Whitney did not know what C.O.D. meant."

"He knows now! Cash on delivery. He could have looked it up." He said it so loudly we all shivered.

"Jacob," said Miss Pitchford in a softer voice, "give the boy his job again, please. He's learned his lesson. He won't do it again."

"He sure won't. I wouldn't let him near an order again."

"Then he can have his job back?"

"Don't go putting words in my mouth, Jenny!"

Miss Pitchford was quiet for a long while.

"All right, Jacob. But what about the stove? What are you going to do about the stove?" She wasn't through with Mr. Willard yet. I held my breath.

"What do you mean—the stove? I'll sell it. There's room in the storeroom for it. Somebody'll want it pretty soon, bad as the rust is here at the beach."

"The Kimballs need it."

"They ain't getting it. I can't put it on that big bill of theirs, Jenny. Joe Kimball's got to show me the color of his money for it."

"That's not what I had in mind—not right now. What if you held the stove for a while and let the Kimballs work it out?"

He shook his head. "I can't afford to pay more than one Kimball at a time. I haven't got jobs for a crew like that."

I heard Clarrie draw in her breath. Sometimes Clarrie cussed. I stepped on her toe with my shoe. Things were going along pretty well. I didn't want them spoiled.

"Perhaps something will turn up that will let them buy the stove. Whitney meant to give it to his mother in December for her birthday. Can you hold it until then?"

I drew in my breath. Miss Pitchford had told a flat-out

fib. Whit hadn't had any ideas about Mama's birthday at all. I don't know what Whitney had been thinking about when he ordered the Nickel-Plated Beauty C.O.D. I think he thought it would be some sort of present to us from Montgomery Ward, and that he could have Pa take it home in the wagon.

Mr. Willard thought for a while. "Yes, I guess so," he said finally. "I won't put it up for sale until a week before her birthday. That suit you, Jenny?"

"Yes, Jacob, it would."

I don't know what got into me then. Just as bold as brass, I spoke out. "Thanks, Mr. Willard, for giving Whit his job back. We'll pay for the stove, all right. Just don't tell Pa about it."

Jacob Willard wasn't pleased. "*Who's* going to pay for it, Missie?"

I went on like a spooked horse. All those months from May to December had gone to my head. "We kids will, Mr. Willard. We got a long time to do it in." I turned to my brothers and sisters. Their eyes were as round as marbles. Their mouths were wide open. "Can we do it?" I asked. "We'll have to earn twenty-five dollars ourselves. It's a lot of money."

Clarrie said, "It's a whole lot of money."

"Aw, we can do it," Cameron bragged.

"Good," I said. "It's just like in *The Three Musketeers.* You know the part I read you — where D'Artagnan and the musketeers say, 'One for all, all for one.' "

Whit broke into a smile. One by one the others did, too. Mr. Willard threw back his head and laughed, but I didn't care what he thought. We'd show him.

Miss Pitchford looked surprised, and then she smiled at me like a sunrise.

"Good luck, Hester," she told me.

The Treasure

by CHARLOTTE ANKER

Mommy came dashing into the house. "Jenny! Guess what? I sold a house this morning. The Terrells are moving here from California," she said. "They have a son about your age."

Well, that was news. It was about time somebody my age moved into Maple Hills.

Mommy fixed some egg-salad sandwiches. She sat down at the table, still going on about the Terrells. I was only half-listening, but I caught a few words. Mr. Terrell was an architect. He was going to design a new section for the house Mommy sold him. Mrs. Terrell wrote poetry.

All the while Mommy was talking, I was thinking of the oyster shells I had found in the hillside.

"How far are we from the ocean?" I asked Mommy, suddenly.

"About a hundred miles," she said. "Why?"

"What was here before they started building the houses?" I asked.

"Partly a wilderness, partly farmland. I think," she replied. "There were the woods, and some low marshy sections, and maybe some wild grassy meadows. Possums and raccoons lived in the forests. Snakes and beavers lived around the creek. And wild birds nested. . . ."

Once she starts something, Mommy has a lively imagination. Usually I like to listen. This time I wanted facts.

"You don't suppose the ocean ever came this far inland?" I asked, doubtfully.

"Not for quite a few million years," she said.

A few million years! I remembered what we had learned in school. Some places where there are now oceans were once dry land where animals roamed. But more important, in certain places where there is now dry land, there were once great oceans. Suppose this whole area was once an ocean with oysters burrowing into the bottom.

That afternoon I made the first big discovery that was not a shell. It was a shark's tooth. When Susie Becker, my best friend at school, came back from her trip to Florida last winter, she wore a shark's tooth on a silver chain. Hers was white, and only about a half-inch long. This one was dark gray, and almost two inches long.

I knew the ocean had been here now! I sat on the bank of the stream a long time. The shells and the shark's tooth were spread out around me. I watched the bubbly water play around the rocks.

I tried to imagine the shark who owned this tooth swimming in the creek. I had to laugh. It would have looked so silly, splashing in that foamy, polluted water. Then I thought: it lived here all the same. Here is its tooth.

I dug a hole deep in the side of the hill and buried the shells and the shark's tooth in it. I covered the hole with a large rock.

Throughout the next two months, I dug often along the creek. I followed the power shovels wherever they were digging foundations for houses. After the workers left for the day, I searched the huge holes they had bitten out of the ground. I found lots of different kinds of shells, teeth, and bits of bone.

The library was only three hills away by bike. I looked through the children's section for books about fossils. That's what I knew I had—fossils. They are the remains of plants and animals that lived millions of years ago.

I had an idea. It wasn't that I thought I'd find a whole dinosaur. But I kept finding so many exciting things. I was sure that somewhere in that jumble of trees and mud and rocks and stream, there was a really super Treasure. And I would find it—me, Jenny Berger, scientist.

One hot August Sunday, I woke up with just one thing on my mind. The Treasure.

After breakfast, I went to my room to get the big metal box Mommy had given me to store my collection.

On the way out of the house, I picked up a stack of news-
papers.

I went down to the hole by the creek to dig out the
Treasure. I took the fossils out carefully, one at a time, so
as not to break them. I wrapped each one in a piece of
newspaper. Then I put them into the metal box. They
just fit. I started up the slope, thinking about a new place
to hide the Treasure. The hillside was too risky. I was
always worrying about floods or dogs or landslides.

It was then that I saw Toby Terrell for the first time.
As I was climbing up the hill, he was racing down it.

"Hi!" he shouted, as he zoomed by. "Any snakes?"

That was too good an opener to ignore. I turned
around and followed him back down the hill. By the time
I reached the stream, he was wading slowly. He didn't

care if his sneakers were getting soaked. His eyes searched the water and rocks.

He was shorter than I was. But he was a lot bulkier. His skin was almost the same color as his brown pants. The best thing was his bright orange T-shirt. It showed an insect buzzing across his chest. Printed on it in large black letters was "Don't kill a fly. It may be somebody's National Bird."

That struck me so funny, I started to laugh.

"Don't laugh," he said solemnly. "I'll bet there are plenty of snakes around here. You have to know how to catch them. You probably scare them away."

I scare *them* away? I had never thought that it could be anything but the opposite. I knew the pretty, green garter snakes that darted across the water every now and then were harmless. But the people building the houses had talked about how dangerous the poisonous copperhead snakes are.

"Why do you want to find snakes?" I felt dumb asking. It was the kind of question grown-ups ask when things seem so obvious to children. With this boy I couldn't tell what kind of answer I might get.

"I'm a herpetologist," he said.

I didn't know what a herpetologist was. But I knew it was a scientific person, which I also now was.

"I used to collect insects," he continued. "They were great. Now I only collect snakes."

"Why did you stop collecting bugs?" I asked.

"I found out they didn't live well in captivity. They usually died after a few weeks," he explained. "My mama said *she* didn't live well in captivity, either. She felt like she was being kept in a zoo. She said all the insects around the house were staring at her as if she were an interesting specimen."

"What's a herpetologist?" I asked. I decided I could risk another dumb question.

"Somebody who studies snakes."

Of course. What else?

In a burst of confidence, I said, "I am a paleobiologist."

A paleobiologist is somebody who studies fossils. At first I thought he was showing off by not asking what that was. Later, I found out he was a super scientist—for his age.

His brown eyes hit my metal box as if they could see through the gray steel.

I don't know what made me say, "Do you want to see my fossils?" Maybe it was the eerie feeling that he could see them anyway.

"Sure!" He said it with so much enthusiasm that I was glad I was going to show him.

We sat down on the hillside. I opened the box and took each fossil out of its newspaper wrapping.

He examined every fossil carefully, more closely than I had. Sometimes he would hold one in his hand. Then he let his hand go limp. He acted as if he were a scale weighing the piece.

"Here are my notes," I said proudly. I showed him my notebook. I had written down everything I had found and exactly where I had found it: "Twenty feet from the third oak tree on lot number seven" or "Seventy steps from the telephone pole near lot number four."

"Good thinking! You really are a paleobiologist," he said.

Although I was already two inches taller than he was, I felt taller than ever.

I must have seemed taller to him, too. He then remembered to ask my name. We exchanged names. It didn't matter that we hadn't before. Herpetologist and Paleobiologist are much more exciting names than Toby Terrell and Jenny Berger.

"We just bought the house at the top of this hill," he said. "We're moving in Saturday. Until then, we're staying with my grandma in Washington."

"I know. My mother told me. She's the real-estate agent who sold your parents the house."

"We're coming here most days this week so my dad can make some drawings. He's an architect. He's going to rebuild the house."

"How old are you?" I was trying to figure out why he seemed both older and younger than I was.

"I'll be eleven in two months."

When Toby said that, I felt completely relaxed with him for the first time. It wasn't because I was older. It's something I know about kids. If they're ten, and they say they're ten, O.K. If, instead, they tell you when they're going to be eleven, they're not really as sure of themselves as they seem to be.

Toby looked at the fossils again. He traced his brown finger along the outline of one of the heavily ridged shells.

"Did you really find them right around here?" he asked.

"Yes."

"All of them?"

He became more excited as I nodded my head.

"Let's dig right here," he said. "There must be more."

Soon we had found a half-dozen rocks with fossils stuck in them. We were still digging when Toby suddenly stood up straight.

"Stop digging and don't move," he said in a low voice, almost a whisper. "Get up, but stand still."

Something in his voice scared me. I jumped up.

"What's the matter?" I asked.

"I think we hit a nest of copperheads," said Toby, trying not to look too happy.

I am not afraid of snakes like some people — not ordinary snakes. But *copperhead* is a spine-chilling word to me. I know copperheads have poisonous venom which can kill you. When Toby said "copperhead," it was like he pushed a button in my brain that made my body become stiff as a doll's.

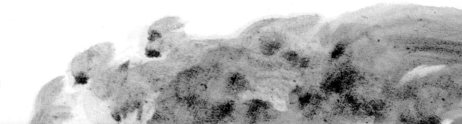

The next moment, a little brown ribbon of a thing came out of the hole where I had been digging. Then it darted across the creek.

"Is that the copperhead?" I asked, amazed. I had expected to see a monstrous serpent, coiled up ready to strike.

"Yes. You can tell by the bands on its back," said Toby.

"I didn't see anything but brown," I admitted.

"That was just the baby," Toby explained. "But they have venom as soon as they're born. Even newborn babies can strike."

Well, I won't go hugging any newborn copperheads, I promised myself. "Do you think, now that it's gone, we could go back to digging?" I asked.

"Tell you what," he said. "Snakes tomorrow. Today let's hunt for more fossils."

There's a person who knows how to make a bargain! I was beaming as we shook hands on it. With Toby's help, I thought, surely I would find that special something I was searching for.

Hay-foot, Straw-foot

by ERICK BERRY

Si Cameron had a mighty clear notion of what he wanted to be. He wanted to be a soldier. The only trouble was the enlisting sergeants in this camp couldn't see it that way. But this one would, by gol! For this time he had made his shirt and breeches look wide and plumped out, kind of, with a padding of hay, and likewise his stockings. When he came to the sergeant's table he intended to stand up on tiptoe, to make himself as tall as possible.

Hot it was, and itchy, this business of being a walking haystack. But it wouldn't be for long, for now there was only one fellow ahead of him, a big fellow who must be all of sixteen or maybe more.

And now his own turn. Si stepped up to the table. He gave a salute the way he'd seen the real soldiers do. Then, balancing himself against the table edge, he rose on his toes. There was a chuckle behind him, but the sergeant didn't so much as lift his eyes from the muster roll, on which he was writing the name and suchlike of the last recruit.

"Name?" His pen slipped a line lower.

"Si Cameron, sir." Si made his voice as gruff as he could, the way he'd been practicing all morning. And it was so almighty gruff it almost frightened him.

The sergeant's pen wrote on. He didn't look up. "Ever been a soldier before?"

"No, sir," said Si truthfully.

"Married?"

"No, sir."

"Hale and hearty?"

"Yes, sir."

"Age?"

That was the critical moment. Si swallowed. "Six–sixteen," he began. But blessed if his voice didn't run up as he said it, like a young'un's.

The sergeant glanced up, under his beetling brows. Then he sat back and roared with laughter. "Well, bless my soul! Where's the rest of ye, Si? Can't just list yer twelve years without them four ye left back to home!"

"But, sir—" Si sank down on his heels again. He still had an argument. "A bigger fellow's easier hit by a musketball. He takes more victuals, and more cloth for his uniform, and more—"

"What's that stickin' out of the hole in your shirt?" asked the sergeant, and before Si could answer, "Hay, I'll be bound! You be off to the commissariat sergeant and he'll buy you to feed the horses."

"But, sir—"

"That'll do, that'll do," said the man, suddenly impatient. "There's twenty more waiting behind you. You go home and grow up, young'un."

"Yes, sir." Si fumbled a salute; he did it without thinking and stumbled off.

Almost in tears he was, for all his twelve years; half anger and half disappointment. For that was the eighth regiment he had tried to enlist in since yesterday morning. He'd claimed to have come from Philadelphia. He'd claimed to hail from Klauverack, down the Hudson; from 'most every place he could think of, according to the home place of the regiment he was trying. And they'd not bothered to disbelieve him, for this army of General Abercrombie's, mustering along the Hudson to attack the Frenchies up at Lake George, needed men badly. But seemingly they were hiring men the way they'd buy draft oxen, by the size and heft. They couldn't be made to understand how handy a little fellow could be. Si was a fellow who could knock a squirrel out of a tree with a

clod of earth. He wasn't liable to be captured by the enemy.

He went over and sat down on a tree stump. He started to unstuff his shirt, feeling sort of hollow and hungry below that shirt, too. Sad he was, but kind of mad, too. All these different regiments in all their different uniforms, drilling, building huts, manhandling carts through the deep spring mud, unloading boats at the wharves on the Hudson below. You'd think there'd be room for one more soldier, even if he wasn't as old as Methuselah and as big as Goliath.

Soldiers would grow, wouldn't they, just like anyone else?

He hugged his thin knees against his empty stomach. That last piece of bread had been a small one. It had been soon eaten. And that was last night. Let's see, it was 'most a week ago he had started out from Litchfield. Hadn't had to walk all the way, either. He'd just sneaked up on a cart that was bringing stores to the army. He'd reached in the back and pitched a bundle that felt like a side of bacon to the road. Then he'd slipped off, let the carter drive on a way, and shouted to him, "Hi, mister! You lose something?"

The carter allowed that he had. And he was grateful enough to give Si a lift. You didn't need to weigh two hundred pounds and be a swamping great blacksmith to know your way about the world. That night, the carter had shared his supper with Si. It had been a good, hot meal too, cooked in a pot over the fire. And Si had whistled to amuse the old gaffer. If there was one thing Si could really do, it was whistle. He whistled like a thrush, like a flute, like the wind down the chimney on a winter's night, like a wet finger ringing a tavern glass, and then again like all the birds you ever heard. There

wasn't a song that, once he'd listened to it, he couldn't whistle again. Pretty soon they had six other carters around them, asking for more. And after that, Si got to ride the rest of the long way. He'd whistle for his supper, for his breakfast too, and dinner.

But it seemed you couldn't whistle up a meal in the army.

Under a cloudy sky the drums beat out orders through the warm, steamy afternoons. On the bare, muddy space before him, a bunch of raw recruits, with sticks on their shoulders instead of firearms, were being marched and wheeled and put through their paces. They looked for a moment as though they were going to march right over him. Then someone barked an order, and they wheeled away. From down on the flats along the river came the repeated pop of musketry. Trained troops were proving their firing pieces.

A plump, red-faced officer cantered up on a tall, raw-boned gray. He slung himself off and tossed the reins toward Si with a "Hold my horse, boy." Then he strode off toward the new enlisted men.

Si caught the reins. He hooked his arm through the loop, sat back again on his tree stump, and watched the officer. It seemed he was some kind of an army surgeon, for he bade the row of men lined up there to stick out their tongues. Then he trotted down their ranks, looking at each in turn. Gol, they looked right comical! A lot of grown men all with their tongues out. They looked like little 'uns making faces at teacher's back. And that didn't content the officer. Next he made them stand first on one leg, then on the other, like a row of herons wading for fish. Well, if that was all there was to getting into the army, Si could do it as well as the next man. And stand on his hands besides, which likely they couldn't.

59

As the officer headed back, Si jumped to his feet. He whipped off his hat. Then he began to make a show of polishing the brown leather of the saddle, as high as he could reach. "Want your saddlery cleaned and your steelwork burnished, mister?" he asked. "Do a real good job."

"Sorry, Yankee, but I've got a groom for that." The plump, young surgeon swung into the saddle and tossed Si a penny. Then he was off. Likely he went to look at some other tongues elsewhere. Kind of a finicky task for a growed man.

And all of a sudden the sun had come out. Si's world had changed color. A penny, a whole penny, had been earned in less than ten minutes. It took Si no more effort than to sit on a stump, which he'd been doing anyhow, and hold the end of some reins in his hands. A penny meant a loaf of bread. A penny meant six buns at a huckster's stall, or three buns and some cider and a piece of pie.

Maybe a penny in the hand isn't pie in the stomach, but it's as good as. And what's more, food meant another whole day in the camp, in which he could try to get into the army. Holding the precious copper in his fist for the heartening feeling of it, Si went in search of that pie.

He ate a large slice of bread and cheese, with even a slice of onion balanced atop it. He had a wedge of pie still in reserve. And he had knotted the ha'penny change in the flap on his shirt. Then he watched his friend drive off with the cart train. The carter shouted to him, "See ye when we get back again, Si!" Si waved in return, but he felt no pang of regret. He turned toward the camp.

It was then that he saw the soldier, out in an open kind of place and marching all by himself. Or that's what he seemed to be doing. He was a big, tall gawk of a fellow.

He had the yellowest hair you ever saw and shoulders so wide they'd get him, easy, past any sergeant in the army. He was kind of stomping up and down and wheeling and muttering to himself. Si stood and watched for a bit. He wondered what in tarnation the fellow thought he was doing.

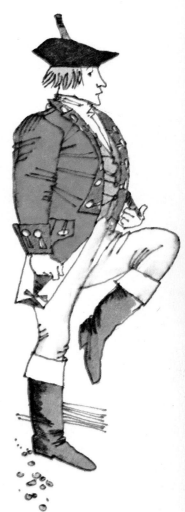

A recruit wasn't anyone to be scared of. Why, a few hours ago or maybe a few days ago this fellow hadn't even been a soldier. Si up and asked him, "What do you think you're doing, mister?"

"Left, right, left, right," said the man, too busy to answer. But he turned a mighty worried face on Si.

Si dropped into step beside him. He had to stretch his pace a heap to keep up. A half hour ago he couldn't have done it. But that bread and cheese and onion had helped a lot. And it was kind of exciting making out you were a soldier at last.

"Left, right, left, right," said the fellow.

"Look," said Si, swallowing the last of his meal, "when you say 'left' put your left foot forward. I know that much about the army. You're putting your right foot forward."

"Oh," said the fellow. And he started out new, the other way. But in a few moments, he was doing it wrong again.

"Your *left*, your *left!*" shrilled Si crossly. "Look, mister, don't you know which is your left foot? It's opposite your left hand, kind of, not catty-corner."

"I *don't* know, for a fact," said the big fellow.

Si stared. Well, that wasn't so funny. Lots of men didn't know their right from their left. If they didn't have to hold a pen, what would they need to know it for? Most tasks around a farm took both hands. It didn't matter which hand you took hold with first.

The big fellow stopped to mop his face on his coat-sleeve. "Down our way, when we walk, we just put one foot forward and then the other. It don't signify which. I joined the army to lick the Frenchies. It seems like I got to learn to dance first, or as good as. Don't know as I'll ever get to be a soldier. Likely they'll send me back home again."

For a big fellow he was mighty upset. But Si could understand just how he felt. It seemed a shame. Here the army wouldn't take you if you were too little, even if you didn't confuse your left foot with your right. And maybe then they'd turn you down for not knowing, even though you were tall as a haystack and 'most as broad as a barn. What he and this soldier ought to do was combine on this, like working both ends of a saw. Then at least one of them would be in the army, and all set to stay there.

"Look," said Si. "What say we mark your feet, so you'll know the two apart? Like taking off one boot, so you'd get 'boot-foot, bare-foot.' Only"—he scratched his head—"maybe the sergeant would sort of notice that."

The big fellow, who had stopped right away to take off one boot, nodded and straightened up. Si looked around him. There wasn't a thing in sight, like a piece of chalk or lime, to mark a boot with. The fellow picked up a piece of straw and began to chew it.

Si hauled a handful of hay out of his own britches and thrust them into the man's left boot. Then he stuck the fellow's straw into his right-hand boot top.

"You know the difference between hay and straw?" Si asked.

"Sure I do. Who don't?" The fellow was indignant.

"Well then, try marching to 'hay-foot, straw-foot, hay-foot, straw-foot'!" And off they went together. Si bawled

out the orders just like those sergeants he'd watched for the past two days.

As soon as the fellow got the notion, Si switched to "hay-foot, right-foot, hay-foot, right-foot." Then he began "left-foot, straw-foot, left-foot, straw-foot." And before long, he had him doing "left-foot, right-foot," and the fellow wasn't fazed at all. He kept right at it, too, you had to hand it to him.

Then Si got another stick to serve as musket, and the big fellow put the two of them through some more drill. Kind of fun it was, too. It was easy to learn when you were dead set on learning. The sun was getting low. Off in the camp there was a sudden roll of drums. From all four corners at once the men began to run.

"That must be the call to victuals," said Si. "Nothing makes a man run so fast as a call to food."

They started back to the camp together. They marched fast, in step with each other. The fellow was still saying, "Left-foot, right-foot," under his breath. Si was hungry again, more hungry than he had been before he had that bread and cheese. Drat all this marching anyway! He'd ought to have sat down and kind of cosseted that last meal, not marched it all away.

Lines were forming up outside the cookhouses. The stew, or whatever it was, smelled like heaven. Si licked his lips.

"You wait here," said the fellow, and rushed off. But Si knew how hopeless it was to try to get into the food line if you weren't part of the army. He'd tried that yesterday, twice, and got cuffed good and plenty. Both times, too.

He waited, though, like he was bid. After a while the big fellow came back. He held a bowl of steaming stew in his hand and a wooden spoon. "Eat hearty," he ordered. "There's more where that come from, and I'll get mine later, soon as they've forgotten me."

So they found another tree stump and sat down on it. Si filled up hearty, like he'd been told. After that the fellow went off and was gone quite a while. But Si, feeling content, still waited. And when the other came back he was wiping his mouth on his sleeve and looked more cheerful than he had all afternoon.

Then they sat down to talk. "What's your name?" the fellow asked.

Si told him. Seemed the fellow's own name was Con, Con Stillman. He was seventeen and came from Connecticut, too. He was one of nine boys. So his pa had said, "All right, you go join the army and lick the Frenchies if you want to, Con. Seems like I can spare you. I got plenty sons to help plow and harvest till you come back." Ma had given him a new coat. And Pa had given him three shillings. Then he'd walked here all the way, on his own feet.

"I could have learned that 'left-foot, right-foot' then, if I'd knowed about it earlier." Con grinned.

Si's story was different. He had only his Uncle Lisha, who was kind of mean anyhow, so he'd just run away without so much as a by-your-leave.

After a while there was another roll of drums. Si had heard that drumming last night, too. That meant you had to turn in and be counted, to see if you'd strayed or run away. And then you could roll up and go to sleep in a tent or a hut with the other soldiers.

Con got up to go. "You got someplace to stay?" he asked.

Si glanced at the sky. It looked like it was going to be a fine night. He recollected a big pile of hay, up by the brick house. Fort Crailo, they called it. The majors and the captains and the generals lived there. It would be nice and warm in that hay.

"I'm staying up at the fort," he said grandly. "See you in the morning."

Curling up in the hay, he savored the last of the stew on his lips and smiled sleepily. He had a full stomach, had found a friend, and there were lots more army orders to learn. Likely if he learned all those drill orders, someday he could borrow a uniform and slip into the army and not a soul would be the wiser.

"Sergeant—no, *General* Si Cameron," he murmured. And went to sleep.

Hisako lives with her grandparents. She thought her parents had died when she was a baby. Then, a mysterious birthday present leads Hisako to discover that her father is alive. After she meets him, Hisako's only wish is to go to Paris to live with her father.

Hisako Decides

by YOSHIKO UCHIDA

It was hard to find just the right time and place to talk to Grandmother and Grandfather about going to Paris with her father. Hisako wanted to say something after supper. But Grandmother hurried outside to water her plants. Grandfather went to watch the news on TV.

This was one time Hisako wanted to say the right thing in the right way instead of blurting everything out

all at once like an exploding volcano. It wasn't that she didn't like living with Grandmother and Grandfather. She must make them see that. It was just that she thought she'd like living with her father better.

The next morning, Hisako hurried down for breakfast. The right words were all shaped inside her head, but Grandfather had already gone to his study to play his lute. And Grandmother was out sprinkling the street.

By lunchtime the right words had evaporated. Hisako decided to wait until suppertime when her father would be here. She would ask in front of him. They could all decide together right then and there.

When Father arrived, however, he had a plan of his own. "I'd like to borrow Hisako for two weeks and take her to Tamba with me," he said. "A friend of mine there is going to Kyushu for two weeks. He has asked me to stay in his house while he is away. Hisako and I could watch his house and enjoy some time in the country as well."

"Oh, Grandmother, could I go?" Hisako asked eagerly. Grandmother nodded quickly as though she had already made up her mind.

"Why, of course," she said. "I think it would be a fine thing for you to have some time with your father. Don't you think so?" she asked Grandfather.

Grandfather seemed agreeable, too. "Certainly," he said. "By all means."

Hisako was so excited about this new vacation that she almost forgot the speech she had planned. She looked at Grandfather and then at Grandmother, swallowed hard, and opened her mouth.

"I have sort of a plan too . . ." she began.

Hisako suddenly felt her father kick her foot. She looked at him quickly and saw him shake his head.

"Yes?" Grandfather asked. "What plan?"

Hisako felt her father kick her ankle again. "Ouch," she said. "It's uh . . . nothing. I guess it's nothing, after all."

Hisako went to the gate with her father when he was ready to leave. "Why did you stop me?" she asked. She felt a little annoyed with him. "I was all ready to talk to them about going to Paris with you."

"I know, Hisa Chan," Father said. "I want you to wait until we get back from Tamba. If you still want to go then, we'll talk about it together. All right?"

It really wasn't all right at all. Hisako wanted to have it settled now. From now on she would be living with her father forever, traveling all over Europe with him. It would be a storybook life. It would be better than any of the wildest daydreams she'd ever dared have.

"I . . . I guess so," she said, without any enthusiasm at all.

"Good," her father said. "Then I'll be by for you about nine o'clock tomorrow morning."

"So early?" Hisako asked. She hadn't even packed yet.

But Father had already started down the street. "See you in the morning," he said. With a wave of the hand, he was gone.

The house of Father's friend was an old farmhouse. He lived alone. The rooms were dark and bare. They looked as though they hadn't been swept or dusted in a long, long time. Water had to be pumped from a well behind the house. The only way to get hot water was to boil some in a kettle. There was nothing in the kitchen for cooking except two charcoal braziers and a few odd

pots and pans. There were only a few dishes in the cupboard. Most of them were chipped or cracked. There was no bathtub. If Hisako wanted a bath, she would have to go to the public bathhouse in the village.

Hisako had to try hard not to show her disappointment at this house. Father didn't seem disturbed at all. He went from room to room, sliding open the paper doors and shutters and letting in some fresh air.

"This would make a fine studio if it had a little more light," he said, looking around. "Can you cook some rice for our supper?"

Hisako glanced at the brazier. "On that thing?" she asked doubtfully.

Father went on as though he hadn't noticed Hisako's dismay. "We'll get some salt fish and bean curd in the village. There's rice in the bin."

Once in a while Hisako cooked the rice at home. But Grandmother had an electric rice cooker, and that made quite a difference. "I'll try," she said, and measured out some rice.

They went to the village to buy some fish and bean curd cake, and soy sauce and tea. Father bought some sweet bean paste cakes for dessert.

"This will be a fine supper," he said. But when they sat down to eat, the fish was burnt. The rice was sandy and half-cooked.

"Never mind," Father said. "There's plenty of pickled radish in the cupboard and lots of tea. You know, if we were in Paris we might be making supper out of just bread and cheese."

"That's all?" Hisako asked.

Father nodded. "Some days I get so wrapped up in my painting I forget to go shopping. Then I have to eat what's in the cupboard. There's usually some bread and cheese."

Hisako wrinkled her nose. She hated cheese. "Well," she said, "I guess I'd like the bread."

The next morning Father woke her up at seven o'clock. "Get up, sleepy head," he called. "Let's go see what we can find to sketch today."

Hisako thought of her nice soft bed at home. But she rolled out of her quilts and tried to shake the sleep from her eyes. She looked at the clock and shuddered. At home she would still be sound asleep. Her father was as bad as a rooster on a farm.

Half asleep, Hisako munched on rice and pickles and tea for breakfast. Father got together the pads and pencils. They stopped in the village for some milk, sweet buns, and apples. They put the food in their knapsacks and started to hike toward the hills. The air was fresh and the sky was a bright blue. As Hisako walked along beside her father, she began to feel better.

"We could do this together every day in France," she said happily.

"Say, wouldn't that be fun?" Father agreed. "I'd like that. And will you cook and clean and keep house for me?"

"Sure," Hisako answered. But deep down, she felt as though she'd swallowed a hot potato. The one thing she hated most in life was cleaning house. Sweeping and dusting seemed such a waste of time. You could spend hours at it, and two days later the whole house would be dirty again. She hardly ever cleaned her room unless someone made her.

"I hope you have a vacuum cleaner," Hisako said.

Father threw back his head and laughed. "I have exactly one broom, a bucket, and a mop," he said. "After all, my studio is just one big room. My paints are on one side, and my living quarters on the other."

Hisako tried to imagine living with her father in his one-room studio. She would have to dust and sweep and mop, and eat cheese and bread for supper. Somehow, it wasn't quite the way she had pictured life with her father. She turned now to look at him. She saw a slight smile around his lips although he was looking straight ahead.

Hisako felt completely out of words. "I'm starving," she said suddenly. She slipped off her knapsack and dug inside for her sweet roll. She took a huge bite.

Toward the end of the two weeks, Hisako longed to see her friends and her grandparents. Not that she wasn't having a wonderful time with Father. Every day they took long walks into the countryside. They found wonderful old houses or crooked trees or fields of rice to sketch together. Father looked at Hisako's work and nodded.

"Not bad at all," he said. He held them out at arm's length and squinted at them. "You have a good eye. There's strength and movement in your line. But you need more practice."

In the evenings, Father would read to her, or she would read to him. Or sometimes they would just sit on the porch and watch the moon come up from behind the dark hills.

Still, Hisako knew she was beginning to long for her own house in Kyoto and her own room. She missed having friends pop in to listen to records with her or plan what they could do together on Sunday. She missed the good smells and the sound of Grandmother puttering in the kitchen. She even missed the sound of Grandfather's lute with her breakfast. She thought about the bread man with his truck of freshly baked bread, the vegetable woman with her cart, and the noodle lady at the market. The fact was, she was very homesick.

How strange it was, she thought. She could be with someone she loved very much and still feel lonely. She knew at last that the very same thing would happen if she went to Paris with her father. Only there she would be thousands of miles, instead of just two hours away from Kyoto. She would be in a foreign land where she could not even speak the language. She could not run home when she got homesick.

On their last night in Tamba, Hisako knew she must tell her father that she had changed her mind. She had burned their rice, and Father had overcooked the fish. Once more they ate bean curd cakes with soy sauce and dried fish.

"I imagine you'll be glad to get back to your grandmother's good cooking," Father said. It was as though he knew what was going on in Hisako's mind.

Hisako grinned. "I'm better at eating good food than I am at making it," she admitted.

Father laughed. "I thought so. And I think I know something else, too. I think maybe you have changed your mind about going to Paris with me, haven't you?"

Hisako's face lit up. "How did you know?" she asked. "I was wondering how to tell you."

"Oh, it wasn't hard to tell," Father said. He patted her shoulder. "I'm glad you decided to stay in Kyoto, Hisa Chan," he said. "It's best for everyone right now."

It had taken the trip to Tamba with her father to make her see that he was right. He had known what was best all along, of course. But he had been wise enough to let her work it out for herself. Now she could say good-by to him and not feel that he had deserted her. She was ready to wait for him until he could come back to Japan.

When she got home to Kyoto, she knew that this was the right place for her to be.

"I think Hisako has had enough of strange new places for this year," Father said to Grandmother. And Hisako saw that he and Grandmother exchanged quick, happy smiles.

Had Grandmother known that she wanted to leave and go to Paris? Had Father told her? Hisako would never know, but this was a mystery she was willing to leave unsolved.

After the Civil War, Dan Riker and his parents leave Tennessee to herd cattle on the Great Plains of Texas. On the way, Mr. Riker breaks his leg and develops a high fever, and Dan must find help—fast. But they are far from any town. Dan rides out on the prairie. There he meets someone who can help: Will Mesteño, the Black Mustanger.

The Black Mustanger

by RICHARD WORMSER

Dan's mother was just lighting the lantern as they rode into camp. Dan swung down from his horse and said, "Maw, this is Will Mesteño. How's Dad?"

His mother said, "That is not the way I taught you to introduce people, Dan. Try again."

"This is Mr. Mesteño; my mother, Mrs. Riker."

"How do you do, Mr. Mesteño."

"I'm fine, Mrs. Riker, and I had a mother who was like you, ma'am. How is your husband?"

"No change since Dan rode out looking for help this morning. I surely do thank you for coming, Mr. Mesteño."

"I told Dan, just plain Will does it. The *mesteño* is a nickname. It means mustang in Spanish—"

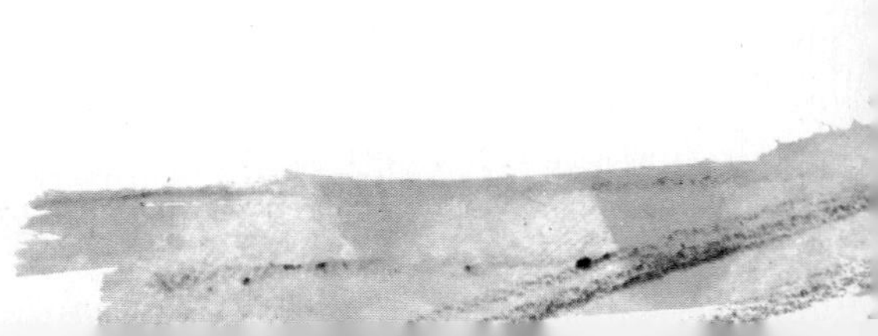

"You are Mexican, sir?"

"Partly. My father was Black. My mother was an Apache from Mexico. I don't promise anything, but I would like to look at Mr. Riker and his leg."

Dan said, "I'll tend your horse, Will. We have grain."

"Blue Streak's not used to it, lad. Don't teach her bad habits." Mesteño Will stepped to Blue Streak's side and stripped away saddle and bridle with two quick motions. The bridle was a notch-ear, made to come away fast.

The horse went off into the darkening prairie, kicking up her heels at the Rikers' horse, Rayo, as she passed, shying away from the mules as though she hadn't seen their like before.

Will looked after them and said, "They'll make friends soon enough."

Mrs. Riker had taken the lantern down from the wagon tongue. Now she held it high to guide Will toward the tent.

Dan didn't go along. He didn't want to see his father lying on a pallet, out of his head and suffering. Instead, he stripped Sherry down and rubbed her back dry carefully. Then he got a split-cane basket and put his pony's evening feed in it. He held the basket in his hands in case Rayo and the mules came back, not to mention Blue Streak. Will might say that his horse didn't eat grain and didn't know grain when she smelled it; still, Dan was going to protect Sherry's supper.

But the pony was not quite finished when Will Mesteño came out. "Dan, you better come and watch all this."

"I have to take care of my pony."

"She is nearly through, and it won't hurt her to miss the last bite or so. I know, it fashes you to see your father sick and raving. But you better watch. If I bring that leg down and save Mr. Riker from being lame or even dead, you will owe the world one life and one leg."

"What?"

"Someday you may have a chance to set someone's leg, save a sick person's life. That will be one debt you won't take to your grave."

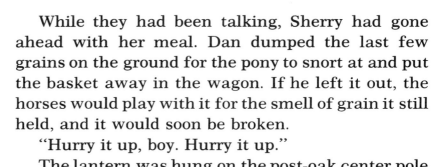

While they had been talking, Sherry had gone ahead with her meal. Dan dumped the last few grains on the ground for the pony to snort at and put the basket away in the wagon. If he left it out, the horses would play with it for the smell of grain it still held, and it would soon be broken.

"Hurry it up, boy. Hurry it up."

The lantern was hung on the post-oak center pole of the tent. It shone clearly on Mr. Riker, laid out on the low cot, rolling around. The straw with which the mattress was stuffed was not rustling; it had been packed down by the sick man's thrashing.

Mr. Riker's eyes were open, bright and staring, but seeing nothing. Dan gulped and felt his stomach drop and wanted to run and run. Will Mesteño's hand closed on Dan's upper arm and held him still. "Look at that leg, Dan, and don't forget it."

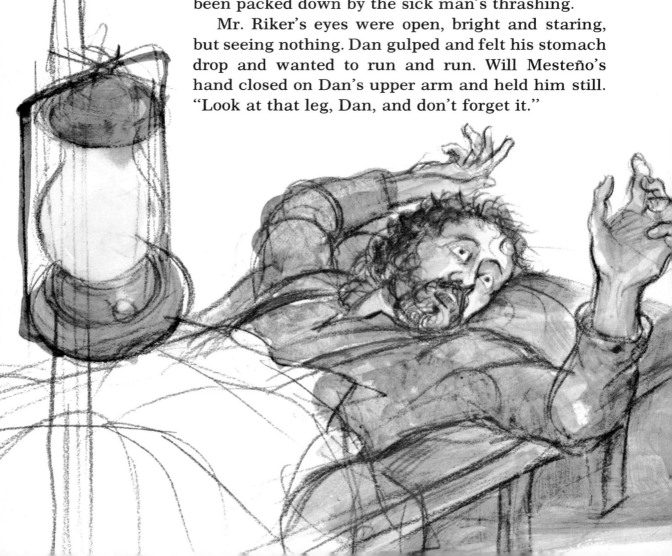

The leg was as big at the ankle as it was where it joined the man's body, a horrible sight. Dan gulped miserably.

"Now," Will said, "we're going to get that limb down to where my fingers can reach the break and feel it. You, Dan. First part is all yours."

Oh, no, Dan thought. I can't.

But the deep voice boomed, "Haul the coldest water you can get from the spring. Usually coldest is right in the middle. Fill two, three buckets. You understand, lad?"

"Yes, sir."

"Go."

As he ran out, almost pushed by the booming voice, he could hear Will say, "Mrs. Riker, I'll thank you for what white cloth you have. Sheets, towels, underwear, anything. If we had ice, none of this would b—"

Grabbing up a pair of buckets, Dan was sprinting for the water hole. He waded in, the sandy bottom firm under his boots, till he was in the center. Will was right; it was coldest there.

His boots squished noisily as he came back up to the camp. Will was kneeling by his saddle, unthonging a pair of pistol wallets from the pommel.

For the first time Dan noticed the peculiarity of that pommel; there was no horn. Many a man back in the South had ridden an old Army saddle, called a McClellan, but everyone in Texas had a horn to rope off.

Will said, "Rest that bucket and come on in the tent."

Dan followed him meekly enough.

Once in the light the mustanger opened the pistol wallets. But they didn't hold guns; instead, he took out a number of strange things: a lump of tar, a bottle that looked as if it held ordinary fire-blackened lumps of wood, another bottle that maybe held sulphur, and finally a leather package, which he unwrapped. There were strips of bark on it. "Cinchona bark," Mesteño Will said. "Some call it Priest's bark, or Peru wood. Mrs. Riker, if you will kindly put this much"—he held out some strips—"in a cup of boiling water, and leave it to stand until it is cold, I do believe it will aid in taking away your husband's heat. Now, Dan. You see this pile of white cloths? You are to take them out to those buckets you have

fetched, and you are to put the cloths in the cold water. When one is drenched clean through, take an end of it, wet as it is, and whirr it around your head, in the air, fast as fast can be. Understand?"

All Dan could say was, "Yes, sir." But he wondered if he had come back with a madman, a tetched-head, as the kids back in Tennessee had called them. Dan looked at his mother.

Mrs. Riker nodded. "Do what he says, Dan."

Dan shrugged and went out of the tent, glad to leave. But he felt like a fool as he put a pair of long drawers in a pail, took them out, and sent them whirling around his head as he held on by the ankles. The horses must have been hanging around on the edge of the firelight. As the flying drops of water spun into the night, there was the clatter of hoofs running away.

Mrs. Riker passed him on her way to the fire and the kettle of hot water. Dan stopped his idiotic work, and said, "Do I have to go on doing this?"

Mrs. Riker said, "I think that man knows what he's doing. I have heard of cinchona bark to take away fever, and he had some."

"But waving wet underwear around in the night?"

Mrs. Riker had mixed the bark and hot water in a mug, and she was shifting it from hand to hand as the heat came through the thick china. "I don't know. I only know that anything that helps your father isn't silly."

So Dan whirled. His mother took the cooling brew into the tent, and he was alone again, glad there was no one to see him making a dunce out of himself. A muslin sheet was soaking in the other basket, a shirt in the first one.

After what seemed a long time, Mesteño Will came out of the tent. "That ought to do for this piece," he said, and took the drawers from him. "Start something else going."

"Mind telling me why I'm doing what I'm doing?"

The mustanger said, "Cold. Knocking the water out of cloth makes it colder, for some reason or other. Since heat wouldn't bring the swelling down, cold may do it. I don't know anything else to try, and cold's worked on horses' legs."

So Dan whirled on, through the slowest passing of time he had ever known. His arms ached, and his back seemed about to break. Every little while Will

came out and put the cloth he had used in the bucket and took the one Dan had whirled and went into the tent. But he didn't say anything.

And then he came and said, "You can quit, Dan." His booming voice was high with something that hadn't been in it before. Hope?

Dan asked, "The swelling's down?"

"Coming down. And the night's cold enough now so's I can just hang the cloths up and they'll dry cold. You better get some sleep. I'll want you strong and ready when I do need you."

Dan carried the buckets nearer the tent door and went in. His father's eyes were closed, and his forehead wasn't much whiter than his cheeks. There was a moist and healthy look to his skin.

Mrs. Riker smiled and said, "The fever's broke, Dan."

"I see. Oh, Will, I—" But there wasn't anything to say.

The dark face looked up, grinning. "I told you to sleep now, boy." The mustanger's hand fell on Mr. Riker's broken leg and the shirt that wrapped it. "Bring me a fresh cloth before you go off to your bed." Will held out the shirt.

Dan could see his father's leg. It did indeed look smaller than it had when Dan and Mesteño Will had ridden into camp.

His mother was paying no attention to him. He went out and pulled his boots off and crawled into his bedroll without washing; he had had all the water he needed for a while.

It was still dark when a hand shook his shoulder, and a voice said, "Boy, the time has come upon us."

Dan sat up so suddenly he cracked his head on the bottom of the wagon bed. "Leg down?"

"Yes. And a man can see where it was misset. If you hadn't gotten help when you did, Dan, your father would be a crippled-up one the rest of his natural life."

Will went away. Dan pulled on his boots, ran his fingers through his matted hair, and stumbled toward the tent. His head felt wide awake, but his body acted as if it wanted to go right back to bed.

The coal-oil lantern had been turned up as high as it would go without smoking. Mr. Riker was wide awake and even managed to smile at Dan. "Son, you certainly picked the right man. Maybe the only right one in all of Texas."

Will chuckled and said, "You'll not be talking so favorable in a few minutes. I'm about to put a grievous hurt on you. Dan, you and your mother are to get down there at the foot of the cot. I surely wish I had something to give you, Mr. Riker. This is going to be an outrageous pain."

There was a leather strap, like a horse hobble, around the ankle of the broken leg. Thongs had been tied to it so that Dan and his mother could both get a hold on it.

Mesteño Will said, "Before we do this thing, I'd like Dan to feel the break, if that is agreeable, Mr. Riker?"

Mr. Riker said, "Sure."

"He may save someone else's leg in the years to come." Will took Dan's fingers and guided them to his father's shin. There was a sharp roughness under the still-hot flesh. "The bone below the break was jumped forward and is trying to creep up. When you are pulling good, I'll push down, like so, and the two pieces should come together."

Dan's mother's whole face was as white as his father's forehead had been in fever. She shut her eyes as she wrapped the rawhide thong around and around her palm, clasped her right hand with her left, and got ready to pull.

But Dan kept his eyes wide open as he took up the other handhold.

"Now," Will said. "With all your strength and weight and heart—*pull!*"

Dan flung himself backward, until all his body was leaning against the thong. Next to him, his mother, her eyes still closed, went back, too. He saw the leg lengthen and Will's hands come down on the break, and then he thought—but could never be sure—that he heard a click as the two pieces of bone came together.

In a moment Will was saying, "You can let go."

Dan opened his hands with difficulty. He had been pulling harder than he had known. Mrs. Riker opened her eyes. She said, "Oh, thank goodness he fainted."

Will was rewrapping the leg with the arrowweeds and torn undershirts. "Worst is over," he said. "I got a lot of faith in the future of that leg. Dan, you pulled like a mosshorn bull climbing out of a mudhole."

Mr. Riker opened his eyes. "When are you going to set the bone?"

Will chuckled. "It's all over."

"But I never felt a thing."

"That's happened before." Mesteño Will stared up at the lantern where it hung on the post. He took it down and blew the flame out. "No use wasting oil. I stitched up a man's liver one time—he had been gored by a range bull—and he talked to me all the time I was working. It's past understanding."

Day was on them. The east and south walls of the tent were turning gold, and Dan felt tired as he'd never felt in his life before.

Will said, "I'm surely glad that I could be of service to you."

"Great service," Mr. Riker said. "We'll never forget you."

The mustanger shrugged. "Anyone would have done it who could." Which wasn't true. "It's a lone, lonesome country here on the plains, and we got to help each other out."

Dan's mother said, "I'll get us all some breakfast."

"I'll be riding on, Mrs. Riker. Don't bother about me."

"Nonsense. We may be between homes, but nobody leaves this camp with an empty stomach."

The man laughed. "All right. You had better feed your husband here light and soft for a while. He's had a bad time."

"I'll do that," Mrs. Riker said. "Dan, you go wash yourself with soap and warm water, and comb your hair and brush your clothes. You're a perfect sight!"

Her words made Dan feel better. Things were back to normal.

More Stories of Then and Now

The Strange Voyage of Neptune's Car by Joe Lasker. Viking Press, 1977.
This story is based on the true adventures of Mary Patten, the first woman to command a clipper ship around Cape Horn.

Journey from Peppermint Street by Meindert De Jong. Harper & Row, 1968.
This book describes the excitement a Dutch boy feels on his first long trip away from home.

Growin' by Nikki Grimes. Dial, 1977.
This is a funny story about the friendship between a poet and a bully.

The Truth About Mary Rose by Marilyn Sachs. Doubleday, 1973.
When Mary Rose Ramirez's father becomes a successful artist, the family moves to New York City.

Jake by Alfred Slote. Lippincott, 1971.
Jake Wrather fights to find a way to keep his Little League baseball team together.

Something to Shout About by Patricia Beatty. Morrow, 1976.
Heather tells the story of how the women of Ottenburg raise the money to buy a new school.

High Elk's Treasure by Virginia Driving Hawk Sneve. Holiday, 1972.
Joe High Elk finds an old Sioux document that involves him in a hundred-year-old mystery.

Dragonwings by Laurence Yep. Harper & Row, 1975.
Moon Shadow leaves China to make a new home in San Francisco shortly before the earthquake of 1905.

How They Told It

How They Told It

Every country in the world has its own folktales. And these tales are more alike than different. Here are some old tales from different countries—and two modern stories that cleverly imitate the old ones.

The Oba Asks for a Mountain

by HAROLD COURLANDER
and EZEKIEL ADEROGBA ESHUGBAYI

It was long ago. There was an Oba, or powerful chief, in the land of the Yoruba. He was not known for any virtues but for his love of war. It came to his ears that the kingdom of Ilesha was rich and prosperous. He decided he would loot Ilesha of its wealth, but he had no excuse to make war. So he sent messengers to Ilesha with a demand for tribute. The messengers arrived. They said, "The great Oba has sent us. He demands that a certain thing be done. If it is not done, his soldiers will come. They will make war. That is all. What is your answer?"

The people said, "What is the thing that is to be done? We will do it. We do not want war."

The messengers said, "The Oba has heard of the fine vegetables that are grown here. He wants a great quantity of these vegetables brought to him by the next festival day. But there is one thing. They must not be wrinkled and dried. They must be as fresh as when they are just taken from the earth."

The people said, "We shall bring them." But when the messengers had departed, the people said, "How can the vegetables be fresh when it takes a person fifteen days to go from here to there? They will be wrinkled and dried, and the Oba will make war upon us."

100

There was a man among them named Agiri-Asasa. He listened thoughtfully to what they said. "There is a way this thing can be done," Agiri-Asasa said. "Bring many pots and bowls. Dig up the vegetables with the earth around them and transplant them into these vessels. In this fashion they can be carried to the Oba."

As he described it, so it was done. They dug up the vegetables, earth and all, and carried them in pots and bowls to the distant town where the Oba lived. There they took the vegetables from the earth and brought them to the Oba's house. He was perplexed, for the vegetables were fresh and sweet. He said nothing. He wondered what task he could give to the people of Ilesha that they could not perform, so that he would have an excuse for war.

The next morning as the people of Ilesha were preparing to leave, the Oba sent for them. He presented them with a thigh of beef, saying, "One thing more must be done if there is to be no war. This thigh of beef I entrust to you to keep for me. Return it to me on the third day before the yam harvest festival. But take care that it is returned to me as fresh as it is now. Do not allow it to become spoiled and moldy. Otherwise I shall send my soldiers to make war against Ilesha."

The people took the thigh of beef. They went out of the town. They talked. One said, "How can we do it? This meat will be spoiled before we reach home. It will soon be nothing but carrion." Another said, "Yes, it is so. The Oba means to destroy us."

Then Agiri-Asasa spoke, saying, "No, there is a way to deal with this matter. Let us take it with us a little way." So they took the thigh of beef and continued their journey. Even before the sun went down, they came to a place where a man was preparing to slaughter a bull. Agiri-Asasa said to him, "Do not hurry to slaughter the bull. Take this thigh of beef instead. We entrust it to your keeping. Three days before the yam festival we will come again. Slaughter your bull on that day and give us the thigh. Thus nothing will be lost, and it will save us from carrying this meat on the road." It was arranged.

On the third day before the festival, the people of Ilesha returned and received the thigh of the newly slaughtered bull. They carried it to the Oba, saying, "See, as you have directed, we return the beef thigh to you. It is as fresh as the day it was given to us." The Oba examined the meat. He was puzzled. He sent the people away.

He was angry. He determined to give Ilesha a task it could not perform. He sent messengers again to Ilesha. They stood in the marketplace and delivered the words of the Oba. "The great Oba has this to say. The people of Ilesha must bring him the mountain called Oke-Umo. Otherwise, he will be compelled to bring war to Ilesha." The people listened. They were worried. But they showed the messengers great respect. They gave them food and drink.

When the messengers slept, the people discussed the matter. Agiri-Asasa had a plan. He said, "When morning comes, let us go to the mountain called Oke-Umo." When day arrived, ten thousand men of Ilesha escorted the messengers to the mountain. Every man had a carrying pad on his head. They surrounded the mountain in a circle. Agiri-Asasa called out, "Now lift the mountain and rest it on your carrying pads!" The ten thousand men tugged at trees and rocks, but they could not lift the

mountain. At last Agiri-Asasa addressed the messengers this way: "Messengers of the great Oba, you see that we are willing to bring the mountain as the Oba has demanded. You see that we have ten thousand men ready to carry it. However, we cannot lift it. If the Oba will send his strongest men here to lift it onto our carrying pads, we will bring it to him without delay."

The messengers went home. They told the Oba. He listened. He said no more about the matter. He put Ilesha out of his mind.

Since that day, there has been a saying in Ilesha:

"There are people to carry the mountain,
But there is nobody to lift it."

Why the Sea Is Salt

by VIRGINIA HAVILAND

Once upon a time—but it was a long, long time ago—there were two brothers. One of them was rich, and one was poor.

On a winter evening, the poor one had not so much as a crumb in the house, either of meat or of bread. So he went to his brother to ask him for something to eat. It was not the first time he had called upon his rich brother for help, and since the rich one was stingy, the poor brother was not made very welcome.

The rich brother said, "If you will go away and never come back, I'll give you a whole side of bacon."

The poor brother, full of thanks, agreed to this.

"Well, here is the bacon," said the rich brother. "Now go straight away to the Land of Hunger."

The poor brother took the bacon and set off. He walked the whole day, and at dusk he came to a place where he saw a very bright light.

"Maybe this is the place," said he and turned aside. The first person he saw was an old, old man, with a long white beard, who was chopping wood for the fire.

"Good even," said the man with the bacon.

"The same to you. Where are you going so late in the day?" asked the man.

"Oh, I'm going to the Land of Hunger, if only I can find the right way."

"Well, you are not far wrong, for this is that land," said the old man. "When you go inside, everyone there will want to buy your bacon, for meat is scarce here. But mind you don't sell it unless you get for it the hand mill which stands behind the door. When you come out again, I'll teach you how to handle the mill. You will be able to make it grind almost anything."

The man with the bacon thanked the other for his good advice. Then he gave a great knock at the door.

When he had entered, everything happened just as the old man said it would. Everyone came swarming up to him like ants around an anthill. Each one tried to outbid the other for the bacon.

"Well," said the man, "by rights it is my wife and I who should have this bacon for dinner. However, since you have all set your hearts on it, I suppose I must let you have it. But if I do sell it, I must have in exchange that mill behind the door."

At first they wouldn't hear of such a bargain. They chaffered and they haggled with the man. But he stuck to his bargain, and at last they had to part with the mill.

The man now carried the mill out into the yard and asked the old woodcutter how to handle it. As soon as the old man had showed him how to make it grind, he thanked him, and hurried off home as fast as he could. But the clock had struck twelve before he reached his own door.

"Wherever in the world have you been?" complained his wife. "Here I have sat hour after hour waiting and watching, without so much as two sticks to lay together under the broth."

"Well," said the man, "I couldn't get back before because I had to go a long way—first for one thing, and then for another. But now you shall see what you shall see!"

Carefully he set the mill on the table. First of all, he ordered it to grind lights. Next he asked for a tablecloth, then for meat, then pie—and so on, till he and his wife had every kind of thing to help them have a good dinner. He had only to speak the word, and the mill would grind out anything he asked for. His wife stood by blessing her stars. She kept on asking where he had got this wonderful mill, but he wouldn't tell her.

"It's all one where I got it. You can see the mill is a good one. That's enough."

The man ground meat and drink and sweets enough to last for weeks. One day he asked all his friends and kin to his house and gave a great feast.

When the rich brother arrived and saw all that was on the table, and all that was stored behind in the larder, he grew spiteful and wild. He couldn't bear it that his brother should have anything. It made him shout: "It was only a few days ago that my brother was so poor he came and begged for a morsel of food! Now he gives a feast as if he were a count or a king!"

The rich man demanded of his brother, "How did you get all this wealth?"

"From behind the door," answered the new owner of the mill. He did not intend to give away his secret. But later on in the evening, when he was quite merry, he could keep his secret no longer. He brought out the mill and said, "There, you see what has given me all this wealth." And he made the mill grind all kinds of things.

When the rich brother beheld this, his heart was set on having the mill. And he got it, after much coaxing. But he had to pay three hundred dollars for it and leave it with his brother until hay harvest. His brother thought that if he kept it until then, he could make it grind meat and drink to last for years.

You may know that the mill did not grow rusty for lack of work to do.

When hay harvest came around, the rich brother got the mill, but the other took care not to teach him how to handle it.

It was evening when the rich brother took the mill home. Next morning he told his wife to go out into the field and toss hay. He would stay at home and get the dinner ready.

When dinnertime drew near, he put the mill on the kitchen table and ordered, "Grind herrings and broth, and grind them good and fast."

The mill began at once to grind the herrings and broth. First, they filled every dish in the house, then all the big tubs, and then they flowed all over the kitchen floor.

Madly, the man twisted and twirled at the mill to get it to stop. But for all this twisting and fingering, the mill went on grinding.

In a little while, the broth rose so high that the man was about to drown. He managed to throw open

the kitchen door and run into the parlor. But it wasn't long before the mill had ground the parlor full, too. It was at the risk of his life that the man reached the doorlatch through the stream of broth.

When he had managed to pull the door open, he ran out and off down the road. A stream of herrings and broth poured out at his heels, roaring like a waterfall over the whole farm.

His wife, who was still in the field tossing hay, began to think it a long time to dinner. At last she said:

"Well, even though the master hasn't called us home, we may as well go. Maybe he finds it hard work to boil the broth, and will be glad of my help."

The men were willing enough to go. But just as they had climbed a little way up the hill, what should

they meet but herrings and broth, all running, and dashing, and splashing together in a stream. The master himself was running ahead for his very life.

As he passed the workers, he bawled out:

"If only each of you could drink with a hundred throats! Take care you are not drowned in the broth."

Away he went, as fast as he could, to his brother's house. He begged him to take back the mill at once.

"If it grinds only one hour more, the whole parish will be swallowed up by herrings and broth."

But his brother wouldn't hear of taking it back until the other paid him three hundred dollars more.

So now the poor brother had both the money and the mill.

It wasn't long before he set up a farmhouse far finer than the one in which his brother lived. With the mill he ground so much gold that he covered the house with it.

Since the farm lay by the seaside, the golden house gleamed and glistened far away to ships at sea. All who sailed by put to shore to see the rich man in his golden house and to see the wonderful mill. Its fame spread far and wide, till there was nobody who hadn't heard tell of it.

One day a skipper sailed in to see the mill. The first thing he asked was whether it could grind salt.

"Grind salt!" said the owner. "I should think it could. It can grind anything."

When the skipper heard that, he said he must have the mill, cost what it would. If only he had it, he thought, he would no longer have to take long voyages across stormy seas for a cargo of salt.

At first the man wouldn't hear of parting with his mill. But the skipper begged so hard that at last he let him have it. However, the skipper had to pay a great deal of money for it.

When the skipper had the mill on his back, he went off with it at once. He was afraid the man would change his mind, so he took no time to ask how to handle the mill. He got on board his ship as fast as he could, and set sail.

When the skipper had sailed a good way off, he brought the mill up on deck and said:

"Grind salt, and grind both good and fast."

Well, the mill began to grind salt so that it poured out like water.

When the skipper had filled the ship, he wished to stop the mill. But whichever way he turned it, and however much he tried, it was no good. The mill kept grinding on, and the heap of salt grew higher and higher. At last it sank the ship.

Now the mill lies at the bottom of the sea. It grinds away to this very day, and that is why the sea is salt.

The Sleeper

by RUTH MANNING-SANDERS

Once upon a time there lived in Ireland a poor widow who had three daughters. The two elder were vain and selfish. But the youngest was a brave, kind little maiden, called Bridget.

One day the eldest girl said, "Mother, bake me a cake, for I'm off to seek my fortune."

So the widow baked a cake. And when it was ready she said to the girl, "Which will you have — half the cake with my blessing, or the whole cake without my blessing?"

"Sakes alive! What do you take me for?" says the girl. "The whole cake of course! And that's little enough."

Well, the girl gets the whole of the cake, and off she goes, walking, walking. And by and by she's tired and hungry. She sits down by the wayside to eat her cake. And there comes an old beggar woman, holding out her hand and asking for a bite.

"Be off with you," says the girl. "It's scarce enough I have for myself." Surprised she is indeed when the old beggar woman vanishes.

After a bit, on goes the girl, walking, walking. She comes at twilight to a fine great house. She knocks at the door, *rat tat*, asking for lodging.

"Yes," says the noble lady of the house, "you shall have lodging and more than lodging. You shall have a spadeful of gold and a shovelful of silver, if you'll sit this night and watch by my son's bed. He lies under an evil spell. He sleeps and sleeps. But wake he must, one time or another time. And when he wakes there's something to do for him that only a brave, kind heart can do.''

You're sure the girl would have done more than sit up all night for a spadeful of gold and a shovelful of silver! So she agreed to watch. The noble lady took her to a room where a young lord lay sleeping. The young lord was handsome as you please. The bed he lay on was none other than gold, with covers of silk and satin. There was a fire in the room and a chair by the fire. There was a table by the chair with two silver dishes on it—nuts in one dish, apples in the other. And on a mat in front of the fire, a little brown dog and a little white cat were playing together. So the girl sat down on the chair by the fire. And the noble lady went away and left her to her watching.

Well, the time passed. The girl ate an apple or two. She cracked some nuts. And she pushed the little dog and smacked the little cat when they came too near her feet in their playing. A clock on the wall went *tick-tock, tick-tock*. It was as much as the girl could do to keep her eyes open after her long walk and all. But keep them open she did. She thought of that spadeful of gold and that shovelful of silver. She planned what she would do with the gold and silver. Now and then she cast a sidelong look on the young lord. He slept and slept and never stirred, till the clock on the wall struck midnight. And then, all of a sudden, the young lord opened his eyes. He got up from the bed and came to stand at the side of the girl.

"All alone, fair maid?" said he.

I tell you, the girl was so frightened she couldn't say a word. There was something wild and strange in the young lord's look that fair took her breath away. She got a grip of the chair with her one hand, and put the other hand before her face, and sat and shivered.

"All alone, fair maid?" said he again.

And again she didn't answer.

"All alone, fair maid?" says he for the third time.

No, she didn't answer even then. But she just peeked at him from under her hand, and—my word—his look was so grim and ghostlike. She made a jump to run out of the room. But he gave her a tap with a cane that was leaning against the bedhead, and she turned into a grey flagstone, and sank down into the floor.

Well now, a week or two later, the widow's second daughter said she also would away to seek her fortune. So she told her mother to bake her a cake. Rather than take half the cake with her mother's blessing, she took the whole cake without a blessing. And she set off walking

on a fine bright morning. And, not to weary you, it happened to this girl as it had happened to the other girl. The second had no more manners and no more sense than the first. She also ended up as a grey flagstone on the young lord's bedroom floor.

Now there's only the youngest girl, Bridget, left at home. And Bridget thinks she'd best be off and see what's become of her sisters. So she asks her mother to bake her a cake for the journey. And when her mother says, "Will you have half the cake with my blessing, or the whole cake without it?" Bridget answers, "Your blessing first, and whatever you choose to give me after it. For without your blessing, little mother, I won't set foot out of the house."

So she gets her mother's blessing and half the cake, and off she goes, walking, walking. By and by she sits down by the wayside to rest a bit and eat her cake. Then comes the old beggar woman, crying that she's hungry, and asking for a bite.

Bridget laughs and says, "It's lucky you came when you did then. Five minutes more and I'd have eaten every crumb! But now—take what's left."

And she gave the old woman what she had left of the cake, and that was the biggest half of the half. The old woman gobbled it up. She smacked her lips, and chuckled a bit, and said, "Now you go your way, dearie, and I go mine. But maybe we shall meet again. And in the meantime—here's a bit of advice for you to be going on with:

> *Answer when you're spoken to,*
> *Do what you are dared to do;*
> *Once on the track,*
> *Never turn back.*

And should you find yourself in a fix, and not know which way to turn to help yourself—maybe that will be the very moment when a woman may thank you for the cake. And don't you believe," says she, wagging a finger at Bridget, "that a woman doesn't know what she's talking about."

Then, before Bridget had time to say anything, the old woman vanished. Bridget got up and walked on, feeling a bit scared and yet proud. She knew now that she'd met with a fairy. And that's something that doesn't happen to anybody very often.

On with her then, walking, walking, and coming at evening to the same fine great house. She knocks at the door, *rat tat*, and asks if she might do some service for a night's lodging. She is told, just as her sisters had been told, that she would get a spadeful of gold and a shovelful of silver if she'd watch in the young lord's room for the night.

So now there's Bridget, seated like her sisters before her, by the fire in the young lord's room. The apples and the nuts are in two silver dishes on the table by her side. The cat and the dog are playing together on the mat. And the clock on the wall is going *tick-tock, tick-tock*. The young lord is fast asleep under the silken covers on the golden bed.

Tick-tock, tick-tock: Bridget helped herself to an apple and cracked a nut or two. *Tick-tock, tick-tock*: she patted the little dog. She stroked the little cat. *Tick-tock, tick-tock*: she glanced round at the sleeper on the bed, and thought how very handsome he was. She pitied him with all her heart for being under a spell, and wondered what, if anything, would wake him. *Tick-tock, tick-tock*. Now the clock struck midnight. All of a sudden the young lord opened his eyes, got up from the bed, and came to stand at Bridget's side.

"All alone, fair maid?"

It's no use to say Bridget wasn't scared, because she was. But she remembered the advice of the old fairy, "*Answer when you're spoken to*," and she spoke up bravely:

> "*All alone I am not.*
> *I've a little dog, Bounce, and Kitty, my cat.*
> *I've apples to roast, and nuts to crack.*
> *And all alone I am not.*"

"Ho, ho!" says the young lord. "You're a brave lass. But not brave enough, I'll warrant, to follow me! I am now going to cross the *Quaking Bog* and go through the

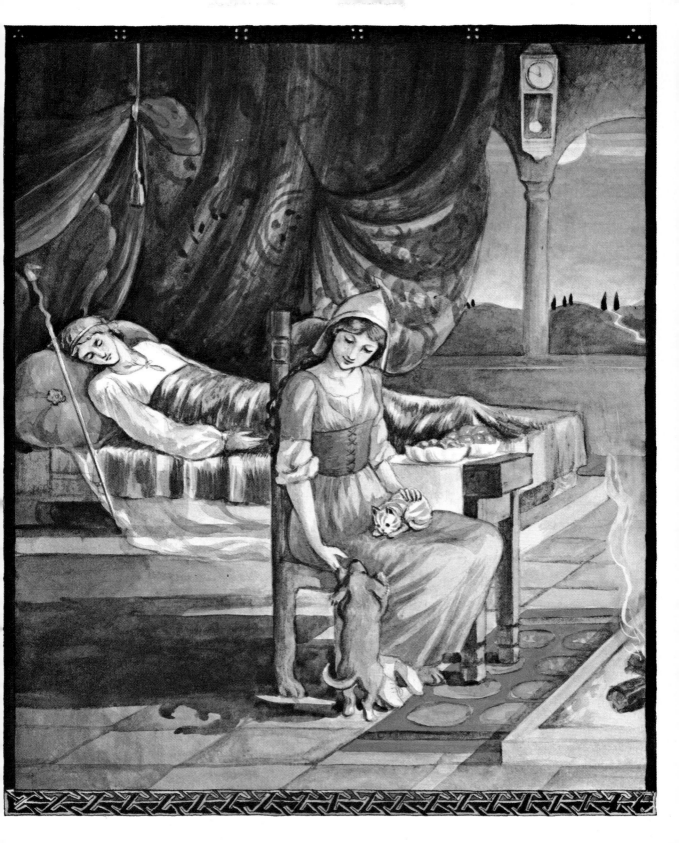

Burning Forest. I must then enter the *Cave of Terror* and climb the *Mountain of Glass*. Ah, and drop from the top of that mountain into the *Dead Sea*. And through all these perils I dare you to follow me," says he. He gave her such a wild look out of his shining eyes as made her heart beat faster than it should. But she remembered the old fairy's advice, "*Do what you are dared to do,*" and she answered, "I'm here to watch over you. So I must go where you go."

But scared and more than scared she was when he gave her a scowling look and sprang out of the window. All the same, she sprang out after him. Away they went, he kind of gliding and she scampering, over fields and through woods. At last they came to a range of great hills that shone green in the moonlight.

Then said he, "Open, open, Green Hills. Let the light of the Green Hills through!"

"Yes," says Bridget, "and let me follow, too."

And the Green Hills opened, and they both went through. And now they were standing on the edge of a great bog with no way round it.

The young lord stepped onto the shaky bits of moss and sod. He went walking over them as if he had no weight at all. And there was Bridget at a stand, looking after him and wondering however she was to get across. All of a sudden the old fairy was at her side. The old fairy touched Bridget's shoes with her stick, and they widened out like boats.

"Now off with you," says the old fairy, giving Bridget a poke in the back.

So off went Bridget, between a slide and a bounce over the bog, easy as you please. And when she got to the other side, her shoes shrank to their proper size again. Then she caught sight of the young lord just entering a forest. But, oh dear me, the trees of that forest were all on fire. The smoke and the flames were being carried by the wind to coil about Bridget's head. And what to do now, she couldn't think. But suddenly a thick damp cloth was dropped over her head, and the old fairy's voice was in her ear:

"Once on the track,
Never turn back."

So through the flames Bridget went. Never a hair of her head was singed.

Now then she was safe through the *Burning Forest*. But she hadn't yet done more than half of the things that she must do if she was to keep the young lord in sight. Beyond the *Burning Forest* was the *Cave of Terror*. The young lord went into that cave with Bridget after him.

I tell you, that cave was echoing with such screams and yells and roarings and howlings as would have deafened the girl for life, if the old fairy hadn't stopped up her ears with wax. So then she was spared the sounds. But she still had to endure the sights. Faces of demons grinned out of a curl of blue smoke. Giant hands moved about with no arms nor bodies fast to them. Fiery serpents went gliding through the air as if they were on firm ground. Swords clashed round her head. And monstrous jaws with snapping teeth appeared on the cave floor just where she was going to tread. Indeed, her heart all but failed her. But since now to turn back would be as bad as to go on, go on she did.

At last she came out through that *Cave of Terror* into moonlight.

There now, shining silver in the moonlight, rose the *Mountain of Glass*, with sides as steep as a house wall. The young lord was going up the mountain like a fly on a window pane. But when Bridget sought to follow him, it was one step forward and two back. She slipped and slid and landed at the bottom again in a heap. So then came the old fairy and gave Bridget's shoe soles a tap with her stick. She made those shoe soles so sticky that Bridget got from the bottom to the top of the mountain almost as easily as the young lord himself.

So there they were, standing side by side on the mountain peak. Half a mile below them was a deep, dark sea. The young lord turned to Bridget and said, "Go home to my lady mother. Tell her how far you came at her bidding. Now farewell!" And with that he gave a spring, and down with him, head first, into the sea.

Well, what do you think? Bridget gave a leap after him. That is more than I would have done, or perhaps you. But she was all worked up to dare anything. And the

next thing she knew, she was going down, down, down through clear green water, until *bump*, there she was, below the sea, sitting in a beautiful meadow, with the young lord sitting beside her.

And the sea was like a green sky above them. She would have spoken then, but he held up a finger and said "Hush!" So she stayed quiet. And by and by she fell asleep.

How long she slept I can't tell you; but when she woke she was back in the noble lady's fine great house. She was lying in bed. The lady and the young lord were sitting beside her. The noble lady was thanking her with tears running down her cheeks. She told her what a brave girl she was, and how the spell was now broken, and how the young lord was only waiting his chance to marry her — that is, if Bridget was agreeable.

But Bridget said that first of all she must find her sisters, because that is what she had left home to do. So now, if she might crave a little food to carry with her, she would set out on her journey again. When she had found her sisters it would be time enough to think about marrying.

The young lord laughed. He told her that her journey should be a very short one. And he took her into the room with the golden bed, where she had sat and watched over him. Then with his cane he struck the two grey flagstones, and they rose up from the floor and turned into the two sisters. They began shouting and scolding. They said that it was an unfair job. They'd been badly treated. But the young lord only laughed the more. So then the noble lady said they should have their rewards, though they hadn't really earned them. She gave them each a spadeful of gold and a shovelful of silver. Then she sent them home.

But Bridget stayed in the noble lady's house, to prepare for her wedding with the young lord.

Her sisters sulked and wouldn't come to the wedding. But Bridget's mother came. And so did the fairy, not in the guise of an old beggar woman now, but all beautiful and shining.

The noble lady took Bridget's mother to live with her in the fine great house. The fairy gave Bridget and the young lord her blessing. She promised that they should live happily ever after.

They did live happily. May we live happily also!

The Mice That Ate Iron

by KATHERINE EVANS

Pablo lived in a fishing village on the coast of Spain.

Pablo's father had been a fisherman. When he died, he left all that he had to his son.

He left Pablo his sturdy fishing boat and his nets as fine as lace. And he left a big iron anchor.

But Pablo was a carefree young man. He played and sang all day.

At night he danced. He had no time to fish.

After a while, Pablo had nothing of what his father had left him—nothing, that is, but the big iron anchor.

And so Pablo left the fishing village and went to another country to make his living.

The big iron anchor was too heavy for Pablo to carry. And what good was it to him anyway?

Pablo took the anchor to his friend Antonio, the innkeeper, and asked him to keep it until his return.

Pablo was gone for a long time. Indeed, Antonio began to think that his friend Pablo would never return.

So one day he sold the big iron anchor to the captain of a sailing ship.

As time went by, Antonio spent the money and forgot about the anchor that had belonged to his friend Pablo.

131

One spring day Antonio stood at the door of his inn enjoying the blue sea and the fishing boats dancing on the waves.

All at once, whom should he see but his old friend!

There was Pablo, tired and dusty, coming down the road from Granada. Over his shoulder he carried his concertina and a trunk.

"Hello, friend Antonio," said Pablo, putting an arm over Antonio's shoulder. "It has been a long time since I left. I have walked far, but at last I have returned to my old home."

"Welcome home, Pablo," said Antonio. "Sit down, and I will bring you something." He helped Pablo put down the trunk and lay aside his concertina.

Off Antonio rushed. He thought to himself, "What shall I tell Pablo about the iron anchor he left with me?" Then he thought of a clever plan.

As Antonio returned, Pablo said, "What a lazy fellow I was—but no longer! I have worked hard all this time. Now I have money to buy a boat and nets. I shall be a fisherman as my father was. And so now I will take my anchor."

Antonio was ready. He made a sad face and said, "Ah, Pablo, the anchor has been eaten by mice. The iron from which it was made was particularly sweet, and so the mice ate it."

"It is a misfortune to me," said Pablo. "It was all I had left. But I know that mice love iron. I have heard of this happening."

Antonio was glad to hear Pablo say this. His plan was working well.

Pablo finished and stood up with a sigh, saying, "Dear friend, could you lend me your burro to carry

my trunk and concertina up the hill to the cottage of my friend? I have been a long time on the road, and my load is heavy."

"Yes, yes indeed," said Antonio, for he did not want Pablo to doubt his friendship. He helped Pablo tie his trunk and concertina on the burro.

Then he watched him set off up the hill.

A few days later Pablo again stopped to see his friend Antonio.

"Where is that burro of mine?" asked Antonio.

"Oh," said Pablo, "let me tell you. A strange thing happened. A big eagle swooped down and carried him off."

Antonio flew into a rage. "That's impossible," he cried. "You have sold my burro and kept the money."

People of the town heard the friends and stopped to watch the quarrel. "I demand that you go with me to the mayor," said Antonio.

Pablo agreed.

Antonio's face was red with rage. Pablo remained calm as he told his story.

"This is impossible," said the mayor. "How could an eagle carry off a burro?"

Pablo answered, "In a country where a large anchor was eaten by mice, an eagle might easily carry off an elephant."

The mayor asked more questions. When he had the whole story, he said, "He who plays a trick must be prepared to take a joke."

And so the mayor decreed that Antonio should buy back the anchor and return it to Pablo.

Pablo, for his part, was to return the burro to Antonio.

The Seeing Stick

by JANE YOLEN

Once in the ancient walled citadel of Peking, there lived an emperor who had only one daughter and her name was Hwei Ming.

Hwei Ming had long black hair smoothed back with ivory combs. She had tiny feet encased in embroidered slippers. And she had small slim fingers covered with jade rings.

But rather than making her happy, such possessions made her sad. For Hwei Ming was blind, and all the beautiful handcrafted things in the kingdom brought her no pleasure at all.

Her father was also sad that his only daughter was blind, but he could not cry for her. He had given up weeping when he ascended the throne. Yet still he had hope that one day Hwei Ming might see. So he resolved that anyone who could help her would be rewarded with a fortune in jewels, and he sent word of his offer to the Inner and Outer Cities of Peking and to all the towns and villages for hundreds of miles around.

Monks came with their prayers and prayer wheels, for they thought in this way to help Hwei Ming see. Magician-priests came with their incantations and spells, for

they thought in this way to help Hwei Ming see. Physi-
cians came with their potions and pins, for they thought
in this way to help Hwei Ming see.

But nothing helped. Hwei Ming had been blind from
the day of her birth, and no one could cure her.

Now one day an old man, his clothes tattered from his
travel, stopped by the gates of the Outer City. Far away in
the south country where he lived, he had heard tales of
the blind princess and of the emperor's offer. And so he
had taken his few possessions—a long walking stick,
made from a single shoot of golden wood, and his whittling knife—and started down the road.

The sun rose hot on his right side, and the sun set cool
on his left as he made his way north to Peking to help the
princess see.

The guards at the gate of the Outer City did not want to let in such a ragged old man. "Grandfather, go home. There is nothing here for such as you," they said.

The old man touched each of their faces in turn with his rough fingers. "So young," he said, "and already so old." He turned as if to go.

Ashamed that they had been unkind to an old man, the guards stared at the ground and shifted their feet uneasily.

The old man smiled to himself at their distress and turned back. Then he propped his walking stick against his side and reached into his shirt for his whittling knife.

"What are you doing, Grandfather?" called out one of the guards.

"I am going to show you my stick," said the old man. "For it is a stick that sees."

"Grandfather, that is nonsense," said the second guard. "That stick can see no more than the emperor's daughter. And she, poor child, has been blind from birth."

"Just so, just so," said the old man, nodding his head. "Still, it is a stick that sees."

"Indeed, Grandfather," said the second guard, "to repeat nonsense does not turn it into sense. You might as well say that the princess has eyes in her fingers."

"Just so, just so," said the old man. "But stranger things have happened." And so saying, he picked up the stick and told the guards how he had walked the many miles through villages and towns till he came with his seeing stick to the walls of Peking. As he told his tale, he carved pictures into the stick: an old man, the two guards, the walls of Peking.

The two guards watched in amazement. They were flattered by their likenesses in the golden wood of the old

man's stick. Indeed, they had never witnessed such skill. "Surely this is something the guards at the wall of the Inner City should see," they said. So, taking the old man by the arm, they guided him through the streets of the Outer City, past flower peddlers and rice sellers, past silk weavers and jewel merchants, up to the great stone walls.

When the guards of the Inner City saw the story stick, they were surprised and delighted. "Carve our faces, too," they begged like children. Laughing and touching their faces as any fond grandfather would, the old man did as they bid.

In no time at all, the guards of the Inner City took the old man by the arm and led him to the wall of the Imperial City and through the gate to the great wooden doors of the emperor's palace.

Now when the guards and the old man entered the throne room of the palace, it happened that the emperor's blind daughter, Hwei Ming, was sitting by his side—silent, sightless, and still. She listened as the guards told of the wonderful pictures carved on the golden shoot. When they finished, the princess clapped her hands. "Oh, I wish I could see that wondrous shoot," she said.

"Just so, just so," said the old man. "I will show it to you. For it is no ordinary stick, but a stick that sees."

"What nonsense," said her father in a voice so low it was almost a growl.

But the princess did not hear him. She had already bent toward the sound of the old man's voice. "A seeing stick?"

The old man did not say anything for a moment. Then he leaned forward and touched Hwei Ming's head and cheek. For though she was a princess, she was still a child. The old man smiled, reached into his shirt, and pulled out his knife.

Then, with the stick in one hand and his knife in the other, he began again to tell the story of his long journey to Peking. As he introduced each character and object, he carved a face and figure into the shoot. And as he finished each one, the old man took Hwei Ming's small fingers in his and placed them on the shoot. Finger on finger he helped her trace the likenesses.

"Feel the long flowing hair of the princess," the old man said. "Grown as she herself has grown, straight and true."

And Hwei Ming touched the carved shoot.

"Now feel your own long hair," he said.

And she did.

"Feel the lines in the old man's face," he said. "Years of worry and years of joy." He put the stick into her hands again.

And Hwei Ming's slim fingers felt the carved shoot.

Then he put her fingers onto his face and traced the same lines there. It was the first time the princess had touched another person's face since she was a very small girl.

The princess jumped up from her throne and thrust her hands before her. "Guards, guards," she cried out. "Come here to me."

And the guards lifted their faces to the Princess Hwei Ming's hands. Her fingers, like little breezes, brushed their eyes and noses and mouths, and then found each face on the seeing stick.

Hwei Ming turned to her father, the emperor, who sat straight and tall and unmoving on his great throne. She reached out, and her fingers ran eagerly through his hair, down his nose and cheek, and rested curiously on a tear they found there. And that was strange, indeed, for had not the emperor given up crying when he ascended the throne?

They brought her through the streets of the city, then, the emperor himself leading the procession. And Princess Hwei Ming touched men and women and children as they passed. Till at last she stood before the walls of Peking and felt the great stones themselves.

Then she turned to the old man, her voice bright and full of laughter. "Tell me another tale," she said.

"Tomorrow, if you wish," he replied,

For each tomorrow as long as he lived, the old man dwelt in the Innermost City. The emperor rewarded him with a fortune in jewels, but the old man gave them all away. Every day he told the princess a story. Some were as ancient as the city itself. Some were as new as the events of the day. And each time he carved wonderful images onto a shoot of golden wood.

As the princess listened, she grew eyes on the tips of her fingers — at least that is what she told the other blind children whom she taught to see as she saw, with her hands. Certainly it was as true as saying she had a seeing stick.

But the blind princess Hwei Ming believed that both things were true.

And so did all the blind children in her city of Peking.

And so did the blind old man.

Fareedah's Carpet

by JEAN RUSSELL LARSON

West of the mighty river Tigris, in the fragrant garden which was ancient Persia, dwelled a wealthy farmer and his family. The youngest daughter of the household was called Fareedah.

"Look after the sheep, daughter," said Fareedah's mother one day.

Fareedah sauntered along behind the flock, fixed her gaze on the far horizon, and allowed the sheep to wander dangerously close to the edge of a steep cliff.

"Stop," cried her mother, running to lead the sheep to safer ground. "I cannot trust you to do the job well so I shall do it myself."

That was exactly the result which Fareedah had desired and she went to lie in the shade of a fig tree. In fact the girl had cunningly avoided all work for many years.

But Fareedah's mother was not easily discouraged.

"Come and help me thresh the grain, Fareedah," she said only a few days later.

So Fareedah went and sat down on the ground beside her mother.

"Shake this back and forth," said the good woman, handing Fareedah a large sieve full of wheat. "The grain will fall through onto the mat and the chaff will be left behind."

"Yes, Mother," said Fareedah, smiling sweetly. Then she joggled and jounced the sieve so vigorously that the golden grain flew in all directions.

"Never mind," sighed her mother. "You will waste more than you save. I shall do it myself."

Fareedah, still smiling, went to lounge beneath the lilac bushes.

For some time Fareedah's mother considered how she might overcome her daughter's distaste for work. At length she settled upon a plan and called Fareedah to her.

"I have had a curtained pavilion set up in the garden. In that pavilion I have placed a large loom and weaving materials. You will retire to the pavilion and remain there until you have completed a large carpet."

Fareedah scowled. Try as she would, she could think of no way of escaping the task her mother had set.

"You have seen me working at the loom," said Fareedah's mother, conducting the girl to the pavilion. "Simply do as you have seen me do and all will be well."

"Yes, Mother," said Fareedah crossly.

Sitting down upon the mat, she glowered at the huge
loom.

"Begin work now," instructed Fareedah's mother.
"Meals will be brought to you and you may sleep here on
the mat. When the carpet is finished you may rejoin the
family and receive our praises."

Whereupon the good woman went out of the pavilion,
leaving lazy Fareedah alone with the loom.

If there were a way to avoid weaving the carpet,
Fareedah could not think of it, though she scratched her
head and pursed her lips tight. At last, resigned to
her fate, the girl began to work.

"Good morning," a voice behind Fareedah suddenly
thundered.

She turned to see a large camel looking in through
the curtains.

"Who spoke?" demanded Fareedah.

"It was I," said the camel. "Do you see anyone else
here?"

"Camels cannot speak!" declared Fareedah impatiently.

The camel rolled his big eyes skyward and sighed.

"Then why are you talking to one?" he asked.

"You need not be rude," Fareedah snapped. "I only
meant to say that I had never heard a camel talk, so I did
not believe such a thing could happen."

The camel shrugged.

"I have been told," he said, "that there is a land where
the ground is covered with ice and snow all year round. I

myself have never seen such a place, but I will not deny the possibility."

"I see what you mean," said Fareedah. "However I have no time for talking camels and idle conversations. I must work."

At the word *work* the girl made such a sad face that the camel laughed.

"This is no laughing matter!" Fareedah cried, jumping up and facing the camel angrily. "I long to wander the hillsides, plucking flowers and resting in the shade of tall trees. Instead I must remain here in this terrible place until I have completed a carpet."

Sinking down upon the mat once more, she rested her chin in her hands.

"That," she sighed mournfully, "may take forever."

The camel brushed the curtains aside and moved into the pavilion.

"Would you like me to weave the carpet for you?" he asked.

Fareedah stared at him.

"That is the silliest thing I ever heard," she said. "Camels do not weave carpets."

The camel rolled his great eyes again.

"You told me that camels do not talk," he said. "Yet we are having the pleasantest of conversations, you and I."

"That is true," Fareedah admitted. "But how could you weave a carpet? It seems quite impossible."

"Let me show you," said the camel.

Taking the brightly colored threads in his mouth, he began, in a most wondrous manner, to weave them in and out among the threads which Fareedah had hung on the loom. Before the girl's startled eyes a beautiful design began to take shape.

"How marvelous this is!" Fareedah clapped her hands for joy. "Will you weave the entire carpet for me?"

"Yes, the entire carpet," the camel assured her, dropping the threads from his mouth.

"Oh," squealed Fareedah, dancing around, "how can I ever repay you?"

The camel seemed to consider for a moment.

"Well," he said at last, "it seems only fitting that you should make me comfortable while I work."

"Yes," agreed Fareedah, "that is right and proper. Simply tell me your needs and I will fly to your service!"

"Very well," said the camel, "it is a bargain. First I shall need a place to sleep."

"But," Fareedah inquired, "won't you sleep outside, as camels always do?"

The camel stared at her coldly.

"What?" he asked. "Sleep outdoors and risk getting a chill? The nights are cold; and if I should become ill, then you would need to finish the carpet."

"Oh," Fareedah replied hastily, "in that case you may sleep here and I will sleep outside."

She bustled about, smoothing the large mat and plumping the scarlet cushions.

"That will do nicely," said the camel.

"Now you will begin work?" asked Fareedah.

"Yes," the camel replied, "and while I work you may fetch me a drink. I have had no water for several days and I am thirsty."

"I shall go at once," said Fareedah.

Slipping from the pavilion, she crept along behind the shrubbery which edged the garden. At length she reached the well. She found a jar there, filled it with water, and then returned the way she had come.

"Refreshing," declared the camel when he had finished drinking. "I should like more."

"Very well," said Fareedah, and went to refill the jar.

"Tasty water," the camel remarked when he had finished the second jarful. "I should like more."

151

Fareedah stared at him in surprise. How could he drink yet another jarful? Where was he putting all that water?

Once again Fareedah went to the well. The sun was hot and the water jar, which had been no burden on the first two trips, seemed exceedingly heavy. Fareedah set it down and mopped her brow with a corner of her veil. Surely this would be the last trip.

But it was not. Three times more the camel demanded water, and three times more poor Fareedah returned to the well to fill the jar.

When the camel had drunk his fill, Fareedah sank down upon the mat at his feet and sighed heavily. How her arms ached. She was also very hungry and was pleased to hear, at just that moment, a servant approaching through the garden.

"I bring your meal," he announced.

"I am ready for it," called Fareedah, leaping up and going to meet him.

Taking the silver platter from his hands, she went back into the pavilion and sat down once more upon the mat.

"This looks delicious!" she said happily.

The camel dropped the threads from his mouth and turned to look at the platter.

"Yes," he agreed, "it does. Move aside and let me dine."

"You?" cried Fareedah. "This is for me!"

The camel sniffed.

"I am doing the work here," he said. "Therefore I need nourishment. You are not thinking of breaking our bargain?"

"Oh no," Fareedah assured him, "you are most welcome to the food."

"That's better," said the camel.

"I—I was only wondering," stammered Fareedah, "what I shall eat."

"That," replied the camel, "is entirely your affair and no concern of mine!" And having spoken, he fell to eating.

Remembering an apple tree which grew nearby, Fareedah left the pavilion and crept quietly along behind the shrubbery. When she reached the tree she caught a low-hanging bough in her hands and swung herself up to the branches. The finest fruit was near the top of the tree, so Fareedah inched her way higher. Suddenly the branch on which she was standing gave way, causing her to plunge to the ground, bumping her head. For an instant she was senseless. Then, rubbing her head, she rose unsteadily and picked up an apple which had fallen to the ground with her. It was bruised, but better than nothing. Munching the apple, she made her way slowly back to the pavilion.

In the pavilion the camel was busy creating a carpet

of brilliant colors. There were crimson blossoms, purple plums and grapes, and golden grains. There were strange, beautiful patterns which seemed to shift and sway before the eyes. When she saw it, Fareedah was encouraged. What a lot of work it must require, and how fortunate that she did not have to do it!

As the camel had eaten the noon meal, so did he consume the evening meal, causing Fareedah to retire with an empty stomach, for she did not relish another fall from the apple tree.

As had been agreed, the camel slept within the pavilion while poor Fareedah huddled outside, rubbing her hands to warm them. Stars glittered like chips of ice in the velvety black sky, and a chill wind blew.

"There is this much about it," Fareedah reasoned, comforting herself, "at least I do not have to weave that carpet!"

Days passed, each one much like the one before. The carpet increased, and so did the demands of the camel.

"I feel the need of a stiff brushing," he said one morning.

Fareedah obligingly took up a brush and began to stroke him. The camel sank lazily down upon the mat and hummed a happy tune.

"Behind the ears," he directed. "Harder, if you please!"

Fareedah stood for hours, brushing and grooming the camel until her arms ached. The animal so enjoyed the brushing that it became a part of the daily routine. The camel looked forward to it, but lazy Fareedah did not.

Each day, too, the camel required Fareedah to cool him. The heat of the day, he declared, took his strength, and he could accomplish much more if she would stand at his side and wave a large fan. So Fareedah wagged the fan back and forth for hours on end while the camel plied the brightly colored threads.

"Faster!" he would urge from time to time, putting down the threads. Though he rested often, Fareedah was not allowed to stop fanning.

The camel continued to eat all of the food which came into the pavilion. In addition to that, he had developed an almost unquenchable thirst. When the unfortunate Fareedah was not waving the fan, she was making trip after trip to the well for the cool water which the beast demanded.

Though the nights were as cold as ever, Fareedah no longer slept outside the tent.

"Each night as I sleep," said the camel one day, "the coverlet slides off my back, and I fear I shall become chilled."

"That is too bad," Fareedah murmured.

"I knew you would think so," said the camel. "I know, too, that you will want to help me, so henceforth you must stand at my side each night and replace the coverlet when it slips from me."

So poor Fareedah did as she was told, comforting herself with the thought that at least she did not have to weave the carpet.

At last the carpet was finished.

"It is the most beautiful carpet I have ever seen!" cried Fareedah, joyfully.

"It is rather nice," agreed the camel. "In fact, I don't know when I have seen a finer one."

"I will go and get my mother now," said Fareedah. "If you stand just outside, you will be able to hear what she says about the carpet."

Fareedah went to fetch her mother, and that good woman praised the carpet, marveling at its patterns and

colors. Then, summoning two servants, she ordered them to carry the carpet from the pavilion.

"Thank you for helping me," said Fareedah to the camel as she watched her mother and the servants go across the garden toward the house. "I believe my mother liked the carpet, don't you think so?"

"Yes," said the camel. "I think she did. But we can discuss that matter at length this evening when you bring me water."

"Bring you water!" cried Fareedah. "Why should I do that? The carpet is finished, and so is our bargain. What reason could I possibly have for bringing you water?"

"Why," said the camel, in a silky voice, "the same reason which will cause you to fan me each day, keep me covered each night, and feed me in the manner to which I have become accustomed. That reason is this: If I go to your mother and tell her of our bargain, things will not go well with you."

Fareedah could scarcely believe her ears. The plan which worked so well had now turned upside down, trapping her. She could do as the camel said, and her mother would never learn the truth about the carpet. She sighed, remembering how heavy a water jar became after the third trip to the well, and how weary her arms grew when she waved a fan hour after hour. There was another thing to consider. She had no guarantee that the camel would not add still more duties to the list. Every moment of her day might be spent in serving him.

"I think I should like a stiff brushing," declared the camel arrogantly.

"Then I suggest," cried Fareedah, stamping her foot crossly, "that you go and roll over in the thorn bushes!"

"Ah, ah," said the camel, "I may be forced to speak to your mother."

"No, you won't," announced Fareedah, "for I mean to speak to her myself."

So saying, the angry girl turned and stalked off across the garden, leaving the camel surprised and confused. Things had not turned out as he had intended.

When Fareedah's mother heard the story of the carpet, a slow smile spread over her face.

"You are not angry?" asked Fareedah.

"No," replied her mother, "for you have learned a valuable lesson. You labored to escape work, and for that labor you have nothing to show. With only half the amount of work you yourself could have produced the carpet."

"You are right," agreed Fareedah solemnly. "I have indeed learned a lesson."

From that day on Fareedah did her share of tasks without complaining, and the camel, having received a thorough scolding, forsook his roguish ways and became Fareedah's pet, fetching, carrying, and weaving at her command.

Thunder Appoints the Eagle Ruler of Earth

by TRAVELLER BIRD

I have known of eagles, our sacred keeper of the land.

One May morning when I was eight, I went with my father and grandfather to Snowbird Peak. The clouds hung low on the mountaintop. They were white and billowy and it seemed that you could reach right up and touch them.

While we stood there looking out over a timeless landscape of iron mountains and budding timber that stretched away into the four cardinal directions, we saw two eagles flying over the canyons in the distance. They would soar in wild and silent flight, and then swing across the blue skyline, spinning and spiraling. They were Bald Eagles, a male and a female. My grandfather said they were in their mating flight. They were exciting to watch; free and just beautiful.

Long ago when the Earth was new and all things could talk, Thunder went searching for his friend, the Eagle. Thunder was the Ruler of all the Universe, and the

159

Eagle was his best friend. Thunder found the Eagle sitting on Looking-Glass Peak. They had a conference.

Thunder said to the Eagle, "I appoint you Ruler of all the animals. You are to rule over all creatures that fly, all creatures that walk on four legs, and all creatures that crawl on Earth. You must have a council with all the wild animals. You must ask them what they want to be able to do, and you must grant them their request if you think it right they should be that way. You are to be my helper on Earth."

So the Eagle called a council of all the animals. They met in the animal council house on Little Snowbird Mountain. All kinds of birds came, and all the four-legged animals, and the animals that crawl.

When they arrived, they took seats on logs in the council house. Each tribe was assigned certain seats. The Eagle stood near a small fire in the center of the council house. He asked each one of them what he wanted to be able to do.

The Yellow Mockingbird (huhu) stood up and said, "I want to be a learner. Can you give me the power to sing all the songs of the other birds, so that when a person hears me sing he will think there are many birds around?"

The Eagle said, "Well, if you wish to be that way, I guess so."

That is how the Mockingbird got his power to imitate all the songs of the other birds.

The little Chickadee (tsidilili) got up and said, "I would like to be a fortuneteller. When people are to have visitors, I want to go and give them a message ahead of time. This I can do by flying to a tree near their house and singing a beautiful song. Would you give me that power?" the Chickadee asked.

"Yes," the Eagle said.

That is why the Cherokees say when they see a chickadee fly into a tree near the house, that someone is coming.

Then the Frog (walasi) got up and went and stood by the Eagle. "See these bumps on my body? People are always stepping on me and causing me to have sores.

Could you give me the power to blow myself up so that when a person sees me, he will instantly die of fright?"

"No," the Eagle said. "You are too small. I could not give you that power. But I will do this—I will let you jump a long distance, and when a person sees your blown-up body jump, he will become frightened."

The Beaver (doi) got up and said, "I want to make a poison that will kill people because they take my coat. Can you give me that power?"

"No," said the Eagle. "But I will give you sharp teeth like a knife to bite them with."

"All right," the Beaver said.

Next the Cat (sahoni) stood up and said, "I want to be a great magician, a nightwalker, but I cannot see when the Sun goes to sleep. Will you give me the power to see in the Nightland?"

The Eagle said, "I guess so."

That's why the Cherokees say when they see a cat walking in the darkness, that he is a nightwalker.

Then came the Redbird (totsuhwa), the beautiful singing bird. He got up and said to the Eagle, "I want to be a truthteller. Let the people trust me. I want to sing joyful songs when it's going to rain."

"All right, you can have that power," the Eagle said.

That is why the Cherokees believe that when they see the beautiful redbird sitting in the top of a tree it will rain.

The Grasshopper (sigigi) said, "I want to be an expert singer and dancer. When people hear me sing and see me dance, they will laugh and become happy."

So the Eagle gave that power to the Grasshopper.

This is what my grandfather Sigigi said the Old Ones told long ago of how the Eagle became the Ruler of the Earth and gave power to the other animals.

The Woodsman's Daughter and the Lion

by RICARDO ALEGRÍA

There was once a woodsman who went every day to the forest to cut wood. One day while he was chopping down a tree, a great, ferocious lion appeared, and the woodsman, fearing for his life, threw himself upon his knees. He begged the lion not to eat him, explaining that he was a poor woodsman who had to work hard to take care of his three daughters.

Hearing this, the lion said, "Very well, I shall not eat you, but you must make a promise to me." The woodsman was pleased at this and agreed to promise whatever the lion asked.

Then the lion said, "I shall not eat you if you promise to bring me tomorrow the first thing that comes to receive you when you get home this afternoon."

The woodsman was even more pleased at this, thinking how easily he had saved his life, for it was his little dog that always ran out to greet him. So he made the promise.

That afternoon the woodsman gathered the wood he had cut and set off for home, feeling very lucky. But his happiness changed to sorrow as he neared home when, instead of the little dog that usually greeted him, he saw his youngest daughter run out. She threw her arms about him. The unhappy woodsman asked her what had happened to the little dog, and she said that the dog had a thorn in his paw, and they had kept it indoors.

When he went into the house, all of his daughters noticed their father's sadness and asked him what had

happened to make him so unhappy. The woodsman, crying, told them about his promise to the lion, and how he
must take his youngest daughter to the lion tomorrow.
He loved her very much, but he must keep his word. He
could not break the pact he had made with the lion. He
didn't know what to do!

The youngest daughter, who loved her father more
than the other two did, told him not to worry, that she
wasn't afraid to go with him tomorrow to meet the lion.

The next morning the woodsman and his daughter
set out. When they reached the place in the forest where
the lion had appeared the day before, there he was, waiting for them. The woodsman begged the lion to release
him from the pact because he loved his daughter so much
that he could not bear to lose her. The lion reminded him
of his promise, then turned to the young girl and said,
"Follow me." But before leaving, he told the woodsman

to dig beneath a tree nearby, and he would find gold at its roots. Then the lion entered a cave, and the young girl followed him, leaving her father alone and in tears. After they had gone, the woodsman remembered what the lion had told him, and he dug beneath the tree and found many golden coins. He took them home and now, with so much money, he and his other daughters lived without having to work so hard.

Meantime, the youngest daughter had come with the lion to an underground palace. There she found many beautiful dresses, jewelry, and all the lovely things she had dreamed of awaiting her. The lion was very kind and gave her anything she asked for. Months passed, and the young girl grew very unhappy because she missed her family. One day the lion asked what was troubling her, and she told him that she was sad because she had not seen her sisters or her father for such a long time. So the lion told her that the next day she might visit them, but that she must return before the rooster crowed. This made her happy again, and the next morning, when she left the cave, there stood a carriage ready to take her to her parent's house. At home, everyone was pleased to see that nothing had happened to her and to hear how happily she was living and how kind the lion was to her.

Before the rooster crowed at sunrise the young girl said good-by to her father and sisters and stepped into the carriage to return to the enchanted palace.

More months passed, and again the girl grew sad, so the lion told her to visit her home once more, reminding her to return before the rooster crowed. Happily she stepped into the carriage to go to her father's house. When she arrived, she found that her father was ill. She gave him his medicine and cared for him. But she was so preoccupied with his illness that she did not notice the

sun had risen and the roosters were crowing to announce a new day. When she realized what had happened, she was frightened, said good-by to her father and her sisters at once, and hurried out to the carriage that had brought her. It was nowhere to be seen! Very upset about having broken her promise to the lion, she walked to the woods and came to the tree where she had first met him. There was nothing there. She continued walking and came to the entrance of the cave, but it was sealed up. She sat down and cried. As she sat there, she heard the voice of the lion telling her that she had broken her promise to him, and that he was a prince who had been bewitched. She had *almost* broken the evil spell that bound him; but now she would have to walk across the world and wear out a pair of iron shoes before she could find him again to break the spell and set him free.

Through her tears, the girl promised that she would do this. She went to the blacksmith and had him make her a pair of iron shoes; she put them on and began walking across the world in search of the lion.

Many years passed in the search. When the iron soles of her shoes were worn as thin as a sheet of paper, she reached the house of the sun. She asked the sun's mother if she knew where the lion was. She didn't know, but said to ask her son when he returned. It wasn't long before a great heat was felt, and the sun arrived. His mother asked him if he knew where the enchanted lion was, and he said, no, he didn't; but perhaps the moon would know. The young girl said good-by to them and went on to find the moon's house. When she arrived, the moon's mother said that her daughter had not come home yet, but to wait and she would ask her. Then the girl felt a chill, and the moon arrived. When the mother asked if she knew where the enchanted lion was, the moon answered that

she had seen him at night in a castle behind a great mountain. The young girl left that very day for the mountain. After walking across the mountain without stopping to rest, she came to a castle with great doors, which were all locked. She knocked and knocked at one of the doors, but no one opened it. In desperation, she pulled off one of her iron shoes and threw it at the door. Instantly, all the doors flew open and, as though by magic, a handsome prince appeared and took her in his arms, explaining that he was the lion who, thanks to her love and loyalty, had been freed from the evil spell a witch had cast upon him.

The young girl was filled with joy and lived happily with the prince, and her father and sisters came to live with them as well.

The Great Minu

by BETH WILSON

Across the ocean and far away, a poor African farmer prepared to make a journey to the big city of Accra. He walked around his small farm, taking note of the yams and corn growing in the garden. Then he fed his chickens and goats, latched his thatched-roof hut, and took off down the narrow, dusty road.

The farmer hummed happily to himself as the morning sun came into view. How exciting to be going to the big city! Nothing much happened in his tiny village, but since Accra was the largest city in Ghana, he would find much excitement there.

After walking for some time, he stopped to rest under a tulip tree. He leaned against the tree trunk and breathed in the morning air. Birds swooped and soared in the sunshine, but no man, woman, or child traveled the dusty road in either direction.

Soon he jumped to his feet and started down the road again. As he reached the first village along the way, he saw a woman on her knees, washing clothes in a stream of water. "Good day!" he called to the woman. "I'm on my way to the big city—I'm on my way to Accra!" The woman just smiled and went on washing her clothes.

Farther down the road he saw some men and boys making iron. They were too busy to look up when he passed, but he called out just the same. "Good day! I'm on my way to the big city—I'm on my way to Accra!" The men and boys stopped for a moment and nodded. Then they went on working as if he hadn't spoken.

Soon he saw a grandmother telling stories to her little grandchildren. The traveler loved a story and was tempted to stop. But he knew he must be on his way. He waved his hand high and called out, "Good day! I'm on my way to the big city—I'm on my way to Accra!" The children turned to look, and the grandmother smiled and waved. Then she went on telling her story.

The traveler trudged along until he felt tired and hungry. Finding a cool spot, he sat down by the side of the road and opened his lunch bag. He ate a piece of chicken and a big red banana. Then he took a short nap under a cocoa tree.

As soon as the traveler woke up, he started off again because he still had quite a long way to go.

At last he approached some farms on the outskirts of Accra. The first thing he noticed was a great herd of cows. He wondered who could own such a herd. Seeing a man with them, he asked, "To whom do these cows belong?"

The man did not know the language of the traveler, so he shrugged his shoulders and said, "Minu," meaning, "I do not understand."

The traveler thought Minu must be a person, and so he exclaimed, "Mr. Minu must be very rich!"

Entering the city, the traveler saw some large new buildings in the town square. He wondered who might own the fine buildings. But the man he asked could not understand his question, so he answered "Minu."

"Good heavens!" cried the traveler. "What a rich fellow Mr. Minu must be to own all those cows and all these buildings, too!"

Soon he came to a great hotel surrounded by beautiful grounds and mahogany trees. A group of fashionably dressed African ladies came down the front steps of the hotel. The traveler stepped up to them and asked them who might be the owner of such a grand hotel.

The ladies smiled and said softly, "Minu."

"How wealthy Mr. Minu is!" exclaimed the astonished traveler.

He wandered from one neighborhood to another. Seeing a large house with many columns and porches, he stopped in surprise. "These homes in Accra are so grand—not a bit like the huts of my village," he said. Just then a servant came out. The traveler stepped up hurriedly and asked, "Please tell me who owns this fine house."

The young woman humped her shoulders. "Minu," she mumbled.

"How foolish of me to ask," the traveler said. "The Great Minu, of course." He stood for a moment, admiring the house and garden. Then he went on.

Finally he came to the harbor, where he saw men loading bananas, cocoa beans, and mahogany onto a huge ship. The blue sky above, the foamy green ocean below, and the sailors rushing about on board ship made quite a sight. Surprised at the great cargo, the traveler inquired of a bystander, "To whom does this fine vessel belong?"

"Minu," replied the puzzled man, who couldn't understand a word the traveler said.

"To the Great Minu also?" the traveler asked. "He is the richest man I ever heard of!"

Just as the traveler was setting out for home, he saw men carrying a coffin down the main street of

Accra. A long procession, all dressed in black, followed the men. People on the sidelines shook their heads slowly. Sad faces looked up now and then. When the traveler asked one of the mourners the name of the dead person, he received the usual reply, "Minu."

"Mr. Minu is dead?" wailed the traveler. "Poor Mr. Minu! So he had to leave all his wealth—his herd of cows, his buildings, his grand hotel, and his fine ship—and die just like a poor person. Well, well, in the future I'll be content to live a simple life, to breathe the fresh air on my little farm, and to help the poor people in my little village."

The long dusty road back didn't seem as long as it had before. When the farmer arrived home, he unlatched the door of his hut and looked around inside. Then he climbed into his own snug bed and dreamed of the good foo-foo he would eat the next day.

Petronella

by JAY WILLIAMS

In the kingdom of Skyclear Mountain, three princes were always born to the king and queen. The oldest prince was always called Michael, the middle prince was always called George, and the youngest was always called Peter. When they were grown up, they always went to seek their fortunes. What happened to the oldest prince and the middle prince no one ever knew. But the youngest prince always rescued a princess, brought her home and, in time, ruled over the kingdom. That was the

way it had always been. And so far as anyone knew, that was the way it would always be.

Until now.

"Now" was the time of King Peter the Twenty-ninth and Queen Blossom. An oldest prince was born and a middle prince. But the youngest prince turned out to be a girl.

"Well," said the king gloomily, "we can't call her Peter. We'll have to call her Petronella. And what's to be done about it, I'm sure I don't know."

There was nothing to be done. The years passed, and the time came for the princes to go out and seek their fortunes. Michael and George said good-by to the king and queen and mounted their horses. Then out came Petronella. She was dressed in traveling clothes, with a sword by her side and her bag packed.

"If you think," she said, "that I'm going to sit at home, you are mistaken. I'm going to seek my fortune, too."

"Impossible!" said the king.

177

"What will people say?" cried the queen.

"Look here," said Prince Michael, "be reasonable, Pet. Stay home and wait. Sooner or later a prince will turn up."

Petronella smiled. She was a tall, handsome girl with flaming red hair, and when she smiled in that particular way, it meant she was trying to keep her temper.

"I'm going with you," she said. "I'll find a prince if I have to rescue one from something myself. And that's that."

The grooms brought out her horse, and she said good-by to her parents. Up she sprang to the saddle, and away she went behind her two brothers.

They traveled into the flat lands below Skyclear Mountain. After many days, they entered a great, dark forest. They came to a place where the road divided into three, and there at the fork sat a little, wrinkled old man covered with dust and spider webs.

Prince Michael said, haughtily, "Where do these roads go, old man?"

"The road on the right goes to the city of Gratz," said the old man. "The road in the center goes to the castle of Blitz. The road on the left goes to the house of Albion the enchanter. And that's one."

"What do you mean by 'And that's one'?" asked Prince George.

"I mean," said the old man, "that I am forced to sit on this spot without stirring, and that I must answer one question from each person who passes by. And that's two."

Petronella's kind heart was touched. "Is there anything I can do to help you?" she asked.

The old man sprang to his feet. The dust fell from him in clouds.

"You have already done so," he said. "For that question is the one which releases me. I have sat here for sixty-two years waiting for someone to ask me that." He snapped his fingers with joy. "In return, I will tell you anything you wish to know."

"Where can I find a prince?" Petronella said promptly.

"There is one in the house of Albion the enchanter," the old man answered.

"Ah," said Petronella, "then that is where I am going."

"In that case I will leave you," said her oldest brother, Michael. "For I am going to the castle of Blitz to see if I can find my fortune there."

"Good luck," said Prince George. "For I am going to the city of Gratz. I have a feeling my fortune is there."

They embraced her and rode away.

Petronella looked thoughtfully at the old man, who was combing spider webs and dust out of his beard. "May I ask you something else?" she said.

"Of course. Anything."

"Suppose I wanted to rescue that prince from the enchanter. How would I go about it? I haven't any experience in such things you see."

The old man chewed a piece of his beard. "I do not know everything," he said, after a moment. "I know that there are three magical secrets that, if you can get them from Albion, will help you."

"How can I get them?" asked Petronella.

"You must offer to work for him. He will set you three tasks, and if you do them you may ask for a reward. You must ask him for a comb for your hair, a mirror to look into, and a ring for your finger."

"And then?"

"I do not know. I only know that when you rescue the prince, you can use these things to escape from the enchanter."

"It doesn't sound easy," Petronella sighed.

"Nothing we really want is easy," said the old man. "Look at me—I have wanted my freedom, and I've had to wait sixty-two years for it."

Petronella said good-by to him. She mounted her horse and galloped along the third road.

It ended at a low, rambling house with a red roof. It was a comfortable-looking house, surrounded by gardens and stables and trees heavy with fruit. On the lawn, in an armchair, sat a handsome young man with his face turned to the sky and his eyes closed.

Petronella tied her horse to the gate and walked across the lawn.

"Is this the house of Albion the enchanter?" she said.

The young man blinked up at her in surprise.

"I think so," he said. "Yes, I'm sure it is."

"And who are you?"

The young man yawned and stretched. "I am Prince Ferdinand of Firebright," he replied. "Would you mind stepping aside? I'm trying to get a sunburn, and you're standing in the way."

Petronella snorted. "You don't sound like much of a prince."

"That's funny," said the young man, closing his eyes. "That's what my father always says."

At that moment, the door of the house opened and out came a man dressed all in black and silver. He was tall and thin and as sinister as a cloud full of thunder. His face was stern but full of wisdom. Petronella knew at once that he must be the enchanter.

He bowed to her, politely. "What can I do for you?"

"I wish to work for you," said Petronella, boldly.

Albion nodded. "I cannot refuse you," he said. "But I must warn you it will be dangerous. Tonight I will give you a task. If you do it, I will reward you. But if you fail, you must die."

Petronella glanced at the prince and sighed. "If I must, I must," she said. "Very well."

That evening, they all had dinner together in the enchanter's cozy kitchen. Then Albion took Petronella out to a stone building and unbolted its door. Inside were seven huge black dogs.

"You must watch my hounds all night," said he.

Petronella went inside, and Albion closed and locked the door.

At once, the hounds began to snarl and bark. They showed their teeth at her. But Petronella was a real princess. She plucked up her courage. Instead of backing away, she went toward the dogs. She began to speak to them in a quiet voice. The dogs stopped snarling and sniffed at her. She patted their heads.

"I see what it is," she said. "You are lonely here. I will keep you company."

And so all night long she sat on the floor and talked to the hounds and stroked them. They lay close to her, panting.

In the morning, Albion came to let her out. "Ah," said he, "I see that you are brave. If you had run from the dogs, they would have torn you to pieces. Now you may ask for what you want."

"I want a comb for my hair," said Petronella.

The enchanter gave her a comb carved from a piece of black wood.

Prince Ferdinand was sunning himself and working at a crossword puzzle. Petronella said, in a low voice, "I am doing this for you."

"That's nice," said the prince. "What's 'selfish' in nine letters?"

"You are," snapped Petronella. She went to the enchanter. "I will work for you once more," she said.

That night, Albion led her to a stable. Inside were seven huge white horses.

"Tonight," he said, "you must watch my steeds."

He went out and locked the door. At once, the horses began to rear and neigh. They pawed at her with their iron hooves.

But Petronella was a real princess. She looked closely at them and saw that their ribs stuck out. Their coats were rough and their manes and tails full of burrs.

"I see what it is," she said. "You are hungry and dirty."

She brought them as much hay as they could eat and began to brush them. All night long, she fed them and groomed them, and they stood quietly in their stalls.

In the morning, Albion let her out. "You are as kind as you are brave," said he. "If you had run from them, they would have trampled you under their hooves. What will you have as a reward?"

"I want a mirror to look into," answered Petronella. The enchanter gave her a mirror made of gray silver.

She looked across the lawn at Prince Ferdinand, who was doing sitting-up exercises. He was certainly very handsome. She said to the enchanter, "I will work for you once more."

That night, Albion led her to a loft above the stables. There, on perches, were seven great red hawks.

"Tonight," said he, "you must watch my falcons."

As soon as Petronella was locked in, the hawks began to beat their wings and scream at her.

Petronella laughed. "That is not how birds sing," she said. "Listen."

She began to sing in a sweet voice. The hawks fell silent. All night long she sang to them, and they sat like feathered statues on their perches, listening.

In the morning, Albion said, "You are as talented as you are kind and brave. If you had run from them, they would have pecked and clawed you without mercy. What do you want now?"

"I want a ring for my finger," said Petronella.

The enchanter gave her a ring made from a single diamond.

All that day and all that night, Petronella slept, for she was very tired. But early the next morning she crept into Prince Ferdinand's room. He was sound asleep, wearing purple pajamas.

"Wake up," whispered Petronella. "I am going to rescue you."

Ferdinand awoke and stared sleepily at her. "What time is it?"

"Never mind that," said Petronella. "Come on!"

"But I'm still sleepy," Ferdinand objected. "And it's so pleasant here."

Petronella shook her head. "You're not much of a prince," she said, grimly. "But you're the best I can do. Come along."

She grabbed him by the wrist and dragged him out of bed. She hauled him down the stairs. His horse and hers were in another stable, and she saddled them quickly.

186

She gave the prince a shove, and he mounted. She jumped on her own horse, seized the prince's reins, and away they went like the wind.

They had not gone far when they heard a tremendous thumping. Petronella looked back. A dark cloud rose behind them, and beneath it she saw the enchanter. He was running with great strides, faster than her horse could go.

"What shall we do?" she cried.

"Don't ask me," said Prince Ferdinand, grumpily. "I'm all shaken to bits by this fast riding."

Petronella desperately pulled out the comb. "The old man said that this would help me," she said. And because she didn't know what else to do with it, she threw it on the ground. At once, a forest rose up between her and the enchanter. The trees were so thick that no one could get between them.

Away went Petronella and the prince. But the enchanter turned himself into an ax and began to chop. Right and left he chopped, flashing, and the trees fell before him. Soon he was through the wood, and once again Petronella heard his footsteps thumping behind.

She reined in her horse. She took out the mirror and threw it on the ground. At once, a wide lake spread out behind her, gray and glittering.

Off they went again. But the enchanter sprang into the water, turning himself into a salmon as he did so. He swam across the lake and leaped out of the water onto the other bank. Petronella heard him coming thump! thump! behind them again.

This time, she threw down the ring. It didn't turn into anything, but lay shining on the ground.

The enchanter came running up. He jumped over the ring. And as he jumped, the ring opened wide and then snapped up around him, holding his arms tight to his body in a magical grip from which he could not escape.

"Well," said Prince Ferdinand, "that's the end of him."

Petronella looked at him in annoyance. Then she looked at the enchanter, held fast in the ring.

"Brother!" she said. "I can't just leave him here. He'll starve to death."

She got off her horse and went up to him. "If I release you," she said, "will you promise to let the prince go free?"

Albion stared at her in astonishment. "Let him go free?" he said. "What are you talking about? I'm glad to get rid of him."

It was Petronella's turn to look surprised. "I don't understand," she said. "Weren't you holding him prisoner?"

"Certainly not," said Albion. "He came to visit me for a weekend. At the end of it, he said, 'It's so pleasant here, do you mind if I stay on for another day or two?' I'm very polite, and I said, 'Of course.' He stayed on and on and on. I didn't like to be rude to a guest, and I couldn't just kick him out. I don't know what I'd have done if you hadn't dragged him away."

"But then—" said Petronella. "But then—why did you come running after him this way?"

"I wasn't chasing him," said the enchanter. "I was chasing you. You are just the woman I've been looking for. You are brave and kind and talented—and beautiful as well."

"Oh," said Petronella.

"I see," she said.

"Hm," said she. "How do I get this ring off you?"

"Give me a kiss."

She did so. The ring vanished from around Albion and reappeared on Petronella's finger.

"I don't know what my parents will say when I come home with you instead of a prince," she said.

"Let's go and find out, shall we?" said the enchanter, cheerfully.

He mounted one horse and Petronella the other. And off they trotted, side by side, leaving Ferdinand of Firebright to walk home as best he could.

The Coming of Legends

by JOSEPH BRUCHAC

Long ago, in the days before people told legends, there was a boy who hunted birds. One day he had been hunting for a very long time and, because it was growing dark, he sought shelter near a great rock. As he sat there, chipping at a piece of flint to make an arrowpoint, he heard a deep voice speak.

"I shall tell a story," the voice said.

The boy was startled and he looked all around him, but could find no one. "Who are you?" said the boy.

"I am Hahskwahot," answered the voice. Thus the boy realized that it was the big standing rock which had spoken.

"Then let me hear your story," said the boy.

"First," said the voice of the stone, "you must make me a present of one of the birds you have killed."

"So be it," said the boy, placing a bird on the rock. Then the deep voice told him a story full of wonder, a story of how things were in the past. When the story was over, the boy went home.

That evening, the boy returned with another bird and, placing it on the rock, sat down to listen.

"Now," said the voice, "I shall tell you a legend. When one is ended, I may tell you another, but if you become sleepy, you must tell me so we can take a rest and you can return the following evening."

Thus it continued. Soon the boy began to bring people with him and together they listened to the legends told by the standing rock. A great many people now went to the place and listened.

Finally, the voice from the rock spoke to the boy who was no longer a boy but now a man. "You will grow old, but you will have these legends to help you in your old age. Now you have become the carrier of these stories of the past, and you shall be welcomed and fed wherever you go."

And so this is how the Seneca people say that legends came into the world.

More Folktales to Read

And It Is Still That Way edited by Byrd Baylor. Scribner, 1976.
In this book, Papago, Navajo, Hopi, Pima, Apache, Quechei, and Cocepah legends of how and why are re-told by today's children of these cultures.

How the People Sang the Mountains Up by Maria Leach. Viking Press, 1967.
How and why stories from all over the world show how different people have explained the same things.

The Toad Is the Emperor's Uncle and Other Stories by Vo-Dinh. Doubleday, 1970.
These folktales from Vietnam are full of animals, trickery, and humor.

The Piece of Fire and Other Haitian Tales by Harold Courlander. Harcourt Brace Jovanovich, 1964.
Here are twenty-six tales that reflect Haiti's European and African heritages.

The Golden Lynx and Other Tales selected by Augusta Baker. Lippincott, 1960.
A well-known storyteller retells tales of spells and enchantment from sixteen countries.

The Enchanted Orchard and Other Folktales of Central America edited by Dorothy Sharp Carter. Harcourt Brace Jovanovich, 1973.
These are tales of magic and adventure that reflect the many cultures that make up Central America.

The Moon Ribbon and Other Tales by Jane Yolen. T. Y. Crowell, 1976.
These six stories are traditional in feeling, yet all are new and original.

PART 3

The Little Riders

The Little Riders

An American girl, Johanna. World War II. An occupied country. An underground movement. And—the little riders. Put these all together and you have a thriller.

This selection is long enough to allow you to get deeply involved with the people and problems it tells about. You will get to know the main character, Johanna, very well indeed. With her, you will experience life in Holland during World War II. And you will learn about the courage that ordinary people can display during wartime.

The Little Riders

by MARGARETHA SHEMIN

Johanna was sitting on the windowsill in her little attic room, waiting for the clock on the church steeple to strike twelve. It was a very warm summer day and her window was opened wide. From her window, Johanna had the best view of the church steeple in the whole town. That was why it was her favorite spot. And twelve o'clock was her favorite hour of the day.

Once when her father was a little boy, he had slept in that same room and had sat on the windowsill waiting for the clock to strike twelve. He had waited for the doors under the church steeple to open, just as Johanna was doing now. And he had counted the twelve little riders as they rode out on their white horses. Johanna always thought of her father at this time of the day, as she sat on the windowsill.

It had been a long time since she had been home in America with her parents. She couldn't even remember her father very clearly. He was a sea captain, and because he had become very lonesome on his long voyages, he had decided to take Johanna's mother with him on one of them. So he had sent Johanna to Holland to visit her grandparents.

She remembered as clearly as if it happened yesterday how she had said good-bye to her father and mother. She had kissed them both and tried very hard to show them a happy face.

While her father had held her in his arms, he had said to her, "Thank you very much, my little Johanna, for giving me Mother for such a long time. Think of me when you are in my country and don't forget to give my very special love to the little riders in the church steeple. Help Grandfather take care of them, so that when I come with Mother to bring you back home, they will ride for us whenever the church clock strikes."

Now Johanna had been in Holland more than four years. Soon after she had come to her grandparents the war in Europe had broken out, and less than a year later, in the early days of May, Holland had been invaded by the German army. For the people of Holland, who had always loved their freedom more than anything else in the world, the presence of the German soldiers was very hard to bear.

From her window seat Johanna looked down over the town. It was an old town with a canal around the center. Behind the canal were the strong fortifications that had once protected the town from enemies that threatened from outside. Her grandparents' house stood at the marketplace where all the old houses were huddled together, as if they were leaning on each other for support. There were few people in the streets, mostly women and children. It was dangerous these days for men to be out in the streets, since at any time they could be seized and taken far away to work for the Germans.

Johanna looked again at the hands of the big clock on the church steeple. Soon it would be twelve o'clock. After the clock had struck twelve times, the little doors under the steeple would open up, and out would come the little riders.

Grandfather had told Johanna all he knew about the history of the little riders. They were as old as the town, and that was many hundreds of years. They were figures of twelve young noblemen who had gone out as crusaders to the Holy Land and who had never returned to the town. Long ago an artisan had made the figures out of lead, and ever since they had ridden over the town, sitting proud and erect on their horses.

When the air was still trembling with the last stroke of the clock, six little riders would come out of each door. They would ride up to each other, lift their swords in a salute, and then go in the opposite door. In and out as many times as the clock had struck. While they rode in and out of the doors, the carillon of the church played old Dutch folk tunes. The music was carried all over town and could be heard in even the farthest street and in every house where the windows were open.

Ever since Johanna's grandfather was a young man, he had taken care of the church, and his most important task was to take care of the little riders. He was the only man in the town who understood the complex mechanism that made the little riders ride out over the town, every hour, day and night. Johanna helped her grandfather take care of the riders just as her father had done when he was a small boy, and Johanna loved the little riders just as much as her father did. She always looked up at them, wherever she was in town, when the hour struck. But she always tried to be in her room, where she could see them best, when the clock struck twelve, because then, of course, they rode the longest. Now the clock was already striking the hour, and the few women and children down on the quiet marketplace looked up at the church steeple to see the little riders. But just when the clock had struck for the twelfth time and the little doors opened up to let out the first riders, and when the carillon started to play its music, the gay melodies were drowned out.

Toward the marketplace came the sound of oncoming marching. It sounded to Johanna like the rolling of heavy thunder. Those hundreds and hundreds of soldiers' boots —they sounded as if they would trample away the cobblestones of the old marketplace. At the same time all the soldiers started to sing. Nothing could be heard any more of the brave little tunes the carillon sent high up into the sky. But the riders kept riding proud and erect on their little horses.

Johanna averted her eyes from the marketplace to avoid seeing the soldiers. She closed the window so that she wouldn't hear how loud their voices were. But the window didn't keep out the noise. While she watched the riders make their salutes and ride busily in and out the little doors, she could still hear the marching and the

singing and the shouting, and she became afraid. She remembered again what she had almost forgotten during her busy morning—how different Grandfather had looked to her that morning and how long it had taken him to walk up the steps to the church steeple. How worried he had seemed as he looked at the riders who were waiting so patiently behind the little doors to ride out.

Now the last rider had disappeared, and Johanna slipped from her windowsill. Dinner was at twelve o'clock and even now, when there wasn't much to eat, Grandmother did not allow anybody to be late. She quickly walked down the stairs. There was nobody in the hall, but the door to the small vestibule was closed, and she could hear voices behind it.

When Johanna entered the living room where they, like most Dutch families, always had their meals, she saw to her surprise that the table hadn't even been set. She went back into the hall to find Grandfather and Grandmother. But she stopped when she saw them. They were standing at the foot of the stairs, and with them was a German soldier. They spoke in low voices, and Johanna couldn't hear what they were saying. They went upstairs, and all she could hear now was the sound of their footsteps and the opening and closing of doors. The stairs to the attic creaked as they went up to her room.

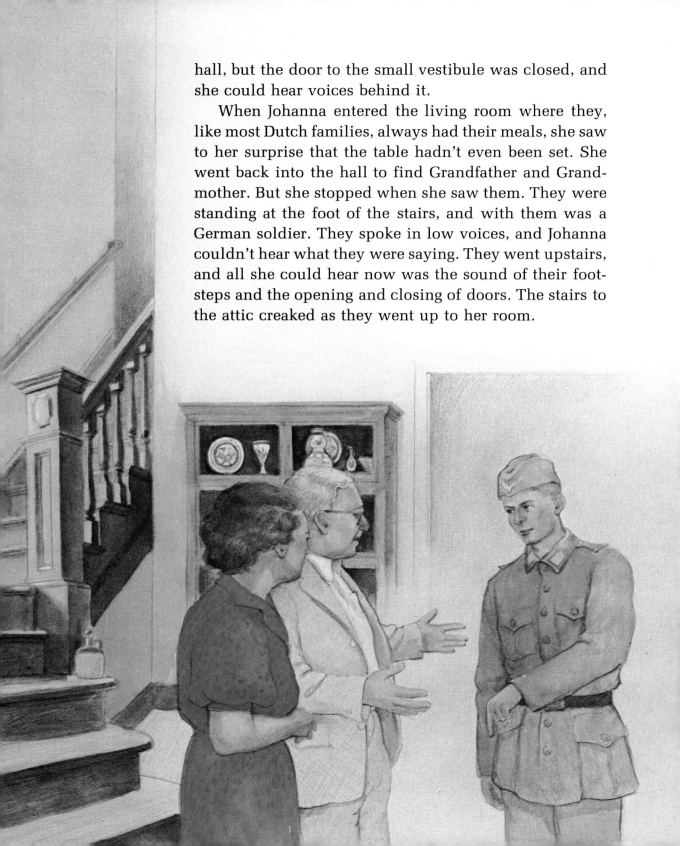

It seemed a long time before they came down again. Grandfather's and Grandmother's voices didn't sound low now. They were loud and angry. The German soldier was walking ahead of them. Then Johanna didn't look any more, and she turned her head away. At the beginning of the war, she had made herself a promise never to look a German soldier in the face because she couldn't bear the sight of them.

Dinner that day was especially good. Grandfather had gone fishing that morning and had caught a big bass. There were, boiled potatoes with the fish, and Grandmother had picked the first red, ripe strawberries from her garden. But nobody ate much. Everybody was quiet. There was only the tinkling of the knives and forks against the plates. A housefly buzzed against the window screen, trying to fly out into the sun. Outside there was no sound to be heard. Everybody ate at this hour of the day, and the marketplace was lying lost and forgotten in the hot sunshine.

Grandfather put down his knife and fork and pushed his only half-empty plate away. He looked straight at Johanna, and his eyes were filled with pride and love.

"There is bad news today, Johanna," he said, "but nothing so bad that we can't bear it. The German soldier you heard talking to us before dinner came to requisition a room in our house for a German officer, a certain Captain Braun. I explained to him that we used all the rooms and didn't have one room to spare. He never listened to me."

Grandfather got up from his chair and walked over to the window. He opened the screen a little to let out the fly that had kept buzzing desperately.

"He took your room," Grandfather continued and sat down again. "There was nothing I could do about it, although I tried very hard for you."

Johanna had to swallow a few times before she could speak. "When will he come?" she asked.

"Late in the afternoon." It was Grandmother who answered. "We'd better finish dinner now. We'll need all afternoon, Johanna, to move your things out of your room. You will sleep on the couch upstairs in Grandfather's den."

Grandmother took the dishes to the kitchen, and Johanna followed her. She was still too stunned to speak. It had all happened so unexpectedly. It would be dreadful to have somebody she really hated in her own house, in her own room. And Johanna hated the German soldiers. She hated the sound of their boots as they marched, always singing, through the narrow streets of the town. She hated their laughing and their loud shouts of "Heil Hitler." She hated the soldiers when they posted the big white bulletins on the corners of the streets, telling of new hostages they had taken and of many hateful orders given by the German town commander. Most of all she hated them because they wouldn't let her go back to her father and mother in America.

It would also be extremely dangerous, Johanna realized, to have one of them in the house. Johanna knew about the radio hidden in Grandfather's den and the weekly meetings Grandfather held upstairs. She knew there were many other dangerous secrets that Grandfather and Grandmother had never told her. All these secrets the house had kept within its walls, and the house had been the only safe place in a world full of enemies and danger. Now the house had been invaded too.

All afternoon Johanna helped Grandmother. She took all her clothes out of the attic closet. Now that the closet was empty she could almost see the cubbyhole hiding all the way at the back of the closet. It had always been Johanna's secret hiding place. She opened the small door that was only big enough for her to crawl through. In the cubbyhole were some of her old toys, her teddy bear that had traveled with her all the way from America to Holland and some seashells her father had once brought back for her from a far country. She never played with them any more, but she didn't want to leave them with Captain Braun. She couldn't take the cubbyhole with her, Johanna thought angrily. She hoped that Captain Braun would never discover it. Last of all she took her books and the pictures of her father and mother and the white house with the shutters, where she had lived in America. Now the room was empty.

Downstairs, Johanna tried to make Grandfather's den look a little like her own room, but it was a small dark room, and Johanna had never liked it. It smelled old and musty. She didn't want even to put the bright, gay pictures on the wall, although Grandfather had made room for them. Her attic room was bright and sunny, but here was only one small window through which the sun never shone. The den looked out on the narrow side street off the marketplace, and right across the street rose the high gray wall of the church. She could see only a small piece of the sky, if she leaned far enough out of the window. And no matter how far she leaned out, she could never see the little riders up under the belfry.

Late in the afternoon Captain Braun arrived. He rang the bell softly. Grandfather went to open the door for him as Grandmother and Johanna stood in the hall. Johanna

thought, "Now he will enter our house, and he will stick out his hand and shout 'Heil Hitler' and what will Grandfather do when he hears those words spoken in his house?"

But Captain Braun only clicked his heels and made a little bow in the direction of Grandmother. She gave him a stiff nod. He stretched out his hand to Grandfather. He and Grandfather were both tall men and could look each other straight in the face without looking up or down. Grandfather looked at Captain Braun and gave him the same stiff nod that Grandmother had given him. He did not take the hand that was stretched out to him.

Captain Braun was looking down at Johanna, but she saw only his big heavy polished boots and the horrible gray color of his uniform. When he tried to speak a few friendly words to her in broken Dutch, she thought more than ever of the promise she had made herself never to look a German soldier in the face. She turned her head away from him. For a moment it seemed that Captain Braun didn't know what to do or say. He clicked his heels again and made another stiff bow in the direction of Grandfather and Grandmother.

"I apologize to you," he said in broken Dutch. "I will try to cause no trouble to you. I wish you all a good evening." Then he turned directly to Grandfather. "Would you be kind, sir, and show me the room?"

Grandfather didn't speak but led Captain Braun to the stairs and mounted them quickly. Captain Braun picked up his heavy sack and followed slowly. Johanna could hear the sack bump heavily on every step till it was carried all the way high up to her attic room. Then she heard the door close and Grandfather's footsteps coming downstairs.

Johanna went to bed early that night. She had felt tired, but now she couldn't fall asleep. She kept tossing in her new bed. There were strange, unfamiliar shadows on the wall. The big gray wall of the church seemed so near, ready to fall on top of the room. Faintly she heard the clock strike ten times. Then the door was opened very softly, and Grandfather came into the room. He sat down in the chair next to Johanna's bed and took her hand in his own.

"Why don't you sleep, Johanna?" he asked. "You should try to sleep now. We have all had a hard day and so much has happened."

"I hate him," Johanna said, "and I hate this room too. From here I can see only the gray wall of the church. I can't see the riders, I can't even hear the carillon very clearly. How can I ever fall asleep without the little riders? I have always watched them just before I went to sleep. In the morning the carillon woke me up. Now he has my room that once was Father's room. He has no right to sit there and watch the riders and listen to the carillon."

Grandfather got up from the chair and walked over to the window. He looked up at the gray wall of the church.

"Captain Braun," he said, "will never see the little riders ride out on their horses and he will never hear the carillon. Today an ordinance came from the town commander. The riders are not allowed to ride any more and the carillon may not play any more. I just went to the church tower."

Grandfather turned away from the window and paced up and down the small room.

"All these years I have taken care of the riders so that they could ride when the clock struck the hour. But tonight I closed the little doors."

Johanna sat up in her bed, her arms around her thin knees. Her face looked small and white, her eyes big and dark.

"Why?" she asked Grandfather. "Why may the little riders not ride out any more?"

"They didn't give us any reasons," Grandfather answered, "but we have seen this coming for a long time. This ordinance is only the beginning. The little riders are made of lead. The Germans need metal, and they may throw them into a melting pot to make munition out of them for their armies. Everywhere the occupied countries are being plundered, their treasures taken away, and the bells of their churches melted down to be made into weapons. Grandmother and I have often talked of what to do if this ever threatened to happen to the little riders."

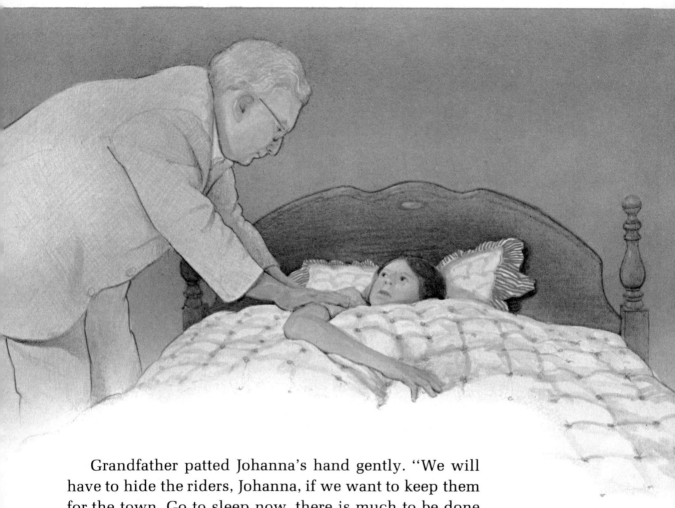

Grandfather patted Johanna's hand gently. "We will have to hide the riders, Johanna, if we want to keep them for the town. Go to sleep now, there is much to be done tomorrow."

Grandfather tucked the blanket around Johanna and left the room, but Johanna didn't want to sleep. She wanted to think about everything Grandfather had told her. The night was cool and quiet. From somewhere she heard the sound of a flute. At first she thought it must come from outside. She pushed her blanket away and stepped out of her bed to look out of the small window. But she saw only the dark street and the high gray wall of

the church across, and she didn't hear a sound. She walked across the room and opened the door to the hall. The sound came from the top of the house. Barefoot, Johanna climbed silently up the attic stairs. Halfway up she could see her room.

Captain Braun had left the door open so that the cool night wind could blow through the warm room. He was sitting on Johanna's windowsill. His back was turned to the door, his long legs dangling out of the window. And he played his flute over the silent marketplace.

Johanna didn't watch him for long. She went downstairs without making a noise. She didn't close her door with a bang, but she closed it very firmly. When she was back in bed, she pulled the cover over her ears so that she couldn't hear a sound that could keep her awake. But it was a long time before she fell asleep.

The next day, everybody looked up at the church steeple, wondering what had happened. It was the first time in many hundreds of years that the little riders had not ridden out and the carillon had not played. Soon the town buzzed with the news of the ordinance from the town commander.

After a few days something happened — something of such tremendous importance that the Germans had suddenly much more urgent and grave matters on their minds that the twelve little riders high up on the church tower. Even Grandfather didn't think any more about hiding them.

Johanna was sitting with Grandfather and Grandmother in the den, listening to the radio hidden behind the books in the bookcase. Then the big news came crackling and almost inaudible, and none of them dared to believe it was true. Allied armies had landed in

France. All morning long, Johanna and her grandparents kept the radio on. They had to hear over and over again the crackling voice that kept repeating the same bulletin.

In the afternoon Grandfather turned off the radio and they went for a walk. It was a clear, cool summer day. People stood together in their front yards, discussing the news in low voices. There were no marching or singing soldiers in the streets of the town today. The few single soldiers who passed by seemed to be in a hurry and did not pay attention to anyone. For one brief moment the town seemed to belong again to its people.

Johanna thought of her mother and father. She had never doubted that her father would come with the liberators. Now maybe he would come soon. He would help free Holland and take her back home with him. At night, lying in bed, she had imagined many different ways that he might come to her. Sometimes she imagined that he would be an officer in the American Navy and he would come on a big battleship. Sometimes she thought of him as a pilot flying a big airplane. But now she hoped that he would be with the first troops that had just landed in France. She always imagined how he would stretch out his arms to her and lift her high up in the air, as he always had done when he came home from his long trips. He would say, "My little Johanna," and she would look into his blue eyes. But then Johanna always had to stop imagining because she couldn't remember the rest of his face.

Grandfather and Grandmother and Johanna spent much time upstairs in the den, listening to the radio. At first the liberating armies advanced fast. The south of Holland was free. Then the days became weeks and the weeks became months. The liberation of the north still seemed sure, but not so near any more. Johanna still dreamed about her father, but she was afraid he would not come soon.

Life went on as it had in the four years before. Grandfather started to think again about a safe hiding place for the little riders because now more than ever the Germans needed every scrap of metal for ammunition.

Every evening Grandfather went up to the church steeple. The last light of the long summer days came through the oval window. He worked with endless patience to take apart the mechanism that for so many years had made the riders ride out on their horses while the carillon played the old folk tunes.

Now Johanna was almost used to the presence of Captain Braun in the house, but still she had never seen his face. In the morning she met him on the stairs, she going down for breakfast, he going up to his room after morning drill. In the evening she met him again, she going up to the den, he going down on his way out for dinner. He always said "Good morning" and "Good evening." Johanna always turned her head away from him and never answered. He walked softly on his heavy boots except when he had to ask Grandfather or Grandmother something. Then he stamped noisily with his boots so that they could hear him long before he knocked on the door. There was always time to hide the radio behind the books in the bookcase.

At night now Johanna sometimes forgot to close the door of her room and she could hear the music of the flute. When the summer nights were quiet, Captain Braun always played. But often now the air outside was filled with the droning sound of heavy airplanes flying over. On such nights Johanna climbed out of her bed and leaned far out the window to see their lights high against the dark sky. She knew that many of them were American planes, and she imagined that her father might be in one of them. They were airplanes flying over to drop their bombs on the towns of Germany. On those nights Captain Braun did not play his flute.

One day when Captain Braun had gone out, Johanna went upstairs and looked at her old room. Her closet was full of coats and army caps with the German eagle on them. Pairs of heavy shiny boots stood in a neat row on her shoe shelf. Johanna had to push aside the heavy uniforms to get to the back of the closet. She wanted to have a look at her secret hiding place. The bolt on the small door seemed untouched and dusty. When she opened it and crawled through the door, the cubbyhole was empty, as she had left it. Captain Braun had probably never discovered it. She had to touch the uniforms again to make them hang as they had before she had pushed them aside. She closed the door quickly and wiped her hands on her skirt.

On the wall, where once her pictures had hung, were now the pictures of Captain Braun's family. In one, an older lady and an older man were standing arm in arm in a garden full of flowers. In another, a young woman and a laughing boy were standing on skis in dazzling white snow. It was strange to see real Germans in a garden full of flowers and with skis on a sunny mountain slope. On the table with some music books was the flute in a black velvet case embroidered with mountain flowers, blue gentians and silver-white edelweiss. Johanna wondered who had made the little case. The old lady from the flower garden, or the young woman on skis? She decided that the old lady would probably be better at embroidering.

Before Johanna left the room she sat down on her windowsill and looked at the church steeple. The little doors were closed now and the steeple looked old and gray, like any other church steeple.

"Don't worry, little riders," Johanna whispered to the closed doors. "It will be all right, the Germans will not get you." Tonight, Grandfather had told her, there would be a meeting in the den about the little riders.

"We cannot hide the riders without asking the townspeople, Johanna," Grandfather had said. "There is too much at stake. If the Germans find the riders gone, they may punish the whole town. This isn't something we

may do on our own." But Johanna was sure that the people of the town would never let the little riders fall into the hands of the German soldiers.

It was a good night to have the meeting, for it was Friday, the night Captain Braun was usually not home. It was a black night outside and raining heavily. Several months ago the town commander had imposed a curfew on the town and no civilians, except a few who had passes, were allowed to be out in the streets from eight o'clock in the evening until six o'clock the next morning.

One by one Grandfather's friends came to the house. They came huddled inside their raincoats, hugging close to the gray walls of the church. The rain and the darkness made them almost invisible. Each one pressed the doorbell six short times and Johanna opened the door just wide enough for one person to creep in. Then she closed the door again. When they had all arrived and gone upstairs, Johanna put on her raincoat and went outside. She left the front door open a little. She sat down behind the lilac bush next to the front door, where she could overlook the whole marketplace but could still get back into the house unseen if she saw something suspicious and needed to warn Grandfather. Grandmother sat at the side entrance of the house, watching the street.

Johanna became cold and wet, sitting behind the lilac bush. The rain fell heavier and dripped from the roof in a little stream down her neck. The night was windy too, and now and then she had to close her eyes when the wet branches of the bush swept against her face. Her legs were stiff and cramped, but she didn't dare to change her position much.

What took the men so long? She had been sure that they would decide to hide the riders, but now she started to doubt. Could there be some among them who didn't think the riders worth the risk of hiding? If she could only go up for a minute and hear what was being said. But she could not leave her post.

And now she heard footsteps coming from the other side of the marketplace and then drawing near. Someone was whistling. It could only be a German, Johanna thought bitterly. No one else could walk so free in the night through the streets of their town, whistling a little tune in the rain. The steps came near and nearer and the tune began to sound familiar. It was Captain Braun coming back earlier than usual. Quickly Johanna went into the house and closed the door behind her. She ran upstairs and knocked on the door of Grandfather's den. Immediately the talking inside stopped and the lights went out. Johanna went all the way to the back of the dark hall and waited. She saw Captain Braun come up the stairs. He had left the lights off and walked softly with his boots in his hands as if he didn't want to wake the sleeping house.

One by one, as they had come, the men left the house. It was still raining and the darkness would protect them until they reached their homes. Johanna was alone now with Grandfather. She didn't dare to ask him what had been decided. Grandmother came in carrying three cups of hot imitation tea and slices of plain bread on a tray. The three of them sat around the table.

"They didn't even give me a chance to deliver the long speech I prepared in advance," Grandfather said. "There was never any doubt in anybody's mind what to do. The Germans will never have the little riders. After the war is over and we are liberated, they will ride again over our town."

Suddenly Johanna felt hungry and she took a big bite from her slice of bread.

"I never doubted that we would decide to hide the little riders," Grandfather continued. "I worked on it all these long summer evenings. Everything is ready now. It will take only a few minutes to bring them down." Grandfather got up from his chair to look out of the window into the dark and rainy night. "There is no moon tonight and it's still raining heavily. There won't be a single German in the streets. We may never have a chance like this again. We'll hide the riders tonight, but we must wait till it's a little later."

"We'll wake you, Johanna," Grandmother said. "Try now first to get some sleep." She left the room with Grandfather.

Johanna didn't undress. She opened the door a little and lay down on top of her bed. The night was loud with the sounds of the wind and the rain, but there were no overflying airplanes. For the first time in many nights Captain Braun played his flute again. The melody was a lazy, drowsy one. It made Johanna feel warm and happy inside and it made her very sleepy.

Johanna must have slept a few hours before Grandfather came to her bed and tugged her arm gently. She got up quickly. Downstairs, Grandmother was already dressed in her coat with a dark scarf tied around her head. They left the house by the side door. The door of the church tower was opposite, but there was the narrow street between that led to the marketplace. Grandfather crossed the street first to open the door. Then came Grandmother and last Johanna.

Inside the tower it was completely dark. Grandfather had climbed the steps so often that he led the way. No one talked, and Johanna could not remember the steps had ever seemed so long and steep. As they climbed higher the sound of the wind and rain came louder and louder. Grandfather had already reached the top of the stairs, and now he handed the riders and the horses to Grandmother and Johanna.

The staircase was so narrow and steep they could take only one rider at a time. It was too dark for Johanna to see the little rider that she carried. She could only feel the cool metal against her hands. The rider was bigger than she had expected, reaching up almost to her waist when for a

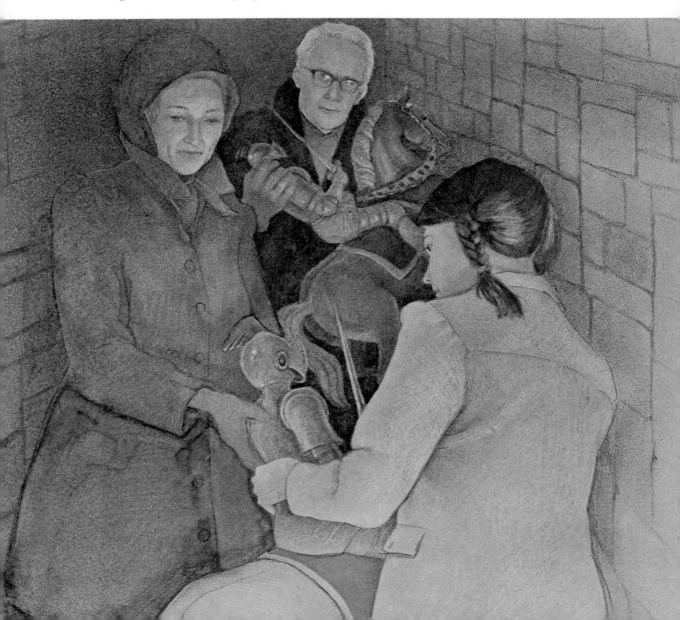

moment she put him next to her on one of the steps. She could feel the hands that held the sword, smaller than her own trembling hands. She started to carry him down. The rider, although made of lead, was hollow inside and not too heavy, but was clumsy to carry on the narrow, steep staircase. Each trip across the street and back up the church tower was harder than the one before. The last

little rider seemed heaviest of all. Grandfather made one more trip to lock the door of the church tower.

In their own house they must be careful to make no noise that could waken Captain Braun, but here the stairs were wider and Grandfather and Grandmother could carry two riders at a time. Johanna felt weak and shaky when the last rider with his horse was finally carried safely into Grandfather's den.

Grandfather locked the door and closed the curtains at the window. He turned on the light. Johanna kneeled down and looked into the proud and brave faces of the little riders.

For that one night the riders were hidden in Grandfather's den under the couch that was now Johanna's bed. The next morning Grandfather would try to find a place where they could stay hidden until the war was over, someplace far away where no German would think of looking.

Johanna went to bed exhausted but happier than she had been in many weeks. The little riders would be safe. If she reached under her bed, she could feel the curly mane of one of the horses. Outside, the night cleared, the rain stopped, and the wind died down. A few stars appeared and with them, like more stars, came the lights of airplanes overhead. Their buzzing sound gave Johanna a safe feeling and made her drowsy. Just before she fell asleep she thought again of her father. He walked toward her, taking long, impatient steps. He lifted her high in the air and said, "Give my very special love to the little riders and help Grandfather take care of them."

The next morning after breakfast Grandfather went to a nearby village where he had a friend who was a farmer. Dirk was one of the few farmers who had been allowed to keep his horse and wagon. Because he delivered eggs and fresh milk several times a week at the house of the German town commander, the German sentries who stood guard at the entrances of the town never searched his wagon. Many times young men who were hiding from the Germans had left town in Dirk's wagon, hidden underneath the tarpaulin between the empty egg boxes and the rattling milk containers. Grandfather and Dirk had often worked together to take such young men to safer places in the country, and Grandfather was sure Dirk would help hide the little riders.

Grandfather was gone most of the day. He came back around teatime. Grandmother and Johanna had just started to worry about what might have delayed him, when Grandfather entered the house. He was happy and pleased. Everything was going to work out beautifully. Dirk had given him twenty-four heavy burlap sacks. In the course of the evening Grandfather's friends would come, unseen through the dark, and each would take home a sack with a rider or horse in it. The next morning they would take the sacks to the small café near the edge of town where Dirk always stopped on his way home for a cup of coffee and a game of billiards with his friends. In the small room behind the bar many people had waited to be taken to safety by Dirk's horse and wagon. The little riders and their horses would wait there now. And they would stay hidden on Dirk's farm until they could return to the church steeple.

It was still a few hours before dark. Grandfather and Johanna went upstairs to put the riders and their horses in the burlap sacks so that they could be taken away without delay when the men came. Johanna looked for the last time at the riders' faces. With her hands she covered their small hands that so many times had lifted the

swords in proud salutes to each other. The Germans will not get them, she thought. They will always ride over the town. Even a hundred years from now.

It was still light when Johanna and Grandfather finished and went downstairs. Grandmother picked up her knitting at the round table in the living room. Grandfather sucked on an empty pipe and Johanna leafed through an old magazine. The curfew would start soon and, except for the bark of a dog and the cooing of the doves that nested under the eaves of the church tower, it was quiet outside.

Then, from the side street that led to the marketplace, came the sound of marching soldiers. It was unusual for a group of soldiers to be exercising at this late hour. Now that they came nearer, they sounded not so much like a group of soldiers exercising as like eight or ten soldiers who, by force of habit, marched instead of walking. They came out of the side street into the marketplace.

"I don't know what they are up to," Grandmother said, "but it's never good if they come by night."

"And there are quite a number of them." Grandfather looked out of the window. "They never use so many for a simple arrest."

"But they do if they search . . ." A house, Johanna was going to say, but she didn't complete her sentence.

One of the soldiers shouted a command and the group stopped still. They were in front of the house. Grandfather stepped quickly back from the window into the dark room.

"They may have come for something else," he tried to reassure Grandmother and Johanna.

The doorbell rang loudly and insistently, and Grandfather went to open the door. Grandmother and Johanna followed him into the hall. Nine soldiers were standing on the doorstep and one of them was the spokesman. Johanna was so frightened that for the first time since the

beginning of the war she forgot all about her promise and looked the soldier straight in the face. She saw a large man with a big, red face and two small shiny eyes under shaggy eyebrows. He spoke to Grandfather in heavily accented but otherwise good Dutch that Johanna could easily understand.

"We are sent by the town commander to requisition from you the key to the church tower." As he spoke he looked around with his shiny little eyes. "We will take the statues of the riders with us tonight and you can get the key back afterward at Headquarters. Hurry, we don't have all night," he concluded.

Grandfather reached up slowly for the big iron key that always hung on a peg near the stairs. He handed the key to the soldier. When they had gone, he closed the door and for a moment leaned heavily against it. Johanna saw small drops of perspiration under his nose and on his forehead.

"They will be back as soon as they have seen the riders are gone," Grandmother said. "We will have to hide them better."

"There is no time," Grandfather said. "They will be back in a few minutes, and where can we hide the riders? No, our only chance is somehow to keep them from going upstairs. If we can tell them something that will make them go away, even if it's only for a short time . . ." Grandfather straightened his shoulders and gave Grandmother and Johanna a sly look.

"There is only one thing for us to do. We must try to fool them. We'll act very surprised when we hear the riders are gone, and we can even suggest that because they are so old and therefore valuable they must have been stolen."

"They will never believe us," Grandmother said.

"They will certainly be back to investigate, but they might believe us long enough to give us a chance to hide the riders."

Grandmother still looked doubtful, Johanna thought, but Grandfather couldn't talk about it further. The soldiers were back. This time they didn't ring the doorbell. Instead they pounded the stocks of their rifles on the door. The spokesman was hot and red and so angry that he could hardly speak Dutch any more. He kept lapsing into heavy German shouts that Johanna couldn't understand.

"The riders may have been stolen." Grandfather's deep, quiet voice tried to interrupt the angry flow of words. "We all know that they are very valuable."

The big red soldier made so much noise that Johanna didn't think he had heard one word of what Grandfather had said. But now he started to laugh loudly. Sneering, he turned to the other soldiers and mimicked Grandfather. "He thinks they may have been stolen because they are so valuable." And all the soldiers roared with laughter. Suddenly the big soldier turned again toward Grandfather and he was not laughing now.

"You old liar!" he barked. For a moment Johanna thought that he was going to hit Grandfather. But Grandfather went on talking as if he had not heard him.

"Take me with you to the church tower and I will show you where I left the riders when I last saw them. I never saw them again after I closed the little doors the night the town commander gave us the order to do so."

Grandfather spoke so convincingly that Johanna was almost ready to believe that the riders were now in the possession of some clever thief instead of upstairs in the den under her own bed. But the big soldier didn't care what Grandfather said. He turned his back to him and gave his orders to the other soldiers.

"The old man and the old woman will come with us to Headquarters. The town commander can conduct the hearing himself. If he orders so, we will search the house later. We will not leave a thing unturned, and if those riders are hidden here," he said, shrugging his shoulders in disgust, "we will find them. And these people will learn what happens to those who dare defy an order given by a German officer."

He looked at Johanna. "The child can stay," he said. But he didn't let Johanna kiss Grandfather and Grandmother good-bye. Johanna was standing near the hall closet, and quickly she slipped down a coat for Grandmother, but she couldn't get Grandfather's coat off the hook. The coat was heavy and the hook too high, and now they were leaving. She could only give Grandfather his hat and his woolen scarf, which weren't enough for the chilly September night. Grandfather and Grandmother walked arm in arm out of the door and the soldiers followed them.

When the last soldier slammed the door behind him, Johanna found that her knees were shaking. She had to sit down on the bottom step of the staircase. The clock in the hall ticked and the minutes passed by.

"If those riders are hidden here, these people will learn what happens to those who dare defy an order given by a German officer," the soldier had said.

They must be hidden more safely, Johanna knew, and she would have to do it. The men would certainly not come now. The neighbors must have seen what happened and they would have warned the men to stay far away from the house. Johanna looked out of the peephole in the door. One soldier was left standing on guard.

"We will not leave a thing unturned and if those riders are hidden here, we will find them," the German had also said.

The riders were big and there were twelve of them and the horses, too. What hiding place would be big enough? Sitting on the bottom step of the stairs, Johanna's mind wandered through the whole house thinking of all the different closets, but not one was big enough to hide the riders safely. At last she thought of her attic room. Of course, her own secret hiding place was there. It was certainly big enough, but it was right in Captain Braun's room. But the more she thought about it now, the more she became convinced that it would also be the safest place to hide the riders. The Germans would certainly not think that the riders might be hidden in the room of a German officer, and they would probably not search his room. Captain Braun apparently had not discovered the cubbyhole and perhaps never would discover it. Anyhow it was the only place in the house where she could hide the riders. She would leave them in the burlap sacks and push them all the way deep in.

Tonight was Friday night and Captain Braun was not home. If she worked fast, the riders would be hidden before he came back. Johanna ran upstairs and started to carry the sacks to the attic room. She didn't put on a light for fear the soldier on guard would see it and come to investigate; instead, she took Grandfather's flashlight. She decided to do the heavy work fast and carry everything upstairs. Putting the riders in the cubbyhole would be easier. She decided also to take the radio from behind the books and put it in the cubbyhole, too.

It wasn't easy. By the time the last horse and rider were in the attic room Johanna was out of breath. Her hair was mussed and her skirt was torn in several places. It had also taken her much longer than she had expected, but if she worked fast there was still time enough before Captain Braun came home. In the closet she pushed Captain Braun's uniforms aside and reached to open the bolt of the little door, but it had become stiff and rusty. She got down on her knees and tried again. The bolt didn't yield. Johanna felt warm and her hands started to tremble. Surely she would be able to open the bolt, it had never given her trouble before. But no matter how hard she tried, she could not open the bolt on the little door. She forgot everything around her, even the riders and Grandfather and Grandmother and the danger they were in at this moment. She thought only of one thing. The door must open. It must.

She was so busy she didn't hear the footsteps on the stairs nor the door of the attic room opening. She first saw Captain Braun when he was standing in the door of the big closet. He had to bend down a little not to hit his head against the low ceiling.

"What are you doing in the dark in my closet?" he asked.

He switched the light on so that Johanna's eyes were blinded by it, and she turned her head away. Around her

on the floor were the sacks with the riders. The radio was right beside her and Johanna pushed it behind her back, but she couldn't hide the riders. Captain Braun kneeled down and opened one of the bags. There was nothing Johanna could do or say. He took out a white horse with gentle black eyes and a fierce curly mane. Then he opened the other bags. The little riders and their horses were lying helpless on their backs on the floor of the closet. The legs of the horses were bent as if they wanted to get up and gallop away. The riders looked more brave and proud than ever, but Johanna knew that no matter how brave and proud they looked, they were forever lost and she could not save them any more.

A feeling of reckless despair came over Johanna. Nothing that she would do or say now could make the situation any worse than it was already. She had tried hard but she had failed; she had failed Grandfather and Grandmother and also the little riders and even her father, whom she had promised to take care of the little riders. If it had not been for Captain Braun, she could have saved them. If he hadn't come home early, the riders would have been hidden and Grandfather and Grandmother would have come back. Now she didn't know what the Germans might do to them. Everything she had ever felt against the Germans welled suddenly up in her.

"I hate you and I despise you," she burst out, "and so does every decent person and you'll never win the war. Grandfather says that you have already lost it." She talked so fast that she had to take a deep breath before she could continue. "And in a few months there will be nothing left of Germany, Grandmother says. You only have to listen every night to the airplanes that fly over."

Then Johanna raised her eyes and looked at Captain Braun for the first time. With his boots and his uniform

he looked like all the other Germans. He looked the same as the soldiers who had taken away Grandfather and Grandmother, but his face was different. Captain Braun did not have a soldier's face. He had the face of a flute player. His face was unmoved and, except for a little heightened color, he appeared not even to have heard what Johanna had said to him.

"So these are the famous little riders," he said quietly. He took one into the room and held it under the light. "They are much more beautiful than I was ever told." He looked again and hesitated for a little while. "I would like to look at them much longer, but it would be safer for them and for you to put them back in the sacks and hide them where they will not be found."

"But I can't," Johanna said. She wasn't feeling angry any more, only very frightened. "The bolt of the door is rusty. I can't open it." She was surprised to hear that she was crying. "And they took Grandfather and Grandmother. They said, 'If we find the riders in this house, you will see what happens to people who disobey an order given by a German officer.' "

Captain Braun kneeled beside Johanna. His hands were strong and quick as he slipped aside the stiff bolt. He took the sacks and started to put the riders back in.

"What will you do to them?" Johanna asked.

"The little riders will be my guests for as long as they want to be," Captain Braun said. "I owe that to them. They are the first Dutchmen who looked at me in a friendly way and did not turn their faces away when I spoke to them."

Johanna felt her face grow hot and red as he spoke. She bent down and started to help him put the riders and the horses back into the sacks.

"There may not be much time," he said. "Crawl through the door and I will hand you the sacks."

Johanna still hesitated. Was he really going to help her?

"Come," he said. "Do as I tell you." There was a faint smile around his mouth, but the rest of his face looked grave. "This is an order given by a German officer." He gave her a gentle push.

In a few minutes the riders were hidden and the radio, too. At a moment when Captain Braun had his back turned, Johanna pushed it deep into the closet. One day when he was out she would come and get it. Grandfather couldn't be without his radio.

"Go down now," Captain Braun said. "It's better for all of us if no one sees us together."

Johanna went downstairs and alone she waited in the dark living room. Outside, the soldier was still standing guard. She pushed Grandfather's big chair near the window and sat down, her tired arms leaning on the windowsill. From there she saw them come across the marketplace.

Grandfather had his arm around Grandmother's shoulders as if to protect her from the soldiers who were all around them. This time there were more than nine. As soon as Grandfather opened the door with his key the soldiers swarmed over the room. The big red-faced soldier was again in charge. At his command the others pushed aside the furniture and looked behind it. They stuck their bayonets into the upholstery and ripped it open, although Johanna couldn't understand why. The riders and the horses were much too big to be hidden in the upholstery of a chair. With their rifles they knocked on the walls, and when Grandmother's Delft-blue plates tumbled from the wall and broke in pieces some of the soldiers laughed. When they left to search the upstairs, the room looked as if a tornado had passed through.

Grandfather and Grandmother went upstairs, too, but they were always surrounded by soldiers, so that Johanna could not speak one word to them. All she could do was follow. The big red-faced soldier told Grandfather to turn on the light and while he fumbled clumsily to find the switch, the soldier pushed Grandfather aside and turned the switch himself. In the soft glow of the lamp the den looked immaculate. Johanna could hear Grandmother give a little gasp of surprise.

The soldiers began with the desk, taking out the drawers and dumping the contents in a heap on the floor. They went through all the papers. Now and then one of the soldiers went over to the red-faced man to let him

read something. He always shook his head and shrugged
his shoulders.

At last they went to the bookcase and began to take
out the books. Johanna saw Grandfather's face grow tight.
She wished she could show him somehow that there was
nothing to worry about, but there was always at least one
soldier standing next to him and Grandmother. The
soldiers reached the shelf where the radio was always
hidden, but there were only the books they kept dumping
on the floor. Now they went down on their knees and
looked under the bed and knocked on the wooden floor.
Over their bent heads Grandfather looked at Johanna
with more pride than she had ever before seen in his eyes.
Grandmother gave Johanna a little wink.

The soldiers finally gave up. They realized that there
was nothing hidden in these rooms. Only the attic room
was left. They climbed the last stairs. Johanna felt weak
and shaky again. Even when they found Captain Braun,

they might still decide to search the room. She was glad now that Grandfather and Grandmother had no idea where the riders were hidden. They walked confidently up the stairs, Grandmother winking again at Johanna behind the soldiers' backs.

The soldiers must not have known that the room was occupied by one of their own officers, because they were taken aback when they found Captain Braun with his legs on the table, writing in his music book. He rose from his chair. The soldiers apologized profusely and the red-faced man especially seemed extremely upset at having intruded so unceremoniously on the room of a German officer. Captain Braun put all of them at ease with a few friendly words and he must have made a joke, for they laughed. For one terrible moment Johanna thought that, after all, Captain Braun's face looked no different from all the other soldiers. What he had done tonight could be a trap and he could betray them. But the soldiers now made ready to go, and they went without searching the room. Captain Braun swung his legs back onto the table and took up his pencil and music book.

The attitude of the soldiers changed during their walk downstairs. When they came they had been sure they would find the riders. Now they seemed uncertain. The big red-faced soldier seemed to take it very much to heart that he had failed to find the riders or even to find any evidence that Grandfather had anything to do with their disappearance. He and the other soldiers seemed suddenly to be in a terrible hurry and left the house without saying a word, except for one young man with a pale complexion and fair hair whom Johanna had hardly noticed before. He stopped on the doorstep to talk to Grandfather.

"We hope you understand, sir, that we only did our duty. Our duty is more important than the little inconvenience we caused you." His pale face started to glow now with enthusiasm and he raised his right hand. "Heil Hitler," he shouted as Grandfather closed the door behind him.

Grandfather picked up Johanna and swung her high in the air, as he had done when she had still been a little girl.

"Oh, Johanna, we are so proud of you, but where in this house did you hide the little riders?"

Grandmother hugged Johanna but she wouldn't let her tell the secret until they were all sitting quietly with a warm drink. "We will clean up the rooms tomorrow," Grandmother said and she didn't even look at her Delft-blue plates. She could look only at Johanna. They talked till deep into the night, and both Grandfather and Grandmother went upstairs with Johanna to tuck her in and kiss her good night.

"Will they ever come back?" Johanna asked Grandfather.

"I don't think so," he said as he sat down on the edge of her bed. "They are convinced that the riders are not hidden here, and they can't prove that I ever had anything to do with their disappearance." He turned off the light and left the room.

As Johanna lay thinking about everything that had happened during the long day, she could hear the airplanes flying over the house. The night was almost gone and, with the daylight, the planes were returning from their mission. Every night it sounded as if there were more planes than the night before. This time Johanna didn't think of her father; instead she thought of Captain Braun. She put on her slippers and walked upstairs. The door of the room stood ajar. Johanna pushed it open. Captain Braun was sitting at the table with his face buried in his hands. He looked up when he heard Johanna.

"I cannot sleep," Johanna said. "If I leave my door open, would you, please, play the flute for me?"

More Stories of Courage

The Bears on Hemlock Mountain by Alice Dalgliesh. Scribner, 1952.
There aren't supposed to be any bears on Hemlock Mountain—but there are. And Jonathan must find a way to escape from them.

Mine for Keeps by Jean Little. Little, 1962.
Sarey isn't pampered because she has cerebral palsy, a condition that makes it difficult for her to control her muscles; instead she learns to lead a normal, independent life.

Call It Courage by Sperry Armstrong. Macmillan, 1940.
A Polynesian boy overcomes his fear of the ocean by journeying alone to a distant island.

Courage to Adventure: Stories of Boys and Girls Growing Up with America selected by Child Study Association of America/Wel-Met. T. Y. Crowell, 1976.
Here are nineteen stories about American children from many different ethnic heritages at many different times in our nation's history.

The Princess and the Lion by Elizabeth Coatsworth. Pantheon, 1963.
About 200 years ago, an Abyssinian princess, followed by her pet lion, sets out to free her brother who is held prisoner in a distant mountain.

Fox Running by R. R. Knudson. Harper & Row, 1975.
A young Apache woman works hard to become a track star at college and later in the Olympics.

Boris by Jaap ter Haar. Delacorte, 1970.
Boris's story reflects the true hardships that World War II meant for many European children.

PART 4

Poetry:
The Poet's Way

Poetry: The Poet's Way

Poetry looks different from prose. Some lines of poetry are long. Others are short. The lines usually are grouped into *stanzas*. In prose, lines are grouped into paragraphs, and most lines in a paragraph are the same length.

Poetry is likely to sound different from prose. The lines of poetry often rhyme, while those of prose do not. You can hear a different kind of rhythm in poetry than in prose.

Here are some poems with lines arranged in many ways. Some of them rhyme, while others do not. Now and then you may want to read a poem several times to find the meaning that seems best to you. Don't be surprised if a poem has a different meaning for someone else. It is the poet's way to say things that can have different meanings for different people. That's what makes reading poetry such an adventure.

Limericks are short nonsense poems
with a special kind of rhyme.

Limericks

by DAVID McCORD

A limerick shapes to the eye
Like a small very squat butterfly,
   With its wings opened wide,
   Lots of nectar inside,
And a terrible urge to fly high.

The limerick's lively to write:
Five lines to it—all nice and tight.
   Two long ones, two trick
   Little short ones; then quick
As a flash here's the last one in sight.

There Was an Old Man with a Beard

by EDWARD LEAR

There was an Old Man with a beard,
Who said, "It is just as I feared!—
Two Owls and a Hen, four Larks and a Wren,
Have all built their nests in my beard."

Howard

by A. A. MILNE

There was a young puppy called Howard,
Who at fighting was rather a coward;
   He never quite ran
   When the battle began,
But he started at once to bow-wow hard.

A Tutor Who Tooted the Flute

by CAROLYN WELLS

A tutor who tooted the flute
Tried to tutor two tooters to toot.
   Said the two to the tutor,
   "Is it harder to toot or
To tutor two tooters to toot?"

Ballads are storytelling poems that people have told and sung for a long, long time.

The Big Rock Candy Mountain

TRADITIONAL

[1]   One summer's day in the month of May
        A weary man came hiking;
     Down a shady lane near the sugar cane
        He was looking for his liking.
     As he strolled along, he sang a song
        Of a land of milk and honey,
     Where a man can stay for many a day
        And never think of money.

[2]   O, the buzzing of the bees in the sycamore trees,
     And the soda-water fountain,
Where the blue bird sings near the lemonade springs
     In the Big Rock Candy Mountain.

[3]   In that Big Rock Candy Mountain
     All cats have wooden legs;
The bulldogs all have rubber teeth,
     And the hens lay soft-boiled eggs.
The trees let down their rich, ripe fruit
     And you sleep on silky hay.
The wind don't blow and there is no snow
     Forever and a day.

[4]   O, the buzzing of the bees in the sycamore trees,
     And the soda-water fountain,
Where the blue bird sings near the lemonade springs
     In the Big Rock Candy Mountain.

[5]   Apple pies grow on bushes below,
     And the crust is flaky and light;
Roast pigeons fly into your mouth
     And the skies are always bright.
There's a lake with stew and dumplings, too;
     Cakes to be had for the asking;
Time seems to fly 'neath a sugar sky
     As you spend your whole life basking.

[6]   O, the buzzing of the bees in the sycamore trees,
     And the soda-water fountain,
Where the blue bird sings near the lemonade springs
     In the Big Rock Candy Mountain.

Colonel Fazackerley

by CHARLES CAUSLEY

[1]   Colonel Fazackerley Butterworth-Toast
Bought an old castle complete with a ghost,
But someone or other forgot to declare
To Colonel Fazack that the spectre was there.

[2]   On the very first evening, while waiting to dine,
The Colonel was taking a fine sherry wine,
When the ghost, with a furious flash and a flare,
Shot out of the chimney and shivered, "Beware!"

[3]   Colonel Fazackerley put down his glass
And said, "My dear fellow, that's really first class!
I just can't conceive how you do it at all.
I imagine you're going to a Fancy Dress Ball?"

[4]   At this, the dread ghost gave a withering cry.
Said the Colonel (his monocle firm in his eye),
"Now just how you do it I wish I could think.
Do sit down and tell me, and please have a drink."

[5]   The ghost in his phosphorous cloak gave a roar
And floated about between ceiling and floor.
He walked through a wall and returned through a pane
And backed up the chimney and came down again.

[6]   Said the Colonel, "With laughter I'm feeling
       quite weak!"
(As trickles of merriment ran down his cheek).
"My house-warming party I hope you won't spurn.
You *must* say you'll come and you'll give us a turn!"

[7]   At this, the poor spectre—quite out of his wits—
Proceeded to shake himself almost to bits.
He rattled his chains and he clattered his bones
And he filled the whole castle with mumbles
      and moans.

[8]   But Colonel Fazackerley, just as before,
        Was simply delighted and called out, "Encore!"
        At which the ghost vanished, his efforts in vain,
        And never was seen at the castle again.

[9]   "Oh dear, what a pity!" said Colonel Fazack.
        "I don't know his name, so I can't call him back."
        And then with a smile that was hard to define,
        Colonel Fazackerley went in to dine.

Here is another kind of storytelling, or *narrative*, poem. Narrative poems may have lines and rhymes arranged in many ways. This narrative poem tells a famous story from American history.

Paul Revere's Ride

by HENRY WADSWORTH LONGFELLOW

[1]   Listen, my children, and you shall hear
Of the midnight ride of Paul Revere,
On the eighteenth of April, in seventy-five;
Hardly a man is now alive
Who remembers that famous day and year.

[2] He said to his friend, "If the British march
By land or sea from the town tonight,
Hang a lantern aloft in the belfry arch
Of the North Church tower, as a signal light—
One, if by land, and two, if by sea;
And I on the opposite shore will be,
Ready to ride and spread the alarm
Through every Middlesex village and farm,
For the country folk to be up and to arm."

[3] Then he said "Good night!" and with muffled oar
Silently rowed to the Charlestown shore,
Just as the moon rose over the bay,
Where, swinging wide at her moorings, lay
The *Somerset*, British man-of-war:
A phantom ship, with each mast and spar
Across the moon, like a prison bar,
And a huge black hulk, that was magnified
By its own reflection in the tide.

[4] Meanwhile, his friend, through alley and street,
Wanders and watches with eager ears,
Till in the silence around him he hears
The muster of men at the barrack door,
The sounds of arms, and the tramp of feet,
And the measured tread of the grenadiers
Marching down to their boats on the shore.

[5]   Then he climbed the tower of the Old North
          Church
       By the wooden stairs, with stealthy tread,
       To the belfry chamber overhead,
       And startled the pigeons from their perch
       On the somber rafters, that round him made
       Masses and moving shapes of shade—
       By the trembling ladder, steep and tall,
       To the highest window in the wall,
       Where he paused to listen and look down
       A moment on the roofs of the town,
       And the moonlight flowing over all.

[6] Beneath, in the churchyard, lay the dead,
In their night encampment on the hill,
Wrapped in silence so deep and still
That he could hear, like a sentinel's tread,
The watchful night wind, as it went
Creeping along from tent to tent,
And seeming to whisper, "All is well!"
A moment only he feels the spell
Of the place and the hour, the secret dread
Of the lonely belfry and the dead;
For suddenly all his thoughts are bent
On a shadowy something far away,
Where the river widens to meet the bay —
A line of black, that bends and floats
On the rising tide, like a bridge of boats.

[7] Meanwhile, impatient to mount and ride,
Booted and spurred, with a heavy stride
On the opposite shore walked Paul Revere.
Now he patted his horse's side,
Now gazed at the landscape far and near,
Then, impetuous, stamped the earth,
And turned and tightened his saddle girth;
But mostly he watched with eager search
The belfry tower of the Old North Church,
As it rose above the graves on the hill,
Lonely and spectral and somber and still.
And lo! as he looks, on the belfry's height
A glimmer, and then a gleam of light.
He springs to his saddle, the bridle he turns,
But lingers and gazes, till full on his sight
A second lamp in the belfry burns!

[8]   A hurry of hoofs in a village street,
      A shape in the moonlight, a bulk in the dark,
      And beneath, from the pebbles, in passing, a spark
      Struck out by a steed flying fearless and fleet:
      That was all! And yet, through the gloom and the light,
      The fate of a nation was riding that night;
      And the spark struck out by that steed, in his flight,
      Kindled the land into flame with its heat.

[9]   He has left the village and mounted the steep,
      And beneath him, tranquil and broad and deep,
      Is the Mystic, meeting the ocean tides;
      And under the alders that skirt its edge,
      Now soft on the sand, now loud on the ledge,
      Is heard the tramp of his steed as he rides.

[10]   It was twelve by the village clock,
        When he crossed the bridge into Medford town.
        He heard the crowing of the cock,
        And the barking of the farmer's dog,
        And felt the damp of the river fog
        That rises after the sun goes down.

[11]   It was one by the village clock,
        When he galloped into Lexington.
        He saw the gilded weathercock
        Swim in the moonlight as he passed,
        And the meetinghouse windows, blank and bare,
        Gaze at him with a spectral glare,
        As if they already stood aghast
        At the bloody work they would look upon.

[12]   It was two by the village clock,
        When he came to the bridge in Concord town.
        He heard the bleating of the flock,
        And the twitter of birds among the trees,
        And felt the breath of the morning breeze
        Blowing over the meadows brown.
        And one was safe and asleep in his bed,
        Who at the bridge would be first to fall,
        Who that day would be lying dead,
        Pierced by a British musket ball.

[13]   You know the rest. In the books you have read
How the British Regulars fired and fled—
How the farmers gave them ball for ball,
From behind each fence and farmyard wall,
Chasing the Redcoats down the lane,
Then crossing the fields to emerge again
Under the trees at the turn of the road,
And only pausing to fire and load.

[14]   So through the night rode Paul Revere;
And so through the night went his cry of alarm
To every Middlesex village and farm—
A cry of defiance and not of fear—
A voice in the darkness, a knock at the door,
And a word that shall echo forevermore!
For, borne on the night wind of the Past,
Through all our history, to the last,
In the hour of darkness and peril and need,
The people will waken and listen to hear
The hurrying hoofbeats of that steed,
And the midnight message of Paul Revere.

The poems in this group will show you some of the many ways that the lines of poems may be arranged. The rhymes may surprise you.

The Hairy Dog

by HERBERT ASQUITH

My dog's so furry I've not seen
His face for years and years:
His eyes are buried out of sight,
I only guess his ears.

When people ask me for his breed,
I do not know or care:
He has the beauty of them all
Hidden beneath his hair.

A Centipede Was Happy Quite

ANONYMOUS

A centipede was happy quite,
    Until a frog in fun
Said, "Pray, which leg comes after which?"
This raised her mind to such a pitch,
She lay distracted in the ditch
    Considering how to run.

261

Autumn Leaves

by EVE MERRIAM

Down
   down
      down
Red
   yellow
      brown
Autumn leaves tumble down
Autumn leaves crumble down
Autumn leaves bumble down
Flaking and shaking,
Tumbledown leaves.

Skittery
Flittery
Rustle by
Hustle by
Crackle and crunch
In a snappety bunch.

Run and catch
Run and snatch
Butterfly leaves
Sailboat leaves
Windstorm leaves.
Can you catch them?

Swoop,
Scoop,
Pile them up
In a stompy pile and
Jump
   Jump
      JUMP!

Pigeons

by LILIAN MOORE

Pigeons are city folk
content
to live with concrete
and cement.

They seldom
try
the sky.

A pigeon never sings
of hill
and flowering hedge,
but busily commutes
from sidewalk to his ledge.

Oh pigeon, what a waste of wings!

View near Robert Frost's home in Vermont

A Time to Talk

by ROBERT FROST

When a friend calls to me from the road
And slows his horse to a meaning walk,
I don't stand still and look around
On all the hills I haven't hoed,
And shout from where I am, "What is it?"
No, not as there is a time to talk.
I thrust my hoe in the mellow ground,
Blade-end up and five feet tall,
And plod: I go up to the stone wall
For a friendly visit.

The poet Robert Frost

Prairie-Dog Town

by MARY AUSTIN

Old Peter Prairie-Dog
Builds him a house
In Prairie-Dog Town,
With a door that goes down
And down and down,
And a hall that goes under
And under and under,
Where you can't see the lightning,
You can't hear the thunder,
For they don't *like* thunder
In Prairie-Dog Town.

Old Peter Prairie-Dog
Digs him a cellar
In Prairie-Dog Town,
With a ceiling that is arched
And a wall that is round,
And the earth he takes out he makes into a mound.
And the hall and the cellar
Are dark as dark,
And you can't see a spark,
Not a single spark;
And the way to them cannot be found.

Old Peter Prairie-Dog
Knows a very clever trick
Of behaving like a stick
When he hears a sudden sound,
Like an old dead stick;
And when you turn your head

He'll jump quick, quick,
And be another stick
When you look around.
It *is* a clever trick,
And it keeps him safe and sound
In the cellar and the halls
That are under the mound
In Prairie-Dog Town.

Knoxville, Tennessee

by NIKKI GIOVANNI

I always like summer
best
you can eat fresh corn
from daddy's garden
and okra
and greens
and cabbage
and lots of
barbecue
and buttermilk
and homemade ice-cream
at the church picnic
and listen to
gospel music
outside
at the church
homecoming
and go to the mountains with
your grandmother
and go barefooted
and be warm
all the time
not only when you go to bed
and sleep

A poem sometimes surprises us because it compares things that we would never think of comparing. You will find some comparisons (and some surprises) in the following poems.

Giraffes

by SY KAHN

Stilted creatures,
Features fashioned as a joke,
Boned and buckled,
Finger painted,

They stand in the field
On long-pronged legs
As if thrust there.
They airily feed,
Slightly swaying,
Like hammer-headed flowers.

Bizarre they are,
Built silent and high,
Ornaments against the sky.
Ears like leaves
To hear the silken
Brushing of the clouds.

Glory, Glory …

by RAY PATTERSON

Across Grandmother's knees
A kindly sun
Laid a yellow quilt.

Check

by JAMES STEPHENS

The Night was creeping on the ground!
She crept and did not make a sound,

Until she reached the tree: And then
She covered it, and stole again

Along the grass beside the wall!
—I heard the rustling of her shawl

As she threw blackness everywhere
Along the sky, the ground, the air,

And in the room where I was hid!
But, no matter what she did

To everything that was without,
She could not put my candle out!

So I stared at the Night! And she
Stared back solemnly at me!

I Go Forth to Move About the Earth

by ALONZO LOPEZ

I go forth to move about the earth.
I go forth as the owl, wise and knowing.
I go forth as the eagle, powerful and bold.
I go forth as the dove, peaceful and gentle.
I go forth to move about the earth
    in wisdom, courage, and peace.

Comma
in the Sky

by AILEEN FISHER

A comma hung above the park,
a shiny punctuation mark;
we saw it curving in the dark
the night the moon was new.

A period hung above the bay,
immense though it was far away;
we saw it at the end of day
the night the moon was full.

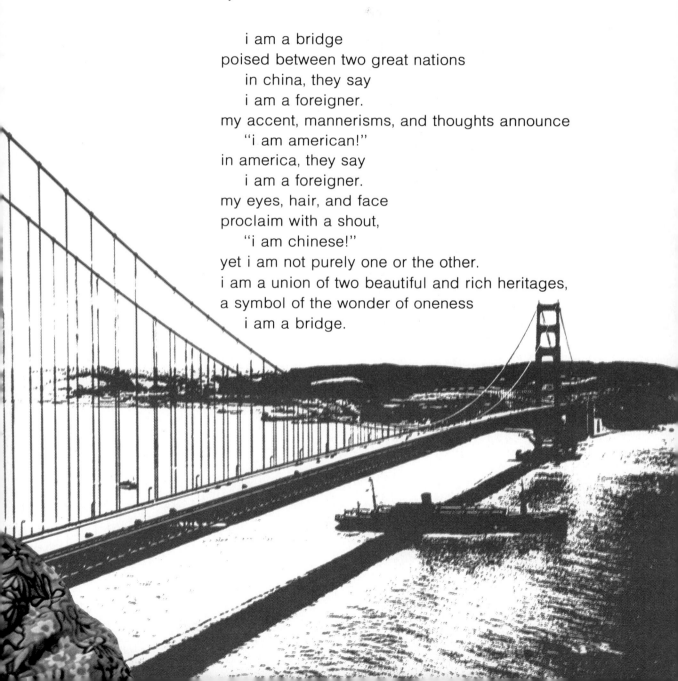

I Am a Bridge...

by CAROLE LIN

i am a bridge
poised between two great nations
    in china, they say
    i am a foreigner.
my accent, mannerisms, and thoughts announce
    "i am american!"
in america, they say
    i am a foreigner.
my eyes, hair, and face
proclaim with a shout,
    "i am chinese!"
yet i am not purely one or the other.
i am a union of two beautiful and rich heritages,
a symbol of the wonder of oneness
    i am a bridge.

Foghorns

by LILIAN MOORE

The foghorns moaned
    in the bay last night
so sad
so deep
I thought I heard the city
    crying in its sleep.

April Rain Song

by LANGSTON HUGHES

Let the rain kiss you.
Let the rain beat upon your head with silver liquid drops.
Let the rain sing you a lullaby.

The rain makes still pools on the sidewalk.
The rain makes running pools in the gutter.
The rain plays a little sleep-song on our roof at night—

And I love the rain.

Different people sometimes get different ideas from the same poem. This is one way that reading poetry may be different from reading other kinds of writing. You may find new things in these poems each time you read them.

Penguin

by MARY ANN HOBERMAN

O Penguin, do you ever try
To flap your flipper wings and fly?
How do you feel, a bird by birth
And yet for life tied down to earth?
A feathered creature, born with wings
Yet never wingborne. All your kings
And emperors must wonder why
Their realm is sea instead of sky.

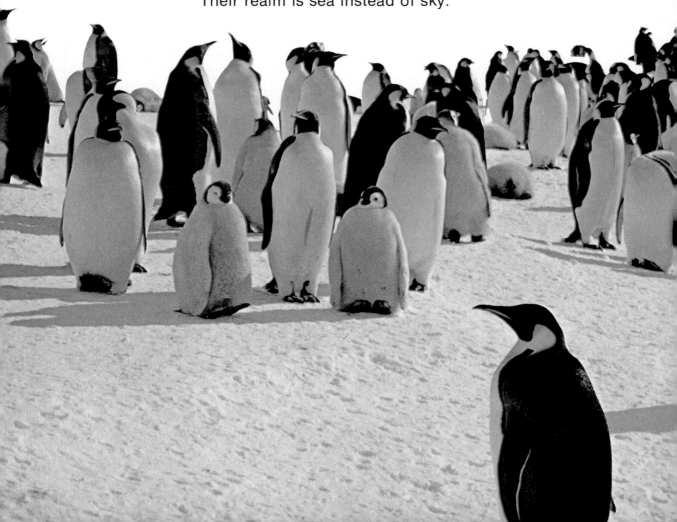

Nancy Hanks

by ROSEMARY BENÉT *and*
STEPHEN VINCENT BENÉT

If Nancy Hanks
Came back as a ghost,
Seeking news
Of what she loved most,
She'd ask first
"Where's my son?
What's happened to Abe?
What's he done?

"Poor little Abe,
Left all alone
Except for Tom,
Who's a rolling stone;
He was only nine
The year I died.
I remember still
How hard he cried.

Four score and seven forth upon this continent in liberty and dedicated are created equal

"Scraping along
In a little shack,
With hardly a shirt
To cover his back,
And a prairie wind
To blow him down,
Or pinching times
If he went to town.

"You wouldn't know
About my son?
Did he grow tall?
Did he have fun?
Did he learn to read?
Did he get to town?
Did you know his name?
Did he get on?"

BY INDUSTRY WE THRIVE

283

Wind Last Night

A KOREAN SIJO POEM

Wind last night blew down
A gardenful of peach blossoms.
A boy with a broom
Is starting to sweep them up.

Fallen flowers are flowers still;
Don't brush them away.

Birdfoot's Grampa

by JOSEPH BRUCHAC

The Old Man
must have stopped our car
two dozen times to climb out
and gather into his hands
the small toads blinded
by our lights and leaping
like live drops of rain.

The rain was falling,
a mist around his white hair,
and I kept saying,
"You can't save them all,
accept it, get in,
we've got places to go."

But, leathery hands full
of wet brown life,
knee deep in the summer
roadside grass,
he just smiled and said,
"They have places to go, too."

My Fingers

by MARY O'NEILL

My fingers are antennae.
Whatever they touch:
Bud, rose, apple,
Cellophane, crutch —
They race the feel
Into my brain,
Plant it there and
Begin again.
This is how I knew
Hot from cold
Before I was even
Two years old.
This is how I can tell,
Though years away,
That elephant hide
Feels leathery grey.
My brain never loses
A touch I bring:
Frail of an eggshell,
Pull of a string,
Beat of a pulse
That tells me life
Thumps in a person
But not in a knife.
Signs that say:
"Please do not touch,"
Disappoint me
Very much.

More Poems to Read

Laughable Limericks compiled by Sara Brewton and John E. Brewton. T. Y. Crowell, 1965.
This is a collection of a favorite kind of funny poetry.

On Our Way: Poems of Pride and Love selected by Lee Bennett Hopkins. Knopf, 1974.
Here are poems by twenty-two black poets, including Gwendolyn Brooks, Nikki Giovanni, and Langston Hughes.

Piping Down the Valleys Wild edited and introduced by Nancy Larrick. Delacorte, 1968.
This book includes popular poems of many moods.

Four Corners of the Sky selected by Theodore Clymer. Little, 1975.
Native American poems, chants, and oratory from many cultures are beautifully illustrated.

Straight on till Morning: Poems of the Imaginary World selected by Helen Hill, Agnes Perkins, and Althea Helag. T. Y. Crowell, 1977.
This book includes poems of magic and mystery.

You Come Too by Robert Frost. Holt, Rinehart & Winston, 1959.
One of America's most famous poets selected many of his favorite poems to share with young readers.

The Moment of Wonder: A Collection of Chinese and Japanese Poetry collected by Richard Lewis. Dial, 1974.
Here is a book of beautiful, imaginative poems.

As I Walked Out One Evening: A Book of Ballads selected by Helen Plotz. Greenwillow Bks., 1976.
Here are 130 ballads of the English-speaking world.

PART 5

You Can't Help Laughing

You Can't Help Laughing

Just about everyone likes funny stories. And there are many kinds of funny stories, each with its own special kind of humor. Some stories are about things that could never really happen. These stories are so exaggerated that they are called *tall tales*. Other funny stories seem almost real, even though they may tell about things that are not likely to happen. Sometimes stories make us smile by teasing us with little jokes. Other times they make us laugh out loud, especially when something totally unexpected happens.

An especially interesting kind of funny story is one that not only makes us laugh, but also makes us think. Such a story is really nudging us gently, as if to warn us not to take ourselves too seriously. Sometimes, that is how we learn to laugh at ourselves.

What kind of book could save the Earth? You'll find out when you read this play about a Martian plan to take over our world.

The Book That Saved the Earth

by CLAIRE BOIKO

Characters

HISTORIAN
GREAT AND MIGHTY THINK-TANK
APPRENTICE NOODLE
CAPTAIN OMEGA
LIEUTENANT IOTA
SERGEANT OOP
OFFSTAGE VOICE

BEFORE RISE: *Spotlight shines on* HISTORIAN, *who is sitting at table down right, on which is a movie projector. A sign on an easel beside her reads:* MUSEUM OF ANCIENT HISTORY: DEPARTMENT OF THE TWENTIETH CENTURY. *She stands and bows to audience.*

HISTORIAN: Good afternoon. Welcome to our Museum of Ancient History, and to my area—things of the good old, far-off twentieth century. The twentieth century was often called the Age of the Book. In those days, there were books about everything from ants to zoology. Books taught people how to, and when to, and where to, and why to. But the strangest thing a book every did was to save the Earth. You haven't heard

about the Martian invasion of 1988? Really, what *do* they teach children today? Well, you know, Mars never did take over the Earth, because a single book stopped it. What was that book, you ask? A great encyclopedia? A book about rockets and missiles? A secret file from outer space? No, it was none of these. It was—but here, let me turn on the historiscope. I'll show you what happened many, many years ago, in 1988. *(She turns on projector and points it left. Spotlight on* HISTORIAN *goes out and comes up down left on* THINK-TANK, *who is seated on a raised box, arms folded. He has a huge, egg-shaped head, and he wears a long robe decorated with stars and circles.* APPRENTICE NOODLE *stands beside him at an elaborate switchboard. A sign on an easel reads:* MARS SPACE CONTROL. GREAT AND MIGHTY THINK-TANK, COMMANDER-IN-CHIEF. BOW LOW BEFORE ENTERING.)

NOODLE *(Bowing)*: O Great and Mighty Think-Tank, most powerful and intelligent being, what are your orders?

THINK-TANK: You left out something, Apprentice Noodle. Go over the whole thing again.

NOODLE: It shall be done, sir. *(In a singsong)* O Great and Mighty Think-Tank, Ruler of Mars and her two moons, most powerful and intelligent being—*(Out of breath)* what-are-your-orders?

THINK-TANK: That's better, Noodle. I wish to talk with our space probe to that silly little world we are going to put under our great rulership. What do they call it again?

NOODLE: Earth, your Intelligence.

THINK-TANK: Earth—of course. You see how insignificant the place is? But first, something important. My mirror. I wish to consult my mirror.

NOODLE: It shall be done, sir. *(She hands* THINK-TANK *a hand mirror.)*

THINK-TANK: Mirror, mirror, in my hand. Who is the most fantastically intellectually gifted being in the land?

OFFSTAGE VOICE *(After a pause)*: You, sir.

THINK-TANK *(Smacking mirror)*: Quicker. Answer quicker next time. I hate a slow mirror. *(He admires himself.)* Ah, there I am. Are we Martians not handsome? So much better looking than those ugly Earthlings with their tiny heads. Noodle, keep on using your mind. Someday you may have a balloon brain just like mine.

NOODLE: Oh, I hope so, Mighty Think-Tank. I hope so.

THINK-TANK: Now, call the space probe. I want to take over that ball of mud called Earth before lunch.

NOODLE: It shall be done, sir. (*She twists knobs and adjusts levers on switchboard. Electronic buzzes and beeps are heard as the curtains open.*)

* * *

SETTING: *The Centerville Public Library*

AT RISE: CAPTAIN OMEGA *stands at center, opening and closing card catalogue drawers in a puzzled fashion.* LIEUTENANT IOTA *is up left, counting books in a bookcase.* SERGEANT OOP *is at right, opening and closing a book, turning it upside down, shaking it, and then rifling the pages and shaking his head.*

NOODLE (*Adjusting knobs*): I can see the space crew, sir. (THINK-TANK *puts on a pair of huge goggles and turns toward the stage to watch.*) They seem to have gone into some sort of Earth building.

THINK-TANK: Very good. Make voice contact.

NOODLE (*Speaking into a microphone*): Mars Space Control calling the crew of Probe One. Mars Space Control calling the crew of Probe One. Come in, Captain Omega. Give us your location.

CAPTAIN OMEGA (*Speaking into a disc which is on a chain around his neck*): Captain Omega to Mars Space Control. Lieutenant Iota, Sergeant Oop, and I have landed on Earth without any trouble. We are now in this (*Indicates room*) — this square place. Have you any idea where we are, Lieutenant Iota?

IOTA: I can't figure it out, Captain. *(Holding up a book)* I've counted two thousand of these odd things. This place must be some sort of storage barn. What do you think, Sergeant Oop?

OOP: I haven't a clue. I've been to seven galaxies, but I've never seen anything like this. Maybe they're hats. *(He opens a book and puts it on his head.)*

OMEGA *(Bowing low)*: Perhaps the Great and Mighty Think-Tank will give us his thoughts on the matter.

THINK-TANK: Very simple my dear Omega. Hold one of the items up so that I may view it closely. *(OMEGA holds a book on the palm of his hand.)* Yes, yes. I understand now. Since Earthlings are always eating, the place in which you find yourselves is surely a refreshment stand.

OMEGA *(To IOTA and OOP)*: He says we're in a refreshment stand.

OOP: Well, the Earthlings certainly have strange taste.

THINK-TANK: That item in your hand is called a sandwich.

IOTA *(Nodding)*: A sandwich.

OOP *(Taking book from his head)*: A sandwich?

THINK-TANK: Sandwiches are an important part of the Earth diet. Look at it closely. *(OMEGO squints at book.)* There are two slices of what is called "bread" and between them there is some sort of filling.

OMEGA: That is correct, sir.

THINK-TANK: To show that I am right, I order you to eat it.

OMEGA *(Gulping)*: Eat it?

THINK-TANK: Do you doubt the Mighty Think-Tank?

OMEGA: Oh, no, no. But poor Lieutenant Iota has not had her breakfast. Lieutenant Iota, I order you to eat this — this sandwich.

IOTA: Eat it? Oh, Captain! It's a very great honor to be the first Martian to eat a sandwich, I'm sure, but — but how can I eat before my sergeant does? *(Handing* OOP *the book; brightly)* Sergeant Oop, I order you to eat the sandwich.

OOP *(Making a face)*: Who, Lieutenant? Me, Lieutenant?

IOTA *and* OMEGA *(Slapping their chests in a salute)*: For the glory of Mars, Oop!

OOP: Yes, Captain. At once, Lieutenant. *(He opens his mouth wide.* OMEGA *and* IOTA *watch him breathlessly. He bites down on a corner of the book, and pantomimes chewing and swallowing, while making terrible faces.)*

OMEGA: Well, Oop?

IOTA: Well, Oop? *(*OOP *coughs.* OMEGA *and* IOTA *pound him on the back.)*

THINK-TANK: Was it not delicious, Sergeant Oop?

OOP *(Slapping his chest in salute)*: That is right, sir. It was *not* delicious. It don't know how the Earthlings can get those sandwiches down without water. They're as dry as Martian dust.

NOODLE: Sir, sir. Great and Mighty Think-Tank. I beg your pardon, but something just floated into my mind about those sandwiches.

THINK-TANK: It can't be worth much but go ahead. Give us your tiny bit of data.

NOODLE: Well, sir, I have seen our films of those sandwiches. I noticed that the Earthlings did not *eat* them. They used them as some sort of communication device.

THINK-TANK *(Haughtily)*: Of course. That was my next point. These are communication sandwiches. Think-Tank is never wrong. Who is never wrong?

OMEGA, IOTA, *and* OOP *(Together; saluting)*: Great and Mighty Think-Tank is never wrong.

THINK-TANK: Therefore, I order you to listen to them.

OMEGA: Listen to them?

IOTA *and* OOP *(To each other; puzzled)*: Listen to them?

THINK-TANK: Do you have rocks in your ears? I said, listen to them. *(OMEGA, IOTA, and OOP bow very low.)*

OMEGA: It shall be done, sir. *(They each take two books from the case and hold them to their ears, listening intently.)*

IOTA *(Whispering to OMEGA)*: Do you hear anything?

OMEGA *(Whispering back)*: Nothing. Do you hear anything, Oop?

OOP *(Loudly)*: Not a thing! *(OMEGA and IOTA jump in fright.)*

OMEGA *and* IOTA: Sh-h-h! *(They listen again.)*

THINK-TANK: Well? Well? Tell me. What do you hear?

OMEGA: Nothing, sir. Perhaps we are not on the correct frequency.

IOTA: Nothing, sir. Perhaps the Earthlings have sharper ears than we do.

OOP: I don't hear a thing. Maybe these sandwiches don't make sounds.

THINK-TANK: What? What? Does someone think that the Mighty Think-Tank has made a mistake?

OMEGA: Oh, no sir. No, sir. We'll keep listening.

NOODLE: Please excuse me, your Brilliance. A cloudy piece of information is rolling around in my head.

THINK-TANK: Well, roll it out, Noodle, and I will clarify it for you.

NOODLE: I seem to remember that the Earthlings did not listen to the sandwiches. They opened them and watched them.

THINK-TANK: Yes, that is quite correct. Captain Omega, those sandwiches are not for ear communication. They are for eye communication. Now, Captain Omega, take that large, bright-colored sandwich over there. It looks important. Tell me what you see. (OMEGA *picks up a very large copy of* MOTHER GOOSE, *holding it so that the audience can see the title.* IOTA *looks over his left shoulder, and* OOP *looks over his right shoulder.*)

OMEGA: It seems to contain pictures of Earthlings.

IOTA: And there seems to be some sort of code.

THINK-TANK (*Sharply interested*): Code? Code? I told you this was important. Tell me about it.

OOP: It's little lines and circles and dots. Thousands of them, next to the pictures.

THINK-TANK: Code. Perhaps the Earthlings are not as stupid as we have thought. We must break the code. We must.

NOODLE: Forgive me, your Cleverness, but did not we give our crew pills to increase their intelligence?

THINK-TANK: Stop! A thought of great brilliance has come to me. Space crew, we have given you pills to increase your intelligence. Take them and then watch the sandwich. The meaning of the code will slowly unfold before you.

OMEGA: It shall be done, sir. Remove pill. *(Crew take pills from boxes on their belts.)* Present pill. *(They hold pills out in front of them, stiffly.)* Swallow pill. *(They pop the pills into their mouths and gulp simultaneously. They open their eyes wide, and they put their hands to their foreheads.)*

THINK-TANK: Excellent. Now, break that code.

OMEGA, IOTA, *and* OOP *(Together)*: It shall be done, sir.
    (They frown over the book, turning the pages.)

OMEGA *(Brightly)*: Aha!

IOTA *(Brightly)*: Oho!

OOP *(Bursting into laughter)*: Ha, ha, ha.

THINK-TANK: What does it say? Tell me this minute.
    Read, Omega.

OMEGA: Yes, sir. *(He reads with great seriousness.)*

Mistress Mary, quite contrary,
How does your garden grow?
With cockle shells and silver bells
And pretty maids all in a row.

OOP: Ha, ha, ha. Think of that. Pretty maids growing in
    a garden.

THINK-TANK *(Alarmed)*: Stop! This is no time for laughing. Don't you see that this is serious? The Earthlings have found a way to combine farming and mining. They can actually grow crops of rare metals such as silver. And cockle shells. They can grow high explosives, too. Noodle, call our invasion ships.

NOODLE: They are ready to go down and take over Earth, sir.

THINK-TANK: Tell them to hold. Tell them new information has come to us about Earth. Iota, go on reading.

IOTA: Yes, sir. *(She reads very gravely.)*

> Hey diddle diddle! The cat and the fiddle,
> The cow jumped over the moon,
> The little dog laughed to see such sport,
> And the dish ran away with the spoon.

OOP *(Laughing)*: The dish ran away with the spoon!

THINK-TANK: Stop laughing. This is more and more alarming. The Earthlings have reached a high level of civilization. Didn't you hear? They have taught their animals music and space flight. Even their dogs have a sense of humor. Why, at this very moment, they may be starting an interplanetary attack of millions of cows! Call our ships. No invasion today. Oop, read the next code.

OOP: Yes, sir. *(Reading)*

> Humpty Dumpty sat on the wall,
> Humpty Dumpty had a great fall;
> All the king's horses and all the king's men
> Couldn't put Humpty together again.

Oh, look, sir. Here's a picture of Humpty Dumpty. Why, sir, he looks like — he looks like — *(He turns a large picture of* HUMPTY DUMPTY *toward* THINK-TANK *and the audience.)*

THINK-TANK *(Screaming and holding his head)*: It's me! It's my Great and Mighty Balloon Brain. The Earthlings have seen me. They're after me. "Had a great fall!" — That means they plan to take Mars and me! It's an invasion of Mars! Noodle, get a spaceship for me. I must escape at once. Space crew, you must leave Earth right now. But be sure to hide all trace of your visit. The Earthlings must not know that I know — *(*OMEGA, IOTA, *and* OOP *rush about, putting books back.)*

NOODLE: Where shall we go, sir?

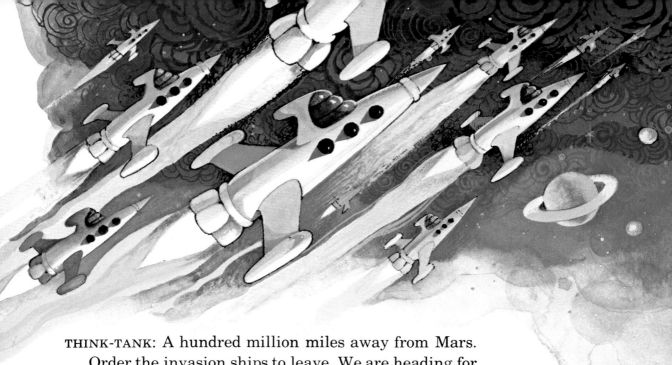

THINK-TANK: A hundred million miles away from Mars.
Order the invasion ships to leave. We are heading for
Alpha Centauri, a hundred million miles away.
(OMEGA, IOTA, *and* OOP *run off right as* NOODLE *helps*
THINK-TANK *off left and the curtain closes. Spotlight
shines on* HISTORIAN *down right.*)

HISTORIAN (*Chuckling*): And that's how one dusty old
book saved the world from a Martian takeover. As
you all know, in the year 2488, five hundred years
after all this happened, we Earthlings resumed contact with Mars. And we even became very friendly
with the Martians. By that time, Great and Mighty
Think-Tank had been replaced by a very clever Martian—the Wise and Wonderful Noodle! Oh, yes, we
taught the Martians the difference between sandwiches and books. We taught them how to read, too.
We set up a library in the city of Marsopolis. But,
as you might expect, there is still one book that the
Martians can never bring themselves to read.
You've guessed it—MOTHER GOOSE! (*She bows and
exits right.*)

The Toothpaste Millionaire

by JEAN MERRILL

One afternoon I stopped by my friend Rufus's house to borrow his bike pump. He had about fifty bowls and pans scattered around the kitchen.

"What are you making?" I asked.

"I already made it," Rufus said.

He handed me a spoon and a bowl with some white stuff in it. I took a spoonful.

"Don't eat it," Rufus said. "Just taste it. Rub a little on your teeth. It's toothpaste."

I tried a little.

"How does it taste?" Rufus asked.

"Not bad," I said. "Better than the kind my mother buys in the pink-and-white striped tube. How'd you get it to taste so good?"

"A drop of peppermint oil," Rufus said. "But I've got other flavors, too."

He pushed three other pots across the table. The first one had a spicy taste.

"Clove-flavored," Rufus said. "You like it?"

"I don't know," I said. "It's interesting."

"Try this one."

The next sample had a sweet taste. "Vanilla," I guessed.

"Right," Rufus said.

"I like vanilla," I said. "In milkshakes. Or ice cream. But it doesn't seem quite right in toothpaste. Too sweet."

"This one won't be too sweet," Rufus said, handing me another sample.

"*Eeegh*," I said and ran to the sink to wash out my mouth. "What did you put in *that*?"

"Curry powder," Rufus said. "You don't like it? I thought it tasted like a good shrimp curry."

"Maybe it does," I said, "but I don't like curry."

Rufus looked disappointed. "I don't suppose you'd like it almond-flavored, either," he said. "I made some of that, too, but I decided not too many people would take to almond."

"What flavor is in that big plastic pan?" I asked. "You've got enough of that kind to frost twenty-seven cakes."

"That's no kind yet," Rufus said. "That's just seventy-nine cents worth of the stuff that goes in the paste. I didn't want to flavor it till I figured out the best taste."

"What does it taste like plain?" I asked.

"Well," Rufus said, "mostly you taste the bicarb."

"Bicarb!" I said. "You mean all this stuff I've been tasting has got bicarbonate of soda in it?"

Rufus grinned. "Yeah," he said. "It's probably good for your stomach as well as your teeth."

"You must have enough for ten tubes in that plastic bowl," I guessed.

"More, I bet," Rufus said.

"Why don't you squeeze the toothpaste in the tube into a measuring cup and then measure the stuff in the bowl," I suggested.

"That would be a waste of toothpaste," Rufus said. "We couldn't get it back in the tube." Rufus hates to waste anything.

"I have a better idea," he said. "I'll pack into a square pan the toothpaste I made. Then I can figure out how many cubic inches of toothpaste we have. And you can figure out how many cubic inches of toothpaste are in the tube."

"But the tube is round, Rufus," I said. "I can't measure cubic inches unless something is cube-shaped."

Rufus thought a minute. "Maybe we can squeeze the tube into a cube shape," he said.

I thought that was brilliant. But then I had another idea.

"Rufus," I said. "It says on the tube that it contains 3.25 ounces of toothpaste. Why couldn't we just weigh your paste and divide by 3.25 to see how many tubes it would make?"

"Hey—we could!" Rufus said. "You are *smart*, Kate. I'm always doing things the hard way."

That's what is really so nice about Rufus. It's not just that he gets great ideas like making toothpaste. But if *you* have a good idea, he says so.

I was pleased that I had thought of a simpler way of measuring the toothpaste, but I told Rufus, "I wish I was smart enough even to *think* of a hard way of doing something."

I *never* would have thought of measuring toothpaste in cubic inches. Partly because I never can remember exactly how to figure cubic inches. And I certainly wouldn't have thought of making a round tube cube-shaped. Would you?

Anyway it turned out Rufus had made about forty tubes of toothpaste for seventy-nine cents.

Before I finished breakfast the next morning, there was a knock on the door. It was Rufus. He was very excited.

"Kate!" he said. "Do you know what the population of the United States is?"

"No," I said. I never know things like that.

My father looked up from his paper. "According to the most recent census—over 200,000,000," he said to Rufus. My father always knows things like that.

"You're right," Rufus said. "And by now, it must be even bigger."

"Probably," my father said.

"Mr. MacKinstrey," Rufus said. "I was thinking that everybody in the United States probably uses about one tube of toothpaste a month."

"Probably," my father said.

"And if they do," Rufus said, "how many tubes of toothpaste are sold in a year?"

My father thought for a second. "Roughly two-and-a-half billion tubes."

"Right!" Rufus said.

I hate people who can multiply in their heads. Except that my father and Rufus are two of the people I like best in the world. How do you explain that?

I really don't like math at all, even when I have a paper and pencil and all the time in the world to figure something out.

And at the same time I look forward every day to Mr. Conti's math class. And how do you explain that, since that's the class where I'm always getting in trouble?

For example, the same day my father answered Rufus's population question, Mr. Conti said in math class:

"Kate MacKinstrey, would you please bring me that note."

"Well, it isn't exactly a note, Mr. Conti."

"I see," says Mr. Conti. "I suppose it's another math problem."

"It looks like a math problem, Mr. Conti."

The message from Rufus that Mr. Conti got to read that day said:

If there are 2½ billion tubes of toothpaste sold in the U.S. in one year, and 1 out of 10 people switched to a new brand, how many tubes of the new brand would they be buying?

The right answer is 250 million. It took the class a while to figure that out. Some people have trouble remembering how many zeros there are in a billion.

Then there was a second part to the note:

If the inventor of the new toothpaste made a profit of 1¢ a tube on his toothpaste, what would his profit be at the end of the year?

And it turns out that the inventor of this new toothpaste would make a two-and-a-half million dollar profit!

Well, that's how Rufus's toothpaste business started. Rufus figured out that if he sold the toothpaste for only a penny more than it cost him to make —it cost him about two cents a tube—he'd soon have millions of customers.

He had to start in a small way, of course. When he started his business, Rufus packed the toothpaste in baby food jars. A baby food jar holds about as much as a big tube, and the jars didn't cost him anything.

People with babies were glad to save jars for Rufus, as nobody had thought of a way of instantly recycling baby food jars before. When Rufus put a sign on the bulletin board at school saying that he could use the jars, kids brought us hundreds of them.

We sterilized and filled the jars. When we had about five hundred jars, Rufus and I stuffed our saddlebags with as many as they would hold and rode our bikes around the neighborhood selling the toothpaste.

We sold quite a few jars. At only three cents a jar, most people felt they could afford to give it a try, and most of the customers said it was good toothpaste.

Still, I could not see how Rufus was going to get rich on three-cent toothpaste unless millions of people knew about it. Then I had this idea about how he could get some free advertising.

Everybody in Cleveland watches a program called "The Joe Smiley Show." On the show, Joe interviews people who have interesting hobbies.

I wrote Joe Smiley a letter telling him I had this friend who had a hobby of making toothpaste and could make about two years' supply for the price of one tube. And Joe Smiley called up Rufus to ask if he would be on the show.

Rufus was very good on the show, though I was afraid that he never would get around to talking about the toothpaste. I was worried because when Joe Smiley asked Rufus how he had learned to make toothpaste, Rufus started telling about his Grandmother Mayflower.

He not only told about how she made scrapbook paste, but about how his Grandma Mayflower had made her own furnace out of two 100-gallon oil barrels. Joe Smiley was so interested in that furnace that it was hard to get him off the subject of Rufus's grandmother.

Rufus told about his grandmother taming raccoons, woodchucks, mice, chipmunks, and catbirds. And, of course, about her brushing her teeth with plain baking soda. You wouldn't think all that stuff about Rufus's grandmother would sell toothpaste. But then, as my father pointed out, you wouldn't

think Rufus's way of advertising the toothpaste would sell toothpaste, either.

Joe Smiley is the kind of guy who is always saying things are the "greatest" thing he ever heard of. Or the most "fantastic." If a girl comes on his show in a pink coat that Joe thinks is attractive, he'll say, "That's the most fantastic coat!" There's nothing that special about the coat. He just means it's nice.

What I mean is, he exaggerates. And everybody Joe has on his show is one of the greatest people he ever met or has done the most fantastic thing.

So when Joe does get to Rufus's toothpaste, he naturally gives it this big build-up. Which is what I was counting on. And what does Rufus do?

The conversation went something like this:

JOE: Now, Rufus, this fantastic toothpaste you make—I suppose it has a special, secret formula.

RUFUS: No. It's made out of stuff anybody can buy for a few cents and mix up at home in a few minutes.

JOE: Fantastic! And, of course, it's much better than the kind you buy at the store.

RUFUS: I don't know about that. But it tastes pretty good. And for about two cents you can make as much as you get in a seventy-nine cent tube.

JOE: Fantastic! And where can people get some of this great toothpaste?

RUFUS: If they live in East Cleveland, I'll deliver it to them on my bike. Three ounces cost three cents—it costs me two cents to make and I make one cent profit. If anyone outside East Cleveland wants some, I'll have to charge three cents plus postage.

JOE: Fantastic! And what do you call this marvelous new product?

RUFUS: TOOTHPASTE.

JOE: Just toothpaste? It doesn't have a name like SPARKLE or SHINE or SENSATION or

WHITE LIGHTNING or PERSONALITY PLUS?

RUFUS: No, it's just plain TOOTHPASTE. It doesn't do anything sensational such as improve your smile or your personality. It just keeps your teeth clean.

Who would have thought that telling people toothpaste wouldn't do one thing for their personality would sell toothpaste?

But three days after Rufus was on "The Joe Smiley Show," he got 689 orders for TOOTHPASTE. One came all the way from Venice, California, from a man who happened to be telephoning his daughter while she was watching the show in Cleveland. The daughter said, "There's a kid here who's selling toothpaste for three cents a jar." And her father ordered three dozen jars.

Fantastic!

McBroom Tells a Lie

by SID FLEISCHMAN

It's true—I did tell a lie once.

I don't mean the summer nights we hung caged chickens in the farmhouse for lanterns. Those hens had eaten so many lightning bugs they glowed brighter'n kerosene lamps.

And I don't mean the cold snap that came along so sudden that blazing sunshine froze to the ground. We pickaxed chunks of it for the stove to cook on.

That's the genuine truth, sure and certain as my name's Josh McBroom.

When I told a lie—well, I'd best start with the time the young'uns began building a hoopdedoodle of some sort in the barn. The scamps kept it covered with a sheet. I reckoned they'd tell us when they were ready.

"Will*jill*hester*chester*peter*polly*tim*to*mmary-larry*andlittle*clarinda!*" my dear wife Melissa called out every evening. "Supper!"

We had hardly sat down to eat, when Jill asked, "Pa, would Mexican jumping beans grow on our farm?"

I hadn't seen anything yet that wouldn't grow on our wonderful one-acre farm. That trifling patch of earth is so amazing rich we could plant and harvest two-three crops a day—with time left over for a game of horseshoes.

"Will you let us grow a crop?" Polly asked. "We need bushels and bushels of jumping beans."

"For our invention," Tom put in.

"In that case," I smiled, "jump to it, my lambs."

They traded with a boy at school who owned a jar of the hopping beans. First thing Saturday morning the young'uns lit out the back door to plant their crop.

Well, that was a mistake. I should have known that our soil was too powerful strong for jumping beans. The seeds sprouted faster'n the twitch of a sheep's tail, and those Mexican bushes shot up lickety-bang. As they quick-dried in the prairie sun, the pods began to shake and rattle, and Chester shouted, "Pa, look!"

Merciful powers! Those buzzing, jumping, wiggle-waggling pods jerked the roots clear out of the ground. And off those bushes went, leaping and hopping every which way.

"Willjillhesterchesterpeterpollytimtommarylarry-andlittleclarinda!" I called out. "After them, my lambs!"

Didn't those plants lead us a merry chase! Most of them got clean away, hopping and bucking and rattling across the countryside. We did manage to capture a few bushes, but the young'uns said it wasn't near enough for their invention. They'd have to think of something else.

At breakfast a day or two later, the older young'uns started breaking fresh eggs into skillets. "Pa—there's something wrong with these eggs," said Will.

"Pa, come look," said Jill from the stove.

"Pa—come quick, but stand back!" my dear wife Melissa exclaimed.

I hopped to the stove as she broke another fresh egg into a skillet. Why, soon as it was fried on one side, that egg jumped up in the air. It flipped over and landed on the other side to fry.

"Well, don't that beat all," I said. "The hens must have been eating your Mexican jumping beans. Yup, and they're laying eggs that *flip* themselves."

"Well, our invention won't run on flip-flopping eggs," Will said gloomily.

After supper my dear wife Melissa tried to jolly everybody up. "Let's pop some corn."

Well, a strange look came over the young'uns' faces. "Popcorn," Jill whispered.

"POPCORN!" Will laughed. "Bet that'll run our invention!"

Didn't those kids light out for the barn in a hurry! In no time at all they were clanking and hammering to do over their contraption to work on popcorn instead of jumping beans.

They were still at it the next day when our neighbor, Heck Jones, came storming along. He was a skinny, rattle-boned man and mean as the law allowed. More'n once he had tried to trick us out of our wonderful one-acre farm.

"I'll have the law on you, McBroom!"

"Do tell," I said.

"You grew them jumping beans, didn't you?"

"I did."

"Look there at my blue ribbon cow, Princess Prunella!"

My eyes nearly shot out of my head. There on the horizon that stupid, worthless cow of his was leaping and high-jumping and bucking.

"Kicked holes right through the barn roof!" Heck Jones snorted. "You allowed them dangerous bushes of yours to get loose, and now Princess Prunella's five stomachs are full of jumping beans!"

"Your roof already had holes in it," I said.

"That cow's ruined. Reckon I'll have to shoot her before she does any more damage," he said, beginning to dab at his eyes.

Well, all that dabbing didn't fool me. Heck Jones could peel an acre of onions without dropping a tear. But I reckoned I was responsible, letting those bushes get away from us.

"Sir," I said. "If you'll guarantee to keep off our farm, I'll pay for a barn roof. And I'll buy that ignorant cow

from you. I reckon when she settles down she'll give churned butter for a month."

"Don't think you're going to slip out so light and easy," Heck Jones snapped. "I intend to see you in jail, McBroom! Unless —"

"I'm listening, sir."

He cleared his throat. "If you want to trade farms, we'll call it fair and square."

"Well, no sir and nohow," I said.

He lifted his thin nose into the wind — that man could sniff things miles off. "Neighbor, I'm a kindly man," he said. "You just grow me a crop of tomatoes to make up for my barn roof, and we'll call it square."

"I'll deliver 'em before supper," I said.

"No, neighbor. Not yet." He whipped out a pencil and piece of paper. "I'll just write out the agreement. Best to do things honest and legal. You deliver the tomatoes when I say so — fresh off the vine, mind you — and I'll guarantee not to set foot on your farm again."

Glory be! We'd be rid of that petty scoundrel at last.

"But fair's fair, McBroom. I'm entitled to a guarantee too. If you don't live up to the bargain — why, this useless, worn-out one-acre farm is mine. Sign here."

Useless? Worn-out? My pride rose up, and I signed. Why, I could grow a crop of tomatoes in an hour. I had the best of the bargain for certain!

But as he ambled off, I thought I heard him snicker through his nose.

Just then the young'uns rolled their invention out of the barn and whipped off the sheet. "It's finished, Pa," Will said.

Glory be! There stood an odds-and-ends contraption on four wheels. A rain barrel with three tin funnels

324

mounted in front and the scamps had fixed up broken chairs to seat all eleven of them.

"It's a Popcornmobile," Jill said.

"That's the exhaust pipe," Chester said, pointing to a black tin stovepipe they'd attached with baling wire underneath the floorboards.

"And look, Pa!" Larry said. "We got headlights, too!"

Indeed, they did! Two quart canning jars were fixed to the front. And the rascals had filled the jars with lightning bugs.

"Pile in, everybody," Will said, "and let's start 'er up."

Mary fetched a clod of frozen sunlight out of the icehouse while Will, Jill, and Hester poured shelled corn through the funnels. Mary pitched the chunk of sunlight into the barrel. They took their seats and waited for the sunshine to thaw and pop the corn and start the machinery they'd rigged up.

It was growing dark, the prairie wind had turned a mite gritty—and suddenly there stood Heck Jones.

"Evenin', neighbors," he said. There was a tricksy look in his eye and a piece of paper in his hand. "McBroom, you guaranteed to deliver a crop of tomatoes on demand. Well, I'm demanding 'em *now.*"

My eyebrows jumped. "Drat it, you can see the sun's down!" I declared.

"There's nothing about the sun in the contract. You read it."

"And it's going to kick up a dust storm before long."

"Nothing in the contract about a dust storm. You signed it."

"Sir, you expect me to grow you a crop of tomatoes *at night in a dust storm?*"

"Hee-*haw*, neighbor. If you don't, this farm's mine. I'll give you till sunup. Not a moment later, McBroom!"

And off he went, chuckling and snickering and *hee-hawing* through his nose.

"Oh, Pa," my dear wife Melissa cried. Even the young'uns were getting a mite onion-eyed.

Just then corn began popping like firecrackers inside the young'uns rain barrel.

"Pa, we're moving!" Jill exclaimed.

Sure enough, the chunk of frozen sunlight had thawed out, and the corn was exploding from the stored-up heat.

I tried to raise a smile. Will grabbed the steering wheel tight and began driving the young'uns around the barn. Popcorn shot out of the exhaust pipe, white as snow.

I knew we didn't have enough of that frozen sunshine left to grow a crop, worst luck! But when I saw those two headlights coming around the barn, my heart leaped back in place. The jars full of fireflies lit up the way like high noon!

"Willjillhesterchesterpeterpollytimtommarylarryandlittleclarinda!" I shouted. "Fetch canning jars.

Fill 'em up with lightning bugs. Quick, my lambs. Not a moment to waste."

Chester said, "The critters have got kind of scarce around here, Pa."

"The thickest place is way the other side of Heck Jones' place," Mary said.

"A powerful long walk," said Larry.

"Who said anything about walking?" I laughed. "You've got your Popcornmobile, haven't you?"

Didn't we get busy! The young'uns fetched all the canning jars in the cellar and bushels of corn for fuel. With a fresh chunk of frozen sunshine in the barrel, off they took—spraying popcorn behind them.

I set to work planting tomato seeds. It was full dark, but I could see fine. My dear wife Melissa held up a chicken by the feet—one of those lantern-glowing hens I was telling you about.

Then I began pounding stakes in the ground for the tomatoes to climb up.

"I do hope the young'uns don't get lost," my dear wife Melissa said. "It's going to blow a real dust storm by morning."

"Heck Jones had sniffed it coming," I declared. "But lost? Not our scamps. I can hear 'em now."

They were still a long way off, but that Popcornmobile sounded like the Fourth of July, loud enough to wake snakes. All the kids were waving and laughing. I reckoned that was the best ride they'd ever had.

"That's a jim-dandy machine you built," I smiled. "And I see you found a lightning bug or two."

Well, it didn't take long to hang those jars of fireflies on the tomato stakes. And glory be? They lit up the farm bright as day.

It wasn't a moment before the tomato sprouts came busting up through the earth. They broke into leaf, and the vines started toward those canning jars. I do believe they preferred that homemade sunshine!

We loaded up the Popcornmobile with bushel baskets of tomatoes. We made so many trips to Heck Jones' place that the popcorn piled up along the road like a snow-bank. Finally, minutes before dawn, I hammered at his door.

"Wake up, Heck Jones!" I called.

"*Hee-haw!*" He opened the door and stood there in his night cap, the legal paper in his hand.

"It's dawn by the clock, McBroom, and that powerful rich, git-up-and-git acre is all mine!"

"Yup, it's dawn," I said. "And there's my end of the bargain."

When he saw that crop of tomatoes he just about swallowed his teeth. His mouth puckered up tighter'n bark on a tree.

The young'uns and I all piled into the Popcornmobile to start for home. That's when I saw Princess Prunella. Only she wasn't jumping anymore.

"Merciful powers!" I declared. "Look there! That numbskull cow mistook all this popcorn for snow and has froze to death!"

We got home for a big breakfast and just in time. That prairie dust storm rolled in and stayed for weeks on end.

Now it's true—I did tell a lie once. That cow of his didn't *really* freeze to death in all the popcorn. But she did catch a terrible cold.

A Wow of a Wedding

by KEITH ROBERTSON

My name is Gloria and I am a turtle. As everyone knows, turtles move very slowly. That isn't a handicap at all as some humans might think. People race around so fast in automobiles that they have no time to look at anything except other cars and road signs. But we turtles move around very slowly and see all sorts of things. And lots of times we sit in one place for hours and contemplate. My Aunt Myrtle says no other species on earth

contemplates as much as we do. Naturally, we have many, many wise thoughts and observations.

My brother Witherspoon and I spend much of our time with Aunt Myrtle. She is very, very old and very, very wise. Turtles live almost forever, you know, and Aunt Myrtle is the oldest turtle I've ever met. She isn't exactly my aunt, but maybe my great-great-great-great-great-great-aunt. Aunt Myrtle explains lots of things, and her stories are usually very interesting.

Aunt Myrtle promised last summer to take us through the university church. We had put it off for one reason or another, and it was yesterday when we finally got around to it. The church has big, heavy doors. Naturally we had to wait until these were open. We found them open yesterday morning, so we walked in and made a complete tour. Aunt Myrtle pointed out what she thought were the nicest windows. Witherspoon almost sprained his neck looking up at them and at the high ceiling.

"They must have built this for very tall people," he said.

"Don't be silly," I told him. "People are never that tall."

"Then why did they build it this way?" Witherspoon asked. He can think of more questions than any turtle I know.

"Just because they do," I said.

"That's not a reason."

"He's right," Aunt Myrtle said. "It probably makes the organ sound better. And it makes the building cool and comfortable in the summer."

She was right about that. It was the coolest spot we'd found. So we went over in the corner and took a nap. When we woke up someone had closed the door, and we had to spend the night there. We weren't worried though, because we knew someone would come sooner or later and open the door. They did early the next morning. However, we didn't leave because we discovered they were having a wedding at ten-thirty.

The wedding was very interesting. Lots and lots of people came and sat in the seats in the front of the church. Meanwhile the organ played soft music, which was very nice. All the people were dressed in their fanciest clothes. Then, finally, the music got much louder. Eight women in blue dresses, all carrying flowers, walked slowly down the aisle. They were followed by a young woman wearing a white dress and carrying flowers.

When the bride got to the altar, a young man came over from one side and stood beside her. The minister asked something, and they answered. I couldn't hear it all, but finally he said, "I pronounce you husband and wife." Then they turned and left the church. Soon everyone else did, too. We were the last ones out.

"Where are they going?" Witherspoon asked.

"To a party, I suppose," Aunt Myrtle said. "They have that in a big room somewhere—sometimes a hotel. Everyone congratulates the bride and groom, and then they all have something to eat and drink."

"That sounds like the best part of the wedding to me," Witherspoon said. He is always hungry.

"They don't have anything very good at these parties," Aunt Myrtle said. "No raw meat or juicy bugs. Just silly little sandwiches usually, junk like egg salad and fish between thin slices of bread."

"I thought the wedding was very nice," I said.

"It *was* a nice wedding," Aunt Myrtle admitted. "But not nearly as exciting as some weddings. It isn't often that there is a wedding like the one my husband Herman and I saw."

"When was this wedding?" I asked. "And where?"

"Right here," Aunt Myrtle said. "But it was many years ago. Back about 1910 or some time like that. Styles and lots of things were much different then."

"You mean they didn't wear fancy clothes?" I asked. "I thought the dresses were pretty."

"Oh, the clothes were much the same, but people's ideas were different. You see almost all the women had long hair. The few who cut their hair short were very daring."

"That's funny," Witherspoon said. "Now lots of boys have long hair, and lots of girls cut theirs short."

"That's right, and people object to that too," Aunt Myrtle said. "Anyhow, the girl who was getting married was named Millicent Sandford. She had cut her hair quite short. She did it as a protest."

"Protest against what?" I asked.

"She was a very active suffragette."

"What's that?" Witherspoon asked. "Some sort of a professor?"

"I guess I'd better explain," Aunt Myrtle said. "You see people are centuries and centuries behind turtles. I have no idea if girl turtles ever had to fight for their rights. If they did it was ages ago, and no one even remembers. As far as I know boy and girl turtles have always been on an equal footing. But people are different. Women in many places of the world have really no rights at all. Men run everything. For a long time, women in the United States didn't have the same rights as men. Back when this wedding took place they could not vote."

"Vote for what?" Witherspoon asked.

"Oh, for President of the United States, for the governor, or even for the mayor of the town. So a group of women worked to change this. They made speeches, wrote papers, marched in the streets, talked to lawmakers, and other things. They called themselves suffragettes. There were some people who felt that no nice girl would be a suffragette. But Millicent Sandford was a suffragette and proud of it. She worked very hard to win women the vote. She cut off her long hair as a protest to show that she felt women had a right to do what they wanted. The man she was marrying claimed he didn't care whether she had short hair or long hair. His name was Jonathan Slurp. He came from a wealthy family who thought they were very important. I believe they were the Long Island Slurps. Now Jonathan was worried about his mother and father. They were quite old-fashioned, and he was certain they would not like Millicent's short hair. He asked her to wear a wig for the wedding. She didn't like the idea very much, but since they expected to move to Colorado after their wedding, she agreed. Of course with all the veil and headdress no one could ever guess she was wearing a wig, so she didn't expect any trouble.

"Everything went wrong from the moment the wedding started. To begin with, the minister came to the entrance of the chapel before the ceremony. He went outside to say something to someone. On his way back, he tripped."

"On what?" Witherspoon asked.

"Well, over Herman as a matter of fact," Aunt Myrtle said. "We were hurrying to get inside and were near the door. But the minister should have seen us. He must have been very clumsy. Anyhow, he fell on the stone steps and cut his forehead. They had to rush him off to the hospital. Most of the people were already inside, and they all had to wait while they found another minister.

"It took about half an hour for a new minister to arrive. Everyone was tired of waiting. One man in one of the rear pews fell sound asleep. He had one foot stuck out

in the aisle. The shoe either had a nail sticking out of it or one of those metal plates that you sometimes see on the toes and heels of shoes. The wedding finally started. Millicent was walking down the aisle, somewhat faster than usual to make up for the lost time, when her long wedding veil caught on this man's shoe. Naturally, it pulled on her headdress and pulled her wig around until the hair was hanging over her face. She was calm and cool. All the people around gasped. Some of them were very shocked to see that she had short hair.

"She simply pulled her wig back on and looked down to see what had caught her veil. The man was still sleeping. In fact he began to snore. Millicent had a very hot temper. She reached over and shook him.

" 'If you will kindly remove your big foot from my veil, we will be able to go on with the wedding,' she said in a clear, loud voice.

"Some people gasped and some laughed. The young minister tried to keep his face straight, but he didn't quite manage. This angered the Slurps, who were already quite shocked by their daughter-in-law's short hair. They thought both Millicent and the minister should be dignified and solemn.

"Herman and I were about halfway toward the altar. I was quite pleased with our spot. We were under a pew where no one was kicking us or stepping on us. But Herman wanted to go nearer the front so he could see better. He waited until Millicent had passed. Then he stepped out into the aisle himself. She had a long train on her wedding gown that was dragging along behind her. As I have said, Herman is a quick thinker. He decided he might as well ride, so he stepped onto her train.

"Having a good-sized box turtle riding on your wedding train doesn't make walking any easier. But

Millicent managed. Some man who was sitting next to the aisle saw Herman. I suppose he thought he would be helpful. He half got to his feet and leaned out to grab Herman. He leaned too far and fell smack on Millicent's train. There was a terrible rip, and the train began to tear. Millicent had to stop. She turned around and saw this man getting up from the aisle. She also saw that her train was almost torn off about six inches above the floor.

" 'I'm certainly not going to drag you to the altar,' she said. She turned, picked up her dress, and tore the train off the rest of the way. She left it there and calmly went toward the altar again as though nothing had happened.

"Herman escaped from the man, and he went on toward the front of the chapel too. However, he stayed out of the aisle, working his way under the benches until he got to the front. He stopped under the front pew right beneath Mrs. Slurp, the groom's mother.

"Mrs. Slurp had slipped off her shoes. I guess they were too tight and pinched her toes. She sat there wiggling her toes. Several things had already happened to make her feel nervous.

"Herman said later that those wiggling toes kept blocking his view, and they made *him* nervous. Finally they got too much for him. He reached out and bit her little toe. He bit it hard, and she screamed. She looked down; she saw just his head as he backed away under the seat. Then she really screamed.

" 'A snake!' she screeched and jumped up on the seat. 'I've been bitten by a snake!'

"Everyone went into a panic. Some people jumped on seats. Others rushed around trying to look brave. The whole place was in an uproar. Most of the people in back ran for the doors.

"Jonathan Slurp left his place beside Millicent and

rushed over to his mother. When a bit of quiet came back to the church, Jonathan went back to the altar and said, 'We'll have to put off the ceremony. Mother is too upset to go on.'

" 'Your mother isn't the one getting married,' Millicent said. 'But I think maybe we'd better put it off. Indefinitely.'

"She stormed down the aisle and out of the church. A big group of people were gathered outside, not knowing what to do. Several of them asked her if they should go back inside.

" 'No. There's not going to be a wedding,' she said. 'But it's a shame to go to all this trouble and get all you fine people together and not have anything happen!' She pulled off her wig and handed it to someone. 'I'd like your attention for a few minutes,' she called. 'There are a few facts I would like to present as to why women should have the same right to vote as men.'

"She made a fine speech. Some of the people cheered. And of course some made remarks and catcalls. Right in the middle of her talk, the young minister appeared with a box for her to stand on so she could see better. Toward the end, Mr. and Mrs. Slurp came out of the church. When Mrs. Slurp saw who was giving the speech, she fainted."

"That sounds like a real wow of a wedding," Witherspoon said. "I wish today's had been like that."

"Did Millicent ever marry Jonathan?" I asked.

"No, she didn't," Aunt Myrtle said. "As a matter of fact, about a week later she eloped with that young minister."

More Books to Make You Laugh

McBroom and the Beanstalk by Sid Fleischman. Little, 1978.
Here's McBroom again in another zany adventure.

The Fast Sooner Hound by Arna Bontemps and Jack Conroy. Houghton Mifflin, 1942.
Here is a tall tale about a dog that was fast enough to outrun a train.

Billy Jo Jive and the Case of the Sneaker Snatch by John Shearer. Delacorte, 1977.
Billy Jo and Susie Sunset search for the missing sneaker that may cost their neighborhood team the basketball championship.

Black and Blue Magic by Zilpha Keatley Snyder. Atheneum, 1966.
Marco is clumsy, so when he receives the gift of wings, it leads to black and blue magic.

Paddington on Stage: Plays for Children by Michael Bond and Alfred Bradley. Houghton Mifflin, 1977.
Some of the funniest adventures of the popular bear called Paddington are presented here in play form.

Miss Bianca in the Salt Mines by Margery Sharp. Little, 1966.
Miss Bianca, aided by her friend Bernard, leads the Mouse Prisoners' Aid Society in a rescue attempt deep in the salt mines.

Ghosts I Have Been by Richard Peck. Viking Press, 1977.
Blossom finds that she has supernatural powers that upset life in her hometown.

PART 6

Robert McCloskey:

An Artist with Words and Pictures

Robert McCloskey: An Artist with Words and Pictures

Meet Robert McCloskey, a man with a rare talent. Through his stories and his pictures, Mr. McCloskey transforms everyday happenings into exciting adventures.

Robert McCloskey: An Artist with Words and Pictures

by SARA KRENTZMAN SRYGLEY

The World He Lives In

An author-artist worth knowing is Robert McCloskey. He has written eight books for young people and illustrated them with his drawings and paintings.

Telling about himself in *The Junior Book of Authors,* Mr. McCloskey said, "It is just sort of an accident that I write books. I really think up stories in pictures and just fill in between the pictures with a sentence or a paragraph or a few pages of words." Probably it isn't quite that easy. A look at his life and the books he has produced shows us that his stories and pictures are more carefully planned than Mr. McCloskey suggests.

Robert McCloskey was born in Hamilton, Ohio, in 1914. This was his home until he was a young man. He enjoyed growing up in a small Midwestern town like Hamilton. Robert played in the parks; visited the barber shop, the stores, and the public library; and went to school. He was interested in music. He learned to play the oboe, drums, and harmonica. His favorite instrument was the harmonica. He even taught his friends how to play it. He also enjoyed building model airplanes and all sorts of mechanical contraptions. He is still good at tinkering with machinery and inventing new gadgets. Recently he has been working on developing a new kind of puppet.

Robert McCloskey with two of his puppets

Very early in his life, Robert McCloskey knew that he wanted to be an artist. This ambition was encouraged when, as a high school student, he won his first national award. He received the prize for a calendar illustrated with woodcuts.

An art career was his dream, but it became a reality only after years of hard work. He studied art for three years in Boston and for two more years in New York. In the summers he often went to Cape Cod and painted.

For a while he had a job drawing cartoon strips, but that work did not satisfy him. He liked to draw old Spanish ships, fierce dragons, or heroic characters from Greek and Roman myths. He knew that he wanted to illustrate books.

When he was studying in New York, Mr. McCloskey had taken some of his work to an editor of children's books, May Massee. When Miss Massee had looked carefully at his drawings, she gave him some good advice. She urged him to stop drawing things he knew little about and to concentrate on things that were familiar to him.

McCloskey took her advice. When he called again on Miss Massee, he had in his portfolio what was to become his first book. *Lentil* is about a boy growing up in a small town in Ohio. Miss Massee was enthusiastic about the book, and it was published in 1940. Robert McCloskey had begun a successful career as an author and illustrator.

Lentil was followed by other books both written and illustrated by Mr. McCloskey. In addition, he illustrated books written by other authors. Some of his books, like *Time of Wonder*, are picture books in which the pictures and the words are of equal importance in telling the story. In others, like *Homer Price* and *Centerburg Tales,* the story is told chiefly in words, with a few pictures to illustrate the people, places, and events of the story.

About the time *Lentil* was published, another important thing happened in Robert McCloskey's life. He married Margaret Durand, a children's librarian.

Two daughters, Sally and Jane, were born to Mr. and Mrs. McCloskey. Most of the time, the family lived on an island off the coast of Maine: Deer Isle in Penobscot Bay. But when Jane was a baby, the whole family went to Italy for a year while Mr. McCloskey studied art at the American Academy in Rome.

Mr. McCloskey was the first illustrator to win the Caldecott Medal twice. This medal is awarded every year for "the most distinguished American picture book for children." In a speech accepting that honor for *Time of Wonder,* he said:

> With everyone clamoring for more scientists, I should like to clamor for more artists and designers. I should like to clamor for the teaching of drawing and design to every child, right along with reading and writing. I think it is most important for everyone really to see and evaluate pictures and really to see and evaluate his surroundings.[1]

The World He Imagines

As you will see, some of Robert McCloskey's own experiences are reflected in his books. The Centerburg in which Homer Price grows up is probably like Mr. McCloskey's hometown. The family's life in Maine inspired the books

[1] *Horn Book,* August 1958, page 245. Used by permission.

with Maine settings, like *Time of Wonder*. But if he had written and drawn everything exactly as it happened, we would not have had stories — we would have had reports of Robert McCloskey's life.

Artists may get ideas from someone they know or a real event, but this is just the beginning of a picture or story. As the artist starts to work, the ideas grow and change. He or she leaves out a bit here, adds a few details there, combines this with that. The picture or the story gradually takes shape in the artist's imagination. Soon he or she has created something entirely new.

When Robert McCloskey began to think about the stories of life in the little town of Centerburg, he had to make up names for his characters. The name Homer Price recalls the ancient Greek poet Homer. He was one of the earliest story-tellers we know about, and one of the greatest. His poems tell of the adventures of a wandering hero, Ulysses, who left his home to fight in the Trojan War. In Mr. McCloskey's books, Homer Price and Uncle Ulysses are not great heroes — they are just ordinary people in an ordinary town. But perhaps Mr. McCloskey wanted to remind his readers of those famous, ancient men and to suggest that the adventures of ordinary people today are also worth writing books about.

When he wrote the story that follows, "Nothing New Under the Sun (Hardly)," Mr. McCloskey also had some other works of literature in mind. As you will see, the mysterious stranger reminds the people of Centerburg of two famous fictional characters. Mr. McCloskey is again inviting his readers to look for magic, adventure, and humor in everyday things.

Nothing New Under the Sun (Hardly)

by ROBERT McCLOSKEY

After the County Fair, life in Centerburg eases itself back to normal. Homer and the rest of the children concentrate on arithmetic and basketball, and the grownups tend to business and running the town in a peaceful way. Election time still being a month away, the Democrats and the Republicans are still speaking to each other. The Ladies' Aid hasn't anything to crusade about at the moment, and Uncle Ulysses hasn't bought any newfangled equipment for his lunchroom recently. There is nothing for people to gossip about, or speculate on, or argue about.

There's always the weather, the latest books and movies, and ladies' hats. But, of course, that doesn't provide nearly enough to talk and think about for a whole month until election time. Uncle Ulysses, the sheriff, and the men around the barbershop usually run out of things to talk about toward the middle of the month. Sometimes during the mornings the conversation is lively. Like today, the sheriff came in beaming and said, "Well, I put on long ullen wonderwear—I mean woolen underwear, this morning."

"Soo?" said Uncle Ulysses. "Guess I'll have to get mine out of mothballs this week."

"Humph," said the barber, "I wouldn't wear woolen underwear for anything on earth. It *itches*!"

Well, that was something to argue about for almost an hour. Then the subject changed to woolen socks, to shoes, to overshoes, to mud, to mud in roads, to mud in barnyards, barns, and chicken coops. Then there was a long pause. Only ten-thirty by the town hall clock, and conversation had already dwindled to nothing at all. Nothing to do but look out of the barbershop window.

"There goes Doc Pelly," said the barber, "I wonder who's sick?"

"Colby's wife is expectin' a baby," said Uncle Ulysses. "I'll ask Aggy this noon. She might know about it."

"There's Dulcey Dooner," said the sheriff.

"He hasn't worked for three years," added the barber disapprovingly.

A few children came into view. "School's out for lunch," pronounced the sheriff.

The door opened, and Homer came in saying, "Hello, everybody. Uncle Ulysses, Aunt Aggy sent me over to tell you to stir yourself over to the lunchroom and help serve blue-plate specials."

Uncle Ulysses sighed and prepared to leave. The sheriff cupped a hand behind his ear and said, "What's that?" Uncle Ulysses stopped sighing, and everybody listened.

The noise (it was sort of a rattle) grew louder, and then suddenly an old car swung into the town square. The sheriff, the barber, Uncle Ulysses, and Homer watched it with gaping mouths as it rattled around the town square once—twice—and on the third time slowed down and shivered to a stop right out front of Uncle Ulysses' lunchroom.

It wasn't because this car was old, old enough to be an *antique*; or because some strange business was built onto it; or that the strange business was covered with a large canvas. No, that wasn't what made Homer and the sheriff and Uncle Ulysses and the barber stare so long. It was the car's *driver*.

"Gosh, what a beard!" said Homer.

"And what a head of hair!" said the barber. "That's a two-dollar cutting job if I ever saw one!"

"Could you see his face?" asked the sheriff.

"Nope," answered Uncle Ulysses, still staring across the square.

They watched the stranger untangle his beard from the steering wheel and go into the lunchroom.

Uncle Ulysses promptly dashed for the door, saying, "See you later."

"Wait for me!" the sheriff called. "I'm sort of hungry."

Homer followed, and the barber shouted, "Don't forget to come back and tell me the news!"

"O.K., and if I bring you a new customer, I get a commission."

The stranger was sitting at the far end of the lunch counter, looking very shy and embarrassed. Homer's Aunt Aggy had already served him a blue-plate special and was eyeing him with suspicion. To be polite, Homer and Uncle Ulysses pretended to be busy behind the counter, and the sheriff pretended to study the menu—though he knew every single word on it by heart. They just glanced in the stranger's direction once in a while.

Finally Uncle Ulysses' curiosity got the best of him, and he sauntered down to the stranger and asked, "Are you enjoying your lunch? Is everything all right?"

The stranger appeared to be very embarrassed, and you could easily tell he was blushing underneath his beard and all his hair. "Yes, sir, it's a very good lunch," he replied with a nod. When he nodded a stray wisp of

beard accidentally got into the gravy. This made him more embarrassed than ever.

Uncle Ulysses waited for the stranger to start a conversation but he didn't.

So Uncle Ulysses said, "Nice day today."

The stranger said, "Yes, nice day," and dropped a fork. Now the stranger *really was* embarrassed. He looked as though he would like to sink right through the floor.

Uncle Ulysses quickly handed the man another fork, and eased himself away, so as not to embarrass him into breaking a plate, or falling off his stool.

After he finished lunch, the stranger reached into the pocket of his ragged, patched coat and drew out a leather money bag. He paid for his lunch, nodded good-bye, and crept out of the door and down the street with everyone staring after him.

Aunt Aggy broke the silence by bouncing on the marble counter the coin she had just received.

"It's good money," she pronounced, "but it looks as though it had been *buried* for *years!*"

"Shyest man I ever laid eyes on!" said Uncle Ulysses.

"Yes!" said the sheriff. "My as a shouse, I mean, shy as a *mouse!*"

"Gosh what a beard!" said Homer.

"Humph!" said Aunt Aggy. "Homer, it's time you started back to school!"

By midafternoon every man, woman, and child in Centerburg had something to gossip about, speculate on, and argue about.

Who was this stranger? Where did he come from? Where was he going? How long was his beard and his hair? What was his name? Did he have a business? What could be on the back of his car that was so carefully covered with the large canvas?

354

Nobody knew. Nobody knew anything about the stranger except that he parked his car in the town parking space and was spending considerable time walking about town. People reported that he paused in his walking and whistled a few bars of some strange tune, a tune nobody had ever heard of. The stranger was shy when grownups were near, and he would cross the street or go around a block to avoid speaking to someone. However, he did not avoid children. He smiled at them and seemed delighted to have them follow him.

People from all over town telephoned the sheriff at the barbershop asking about the stranger and making reports as to what was going on.

The sheriff was becoming a bit uneasy about the whole thing. He couldn't get near enough to the stranger to ask him his intentions, and if he *did* ask, the stranger would be too shy to give him an answer.

As Homer passed by the barbershop on his way home from school, the sheriff called him in. "Homer," he said, "I'm gonna need your help. This stranger with the beard has got me worried. You see, Homer, I can't find out who he is or what he is doing here in town. He's probably a nice enough fellow, just an individualist. But, then again, he might be a fugitive, in disguise or something." Homer nodded. And the sheriff continued, "Now, what I want you to do is gain his confidence. He doesn't seem to be afraid of children, and you might be able to find out what this is all about. I'll treat you to a double raspberry sundae."

"It's a deal, Sheriff!" said Homer. "I'll start right now."

At six o'clock Homer reported to the sheriff. "The stranger seems like a nice person, Sheriff," Homer began. "I walked down Market Street with him. He wouldn't tell me who he is or what he's doing, but he did say he'd been away from people for a great many years. He asked me to recommend a place for him to stay, and I said the Strand Hotel, so that's where he went just now when I left him. I'll have to run home to dinner now, Sheriff, but I'll find out some more tomorrow. Don't forget about that raspberry sundae," said Homer.

"I won't," replied the sheriff, "and, Homer, don't forget to keep me posted on this fellow."

After Homer had gone, the sheriff turned to the barber and said, "We don't know one blessed thing about this fellow except that he's shy, and he's been away from people for quite a spell. For all we know he might be a fugitive, or a lunatic, or maybe one of these amnesia cases.

"If he didn't have so much hair I could tell in a second what kind of a fellow he is," complained the sheriff. "Yep! Just one look at a person's ears and I can tell!"

"Well," said the barber, "I judge people by their *hair*, and I've been thinking. This fellow looks like somebody I've heard about, or read about somewhere. Like somebody out of a book, you understand, Sheriff?"

"Well, yes, in a way, but I could tell you definite with a good look at his ears!" said the sheriff. "Here comes Ulysses. Let's ask him what *he* thinks."

Uncle Ulysses considered a second and said, "Well, *I* judge a person by his *waistline* and his *appetite*. Now I'm not saying I'm right, Sheriff, because I couldn't tell about his waistline under that old coat, but judging from his appetite, I'd say he's a sort a person that I've read about somewhere. I can't just put my finger on it. Seems as though it must have been in a book."

"U-m-m," said the sheriff.

Just then Tony the shoe-repair man came in for a haircut. After he was settled in the barber chair, the sheriff asked him what he thought about the mysterious stranger.

"Well, Sheriff, *I* judge everybody by their *feet* and their *shoes*. Nobody's worn a pair of gaiters like his for twenty-five years. It seems as though those shoes must have just up and walked right out of the pages of some old dusty book."

"There!" said the sheriff. "*Now*, we're getting somewhere!"

He rushed to the phone and called Mr. Hirsh of the Hirsh Clothing Store, and asked, "Say, Sam, what do *you* think about this stranger? . . . Yes, the one bith the weard, I mean beard! . . . uh-huh . . . storybook clothes, eh? . . . Thanks a lot, Sam, good night."

Then he called the garage and said, "Hello, Luke, this is the sheriff talking. What do you make of this stranger in town . . . Yes? . . . literature, eh? Durned if I kin see how you can judge a man by the car he drives, but I'll take your word for it. Good night, Luke, and thanks a lot."

The sheriff looked very pleased with himself. He paced up and down and muttered, "Getting somewhere! Getting somewhere at last!" Then he surprised everyone by announcing that he was going over to the *library*!

In a few minutes he was back, his mustache twitching with excitement. "I've solved it!" he shouted. "The librarian knew right off just what book to look in! It's *Rip Van Winkle*! It's Rip Van Winkle this fellow's like. He must have driven up into the hills some thirty years ago and fell asleep, or got amnesia, or something!"

"Yeah! That's it!" agreed the barber along with Uncle Ulysses and the shoemaker.

Then Uncle Ulysses asked, "*But* how about that 'what-ever-it-is' underneath the canvas on the back of his car?"

"Now look here, Ulysses," shouted the sheriff, "you're just trying to complicate my deduction! Come on, let's play checkers!"

Bright and early the next morning the Rip-Van-Winklish stranger was up and wandering around Centerburg.

By ten o'clock everyone was referring to him as "Old Rip," and remarking how clever the sheriff was at deducing things.

The sheriff tried to see what was under the canvas, but couldn't make head or tail of what it was. Uncle Ulysses peeked at it too and said, "Goodness only knows! But never mind, Sheriff. If anybody can find out what this thing is, Homer will do the finding!"

That same afternoon after school was dismissed, Uncle Ulysses and the sheriff saw Homer strolling down the street with "Old Rip."

"Looks like he's explaining something to Homer," said the sheriff.

"Homer'll find out!" said Uncle Ulysses proudly. Then they watched through the barbershop window while the stranger took Homer across the square to the parking lot and showed him his car. He lifted one corner of the canvas and pointed underneath while Homer looked and nodded his head. They shook hands and the stranger went to his hotel, and Homer headed for the barbershop.

"Did he talk?" asked the sheriff the minute Homer opened the door.

"What's his name?" asked Uncle Ulysses.

"What is he doing?" asked the barber.

"Yes, he told me everything!" said Homer. "It sounds just like a story out of a book!"

"Yes, son, did he get amnesia up in the hills?" asked the sheriff.

"Well, no, not exactly, Sheriff, but he did *live* in the hills for the past thirty years."

"Well, what's he doing here now?" the barber demanded.

"I better start at the beginning," said Homer.

"That's a good idea, son," said the sheriff. "I'll take a few notes just for future reference."

"Well, to begin with," Homer started, "his name is Michael Murphy—just plain Michael Murphy. About thirty years ago he built himself a small vacation cabin out in the hills, some place on the far side of the state forest reserve. Then, he liked living in the cabin so much he decided to live there all of the time. He packed his belongings on his car and moved out to the hills."

"He cided ta be a dermit?" asked the sheriff.

"Not exactly *a hermit*," Homer continued. "But yesterday was the first time that he came out of the hills and saw people for thirty years. That's why he's so shy."

"Then he's moving back to civilization," suggested Uncle Ulysses.

"That comes later," said Homer. "I've only told as far as twenty-nine years ago."

"Can't you skip a few years, son, and get to the point?" demanded the sheriff.

"Nope! Twenty-nine years ago," Homer repeated firmly, "Mr. Murphy read in an almanac that if a man can make a better mousetrap than anybody else, the world will beat a path to his house—even if it is way out in the hills.

"So-o-o he started making *mousetraps*."

There was a pause, and then the sheriff said, "Will you repeat that again, son?"

"I said, Mr. Murphy started making *mousetraps*. He made good ones too, the very best, and when one of Mr. Murphy's traps caught a mouse, that was the end of that mouse for all time."

The sheriff forgot all about taking notes as Homer continued, "But nobody came to buy the traps. But that was just as well, you see, because twenty-eight years ago Mr. Murphy began to feel *sorry* for the mice. He came to realize that he would have to change his whole approach. He thought and thought and finally he decided to build mousetraps that wouldn't hurt the mice.

"He spent the next fifteen years doing research on what was the pleasantest possible way for a mouse to be caught. He discovered that being caught to music pleased mice the most, even more than cheese. Then," said Homer, "Mr. Murphy set to work to make a *musical* mousetrap."

"That wouldn't hurt the mice?" inquired Uncle Ulysses.

"That wouldn't hurt the mice," Homer stated. "It was a long, hard job too, because first he had to build an organ out of reeds that the mice liked the sound of, and then he had to compose a tune that the mice couldn't possibly resist. Then he incorporated it all into a mousetrap. . . ."

"That wouldn't hurt the mice?" interrupted the barber.

"That wouldn't hurt the mice," Homer went on. "The mousetrap caught mice, all right. The only trouble was, it was too big. What with the organ and all, and sort of impractical for general use because somebody had to stay around and pump the organ."

"Yes, I can see that wouldn't be practical," said Uncle Ulysses, stroking his chin. "But with a small electric motor. . . ."

"But he solved it, Uncle Ulysses! The whole idea seems very practical after you get used to it. He decided since the trap was too large to use in a house, he would fasten it onto his car, which he hadn't used for so long anyway. Then, he could drive it to a town, and make a bargain with the mayor to remove all the mice. You see he would start the musical mousetrap to working, and drive up and down the streets and alleys. Then all of the mice would run out of the houses to get themselves caught in this trap that plays music that no mouse ever born can possibly resist. After the trap is full of mice, Mr. Murphy drives them past the city limits, somewhere where they can't find their way home, and lets them go."

"Still without hurting them?" suggested the barber.

"Of course," said Homer.

The sheriff chewed on his pencil, Uncle Ulysses stroked on his chin, and the barber ran his fingers through his hair.

Homer noticed the silence and said, "I guess the idea *is* sort of startling when you first hear about it. But, if a town has a water truck to sprinkle streets, and a street-sweeping truck to remove dirt, why shouldn't they, maybe, just hire Mr. Murphy's musical mousetrap once in a while to remove mice?"

Uncle Ulysses stroked his chin again and then said, "By gum! This man Murphy is a genius!"

"I told Mr. Murphy that *you* would understand, Uncle Ulysses!" said Homer with a grin. "I told him the mayor was a friend of yours, and you could talk him into anything, even hiring a musical mousetrap."

"Whoever heard of a misical moostrap!" said the sheriff.

"That doesn't hurt the *mice!*" added the barber, as

Homer and Uncle Ulysses went off arm in arm to see the mayor.

It scarcely took Uncle Ulysses and Homer half an hour to convince the mayor that Mr. Murphy's musical mousetrap should be hired to rid Centerburg of mice. While Uncle Ulysses chatted on with the mayor, Homer dashed over to the hotel to fetch Mr. Murphy.

Homer came back with the bearded inventor and introduced him to the mayor and to Uncle Ulysses. The mayor opened a drawer of his desk and brought out a bag of jelly beans. "Have one," he said to Mr. Murphy, to sort of break the ice and to make his shy visitor feel at home. Mr. Murphy relaxed and answered the mayor's questions without blushing too much.

"How do we know this *thing of a jig* of yours will do what you say it will?" asked the mayor.

Mr. Murphy just whistled a few bars, "*Tum tidy ay dee,*" and a couple of mice jumped right out of the mayor's desk!

"Of course," Homer explained, "the mice come *quicker,* and get *removed* when the mousetrap plays that tune through the streets. Mr. Murphy guarantees to remove every single mouse from Centerburg for only thirty dollars."

"It's a bargain!" said the mayor. "I wondered where my jelly beans were disappearing to!" And he shook hands with Mr. Murphy. Then he proclaimed Saturday as the day for de-mousing Centerburg. By this time everyone knew that the shy stranger's name was Michael Murphy, but people still spoke of him as Rip Van Winkle (Rip for short), because of the sheriff's deduction. Everybody talked about the musical mousetrap (that didn't hurt the mice) and the mayor's de-mousing proclamation.

362

The children, especially, were looking forward to the great event. They watched with interest while Mr. Murphy went over his car and his musical trap to be sure everything was in perfect working order. Homer and Freddy and most of the other children were planning to follow the trap all around town Saturday and see the mice come out and get caught in Michael Murphy's musical trap.

"Gosh, Homer," said Freddy, "let's follow him until he lets them loose out in the country! That *will* be a sight, seeing all those mice let loose at once!"

"Well, Freddy, I've been thinking it might not be a good idea to follow the mousetrap past the city limits," said Homer, to Freddy's surprise.

"You know, Freddy, I've been over at the library reading up on mice and music—music can do funny things sometimes. It can soothe savage beasts and charm snakes and *lots* of things. If we're going to follow this musical trap till the mice are let loose, we better make some plans."

Homer and Freddy spent all Friday recess period making plans. They decided that all the children should meet in the schoolyard before the de-mousing started on Saturday. They arranged a signal, thumbs up, if everything was going along all right; and thumbs down if anyone was in trouble.

"It's just to be on the safe side," Homer explained.

Saturday dawned a beautiful crisp fall day, fine weather for the grand de-mousing of Centerburg. Mr. Michael Murphy came forth from the Strand Hotel, and after carefully slinging his long gray beard over his shoulder, he cranked his car and warmed up the engine. He carefully removed the canvas covering from the musical mousetrap and ever so painstakingly arranged the spiral ramps and runways so that no mouse, no matter how careless, could stub a toe or bump a nose. He then climbed behind the steering wheel, and the musical mousetrap was under way!

A loud cheer arose from the crowd of children as Mr. Murphy yanked a lever and the reed organ started to play. Even before the cheering stopped the mice began to appear!

Through the streets of Centerburg rolled Mr. Michael Murphy and his musical mousetrap. The mice came running from every direction! Fat, doughnut-fed mice from Uncle Ulysses' lunchroom, thin mice from the churches, ordinary mice from houses and homes, mice from the stores, and mice from the town hall.

They all went running up the ramps and runways and disappeared in Michael Murphy's musical mousetrap. The children followed behind enjoying the whole thing almost as much as the mice.

After traveling down every street in town, the procession came to a stop in front of the town hall, and the mayor came out and presented Mr. Murphy with his thirty-dollar fee—thirty bright, crisp new one-dollar bills.

Just as the mayor finished counting out the bills into Mr. Murphy's hand, the sheriff stepped up and said, "Mr. Murphy, I hope this won't embarrass you too much, in fact, I hate to mention it at all, but this here misical moostrap, I mean mousetrap of yours, has got a license plate that is thirty years old . . . A *new* license will cost you just exactly thirty dollars."

Mr. Murphy blushed crimson under his beard. "It's the law, you know, and *I* can't help it!" apologized the sheriff.

Poor Mr. Murphy, poor *shy* Mr. Murphy! He handed his thirty dollars to the sheriff, took his new license plates, and crept down the city hall steps. He climbed into his car and drove slowly away toward the edge of town, with the musical mousetrap playing its reedy music. The children followed along to see Mr. Murphy release all of the mice.

"I really hated to do that, Mayor," said the sheriff as the procession turned out of sight on Route 56A. "It's the law you know, and if I hadn't reminded him, he might have been arrested in the next town he visits."

There's no telling how this de-mousing would have ended if the children's librarian hadn't come rushing up shouting, "Sheriff! Sheriff! Quick! *We guessed the wrong book!*"

"What?" shouted the sheriff and the mayor and Uncle Ulysses.

"Yes!" gasped the children's librarian, "not *Rip Van Winkle*, but *another* book, *The Pied Piper of Hamelin!*"

"And almost every child in town is followin' him this very minute!" the sheriff yelled.

The sheriff and the librarian and the mayor and Uncle Ulysses all jumped into the sheriff's car and roared away after the procession. They met up with the children just outside the city limits. "Come back! Turn around, children!" they shouted.

"I'll treat everybody to a doughnut!" yelled Uncle Ulysses.

The children didn't seem to hear, and they kept right on following the musical mousetrap.

"The music must have affected their minds," cried the librarian.

"Sheriff, we can't lose all these children with election

time coming up next month!" mourned the mayor. "Let's give Murphy another thirty dollars!"

"That's the idea," said Uncle Ulysses. "Drive up next to him, Sheriff, and I'll hand him the money."

The sheriff's car drew alongside the musical mousetrap, and Uncle Ulysses tossed a wad of thirty dollar bills onto the seat next to the shy Mr. Murphy.

"Please don't take them away!" pleaded the librarian.

"Come, Murphy, let's be reasonable," shouted the mayor.

Mr. Murphy was very flustered, and his steering was distinctly wobbly.

Then the sheriff got riled and yelled at the top of his lungs, *"Get 'em low! Get 'em go! Let 'em go!"*

And that's exactly what Mr. Murphy did. He let them go. He pulled a lever, and every last mouse came tumbling out of the bottom of the musical mousetrap. And *such a sight* it was, well worth walking to the city limits to see. The mice came out in a torrent. The reedy organ of the musical mousetrap stopped playing, and the squeaking of mice and the cheering of children filled the air.

The torrent of mice paused, as if sensing direction, and then each Centerburg mouse started off in a straight, straight line to his own Centerburg mousehole. Mr. Murphy didn't pause. He stepped on the gas, and the musical mousetrap swayed down the road. The mayor, the children's librarian, the sheriff, Uncle Ulysses, and the children watched as it grew smaller and smaller and finally disappeared.

Then Uncle Ulysses remembered the children. He turned around and noticed them grinning at each other and holding their thumbs in the air. They paid no attention whatever when they were called!

"That music has pixied these children!" he moaned.

"No, it hasn't, Uncle Ulysses," said Homer, who had just come up. "There's not a thing the matter with them that Doc Pelly can't cure in two shakes! Just to be on the safe side, Freddy and I asked Doc Pelly to come down to the schoolyard this morning and put cotton in all the children's ears. You know, just like Ulysses, not you, Uncle Ulysses, but the ancient one—the one that Homer wrote about. Not me but the ancient one."

"You mean to say Doc Pelly is mixed up in this?" asked the mayor.

"Yes, he thought it was awfully funny, our being so cautious."

Uncle Ulysses laughed and said, "Round 'em up, and we'll all go down to the lunchroom for doughnuts and milk."

"Sheriff," said the mayor, "with election time coming next month *we* gotta put our heads together and cook up a good excuse for spending sixty dollars of the tax-payers' money."

Time of Wonder is quite different from Robert McCloskey's other work. In this book Mr. McCloskey captures both in words and pictures the excitement of a hurricane.

He chooses words carefully to show how the storm affects one small island off the coast of Maine and the people who live there. The beautiful watercolor paintings set the mood and match the story in showing how the storm comes and goes.

The McCloskey family's days in Maine are clearly reflected in this story. Robert McCloskey's daughters, Sally and Jane, were the models for the two girls you will meet in this excerpt from *Time of Wonder*.

Time of Wonder

by ROBERT McCLOSKEY

Out on the islands
that poke their rocky shores
above the waters of Penobscot Bay,
you can watch the time of the world
go by, from minute to minute,
hour to hour, from day to day,
season to season.

You can watch a cloud peep over
the Camden Hills, thirty miles away

across the bay — see it slowly grow
and grow as it comes nearer and
nearer; see it darken the hills with
its shadow; and then, see it darken,
one after the other, Islesboro,
Western Island, Pond Island,
Hog Island, Spectacle Island,
Two Bush Island — darken all
the islands in between, until
you, on your island, are standing
in the shadow, watching the rain
begin to spill down
way across the bay.

    The rain comes closer and closer.
Now you hear a million splashes.
Now you even see the drops
on the water . . .
on the age-old rocky point . . .
  on the bayberry . . .
    on the grass. . . .
      Now take a breath —
IT'S RAINING ON *YOU!*

    Back from the shore
the trees look like ghosts.
The forest is so quiet
that you can hear an insect
boring a tunnel deep inside a log.
And that other sound —
not the beating of your heart,
but the one like half a whisper —
is the sound of growing ferns,
pushing aside dead leaves,
unrolling their fiddle-heads,

slowly unfurling,
slowly stretching.
Now the fog turns yellow.
The bees begin to buzz,
and a hummingbird hums by.
Then all the birds began to sing,
and suddenly
the fog has lifted!
And suddenly
you find that you are singing too,
  With the blue water sparkling
    all around, all around,
  With the blue water sparkling
    all around!

  In the evening,
when the tide is high again,
(and all your guests have gone,)
you row around to the point,
feeling lonely,
until an owl asks a question.
A heron croaks an answer.
  A seal sniffs softly as he recognizes
you, and eider ducks and fishhawks—
all are listening, all are watching
as you row. By the rock, you shine
a light down into the water.
There is a crab on the bottom
where you were playing
this afternoon.
  He tiptoes sideways
through the castle gate
and disappears
into its watery keep.

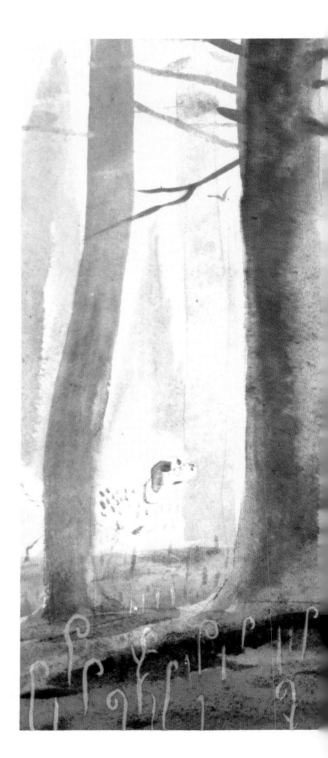

You snap off the light
and row toward the dock
as the stars are gazing down,
their reflections gazing up.
In the quiet of the night
one hundred pairs of eyes
are watching you.

As the days grow shorter and
shorter there are fewer and fewer
boats on the bay, until at last
only the fishing boats are left.
The wind blows brisk
from the northwest, rustling
the birch leaves.
    The ferns change from green
to yellow to brown. The robins are
gone from the lawn and the garden.
The swallows have flown
from their nests in the boathouse.

On some days the wind is so strong
that not even the sturdy fishing boats
are out on the bay.
    Now is the time for being watchful.
    And other times there is not a breath
of wind to ripple the reflection of an
unusual sky.
    Now is the time for being prepared.
    On your island you feel
the light crisp feeling go out of the air
and a heavy stillness take its place.
It's time to make a quick trip
to the mainland for food and gasoline.

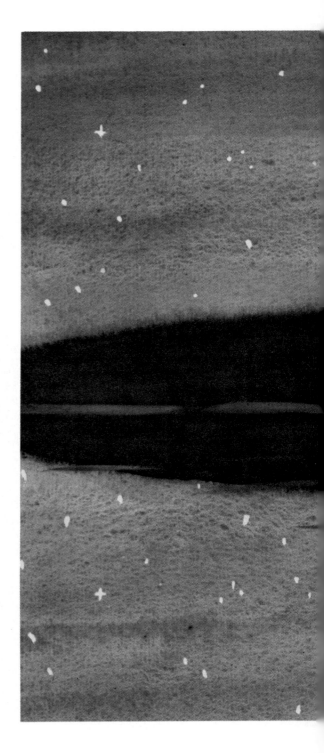

It's time to get ready.
We're going to have some weather.
It's a-comin'.
She's gonna blow.
Take aboard groceries.
Take aboard gasoline.
All of the talk is of
hundred-pound anchors,
two-inch rope,
one-inch chain, and
will it hold?
And the weather . . . and when?
Mr. Gray strokes his chin and says,
"With the next shift of the tide."

Hurry for home,
for there's much to be done
before the tide is too low.

   Home on the island, you pull in
the sailboat, chain the motorboat fast
to its mooring, pull the rowboats
high off the beach.
   Stack the groceries on kitchen shelves.
Bring in wood to build a fire.
Fill the generator with gas.
Then take one last careful look,
while the calm sea pauses
at dead low water.
A mouse nibbles off one last stalk
from the garden and drags it
into his mouse hole.
A spider scurries across his web
and disappears into a knothole.

All living things wait,
while the first surge
of the incoming tide
ripples past Eagle Island,
ripples past Dirigo,
past Pickering,
past Two Bush Island.
The bell-buoy off Spectacle Island
sways slightly with the ripple,
tolling . . .
tolling . . .
tolling the shift of the tide.

Gently at first the wind begins to blow.
Gently at first the rain begins to fall.
      Suddenly the wind whips the water
into sharp, choppy waves.
It tears off the sharp tops and slashes them
into ribbons of smoky spray.
And the rain comes slamming down.
The wind comes in stronger and stronger gusts.
A branch snaps from a tree.
A gull flies over, flying backward,
hoping for a chance to drop
into the lee of the island.
Out in the channel a tardy fishing boat
wallows in the waves, seeking the shelter
of Bucks Harbor.
      A tree snaps.
Above the roar of the hurricane
you see and feel
but do not hear it fall.
A latch gives way.
People and papers
and parcheesi games

are puffed hair-over-eyes
across the floor,
while Father pushes and strains
to close and bolt out the storm.

  Mother reads a story,
and the words are spoken
and lost in the scream of the wind.
You are glad it is a story
you have often heard before.
Then you all sing together,
shouting *"eyes have seen the glory"*
just as loud as you can SHOUT.
With dishtowels tucked by doorsills
just to keep the salt spray out.
  The moon comes out,
making a rainbow in the salt spray,
a promise
that the storm will soon be over.
Now the wind is lessening,
singing loud chords in the treetops.
Lessening,
it hums as you go up to bed.

  And the great swells
coming in from the open sea
say SH-h-h-h . . . SH-h-h-h . . . SH-h-h-h
as they foam
over the old rock on the point.
Lessening,
the wind whispers a lullaby
in the spruce branches
as you fall asleep
in the bright moonlight.

Books by Robert McCloskey

Lentil
When the town finds itself in an embarrassing situation, Lentil and his harmonica save the day.

Make Way for Ducklings
The author got his idea for this book by watching a family of ducks in the Boston Public Garden.

Homer Price
This book follows Homer through several adventures, including a hold-up and an evening with a doughnut-making machine that goes out of control.

Blueberries for Sal
Sal and her mother get mixed up with Little Bear and his mother when they all go out to pick blueberries! The pictures, all printed in blue, capture the lovely Maine landscape.

Centerburg Tales
This book was published nine years after *Homer Price*. Here are Ginny Lee, Uncle Ulysses, the sheriff, and Homer's other friends.

One Morning in Maine
In this story about the McCloskey family, little sister Jane makes her first appearance. Large drawings make the people, the places, and the events seem real.

Time of Wonder
This beautiful book is about a hurricane at the end of a happy summer vacation.

Burt Dow: Deep-Water Man
Here is a tall tale of the sea. A sea captain, swallowed by a whale, escapes by painting his way out!

Glossary

This glossary is a little dictionary. It contains the difficult words found in this book. The pronunciation, which tells you how to say the word, is given next to each word. Sometimes, a different form of the word follows the definition. It appears in boldface type.

The special symbols used to show the pronunciation are explained in the key that follows.

PRONUNCIATION KEY*

a	add, map	m	move, seem	u	up, done
ā	ace, rate	n	nice, tin	û(r)	urn, term
â(r)	care, air	ng	ring, song	yōō	use, few
ä	palm, father	o	odd, hot	v	vain, eve
b	bat, rub	ō	open, so	w	win, away
ch	check, catch	ô	order, jaw	y	yet, yearn
d	dog, rod	oi	oil, boy	z	zest, muse
e	end, pet	ou	out, now	zh	vision, pleasure
ē	even, tree	ōō	pool, food	ə	the schwa,
f	fit, half	ŏŏ	took, full		an unstressed
g	go, log	p	pit, stop		vowel representing
h	hope, hate	r	run, poor		the sound spelled
i	it, give	s	see, pass		a in above
ī	ice, write	sh	sure, rush		e in sicken
j	joy, ledge	t	talk, sit		i in possible
k	cook, take	th	thin, both		o in melon
l	look, rule	th	this, bathe		u in circus

Foreign: *N* is used following a nasal vowel sound:
French *Jean* [zhäN]

In the pronunciations an accent mark (′) is used to show which syllable of a word receives the most stress. The word *bandage* [ban′dij], for example, is stressed on the first syllable. Sometimes there is also a lighter accent mark (′) that shows where there is a lighter stress, as in the word *combination* [kom′bə·nā′shən].

The following abbreviations are used throughout the glossary: *n.,* noun; *pron.,* pronoun; *v.,* verb; *adj.,* adjective; *adv.,* adverb; *prep.,* preposition; *conj.,* conjunction; *interj.,* interjection; *pl.,* plural; *sing.,* singular.

A

a·back [ə·bak′] *adv.* Surprised and confused; upset: taken *aback.*

Ac·cra [a′krə] *n.* The largest city in Ghana, a country in West Africa.

a·ghast [ə·gast′] *adj.* Shocked and scared.

a·gin [ə·gin′] *prep.* Against; a dialect form.

A·gi·ri·A·sa·sa [ä·gi′rē·ä·sä′sä] *n.* The wise man's name in "The Oba Asks for a Mountain."

aisle [īl] *n.* A path through rows of seats.

a·jar [ə·jär] *adj., adv.* A little bit open, as a door.

al·der [ôl′dər] *n.* A small tree that grows well in wet soil.

al·lied [ə·līd′ *or* al′īd] *adj.* Working together; united, as the armies of two or more nations in a war.

Allied armies *n., pl.* The armies (including that of the U.S.) that fought on the same side as Holland against Germany in World War II.

al·ma·nac [ôl′mə·nak] *n.* A calendar in the form of a book or pamphlet. Besides the dates, an *almanac* tells you when the moon will change and what the weather is likely to be. Sometimes it also has wise little sayings or riddles.

am·ble [am′bəl] *v.* To stroll; to walk at a slow and easy pace.

am·ne·sia [am·nē′zhə *or* am·nē′zhē·ə] *n.* Loss of memory. *Amnesia* can be caused by sickness, shock, or a very hard knock on the head.

An·da·le [än′dä·lā] *v. Spanish* Go on; get going; move.

an·tique [an·tēk′] *n.* Something very old, made a long time ago.

An·to·ni·o [än·tō′nyō] *n.* A Spanish male's name. The equivalent of the English name *Anthony.*

ap·pren·tice [ə·pren′tis] *n.* A person who works for another in order to learn that other person's trade or business.

arch [ärch] *n.* A curved structure over an opening.

386

ar·ti·san [är′tə·zən] *n.* A skilled worker, such as a carpenter or plumber.

as·cend·ed [ə·sen′did] *v.* **1** Succeeded to; took over; occupied: *ascended* the throne (became king or queen). **2** Climbed; rose. — **as·cend,** *v.*

a·vert·ed [ə·vûr′tid] *v.* Turned away: *averted* the eyes. — **a·vert,** *v.*

B

bal·ing [bā′ling] *adj.* Used to tie bales. A *bale* is a large, tightly packed bundle.

bal·lad [bal′əd] *n.* A song or poem that tells a story.

bar·rack [bar′ək] *n.* A building in which soldiers live.

bask·ing [bas′king] *v.* Enjoying a pleasant warmth: *basking* in the sun. — **bask,** *v.*

bay·o·net [bā′ə·nit *or* bā′ə·net] *n.* A sharp-pointed weapon that fastens onto the outer end of a rifle.

bee·tling [bēt′ling] *adj.* Overhanging, as eyebrows over the eyes.

bel·fry [bel′frē] **1** *n.* The part of a tower or steeple where a bell is hung. **2** *adj.* Relating to a belfry: the *belfry* arch.

bell-buoy [bel′boi′] *n.* A buoy with a bell that rings when the waves rock it. A *buoy* is a floating object held in place by an anchor and used to mark a place in the water.

be·tray [bi·trā′] *v.* To give away a secret; to help an enemy.

bi·car·bon·ate of soda [bī·kär′bə·nit] *n.* A white powder that fizzes in water. Used in cooking or for an upset stomach. Also called *sodium bicarbonate.*

bil·liards [bil′yərdz] *n., pl.* A game in which hard balls are hit with long rods, played on a cloth-covered table with raised edges.

blue-plate special *n.* A specially priced and prepared meal in a small restaurant or diner: Pot roast is the *blue-plate special* for Thursday.

blurt·ing [blûr′ting] *v.* Saying something all of a sudden or without thinking. — **blurt,** *v.*

bog [bog] *n.* A swamp; wet and spongy ground.

bore [bôr] *v.* To drill a hole or tunnel.

bra·zier [brā′zhər] *n.* An open pan for holding burning charcoal.

Brid·get [brij′it] A female's name, popular in Ireland.

britch·es [brich′iz] *n., pl.* Pants; trousers; a dialect form of *breeches.*

British Regulars [brit′ish reg′yə·lərz] *n., pl.* The best soldiers of Great Britain, who remained in the army in peace as well as war.

broken Dutch *n.* Uncertain Dutch; Dutch not spoken fluently.

bur·lap [bûr′lap] *n.* A rough, loose cloth used for bags, sacks, etc.

bur·nished [bûr′nisht] *v.* Polished by rubbing. — **bur·nish,** *v.*

burr [bûr] *n.* A round, prickly flower head or seedcase. Another form of *bur.*

---

add, āce, câre, pälm;　　end, ēqual;　　it, īce;　　odd, ōpen, ôrder;　　to͝ok, po͞ol;　　up, bûrn;
ə = a in *above*, e in *sicken*, i in *possible*, o in *melon*, u in *circus*;　　y**o͞o** = u in *fuse*;　　oil;　　pout;
　　　check;　　ring;　　**th**in;　　**th**is;　　**zh** in *vision*.

can·tered [kan'tərd] *v.* Moved at a slow, gentle gallop. — **can·ter,** *v.*

Cape Cod [kāp' kod'] *n.* A part of Massachusetts that juts out into the Atlantic Ocean. A *cape* is a long piece of land that reaches out into the water.

car·din·al [kär'də·nəl] *adj.* Of first importance: The *cardinal* directions are north, south, east, and west.

car·il·lon [kar'ə·lon] *n.* A set of bells on which a tune can be played.

car·ri·on [kar'ē·ən] *n.* Dead and rotting flesh.

cas·u·al·ly [kazh'ōō·əl·ē] *adv.* In a cool manner, showing no excitement or worry.

cat·ty·cor·ner [kat'ē·kôr'nər] *adj., adv.* On a slant from corner to opposite corner; diagonally.

cen·sus [sen'səs] *n.* An official counting of the people living in a particular place.

chaff [chaf] *n.* The outside husks or shells of grain; the part of the grain that cannot be eaten.

chaf·fered [chaf'ərd] *v.* Bargained over a price: We *chaffered* and haggled. — **chaf·fer,** *v.*

chest·nut [ches'nut] *n.* **1** A horse with a reddish brown coat. **2** A kind of nut than can be eaten.

cin·cho·na [sing·kō'nə *or* sin·chō'nə] *n.* A tree, of which the dried bark is used to make a medicine for treating fever.

cit·a·del [sit'ə·dəl] *n.* A building which overlooks a town or city in order to protect it.

ci·vil·i·za·tion [siv'ə·lə·zā'shən] *n.* The art, skill, science, knowledge, and culture of a particular group of people at a particular time.

cla·mor [kla'mər] *v.* To make noise; shout for attention.

clasped [klaspt] *v.* Held firmly; fastened. — **clasp,** *v.*

clod [klod] *n.* A lump of earth or clay.

col·umn [kol'əm] *n.* A tall post or pillar, used as a support in or around a building, or for decoration.

comida mexicana [kō·mē'dä mā'hē·kä'nä] *n. Spanish* Mexican food.

com·mis·sar·i·at [kom'ə·ser'ē·ət *or* kom'ə·sâr'ē·ət] *n.* The department of an army that provides food and daily supplies.

com·mis·sion [kə·mi'shən] *n.* Payment based on a percentage of the profits.

com·pelled [kəm·pəld'] *v.* Forced; driven. — **com·pel,** *v.*

com·plex [kəm·pleks' *or* kom'pleks] *adj.* Made up of many parts.

con·ceive [kən·sēv'] *v.* To form or get an idea.

con·cer·tin·a [kon'sər·tē'nə] *n.* A small musical instrument like an accordion.

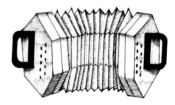

con·fi·dent·ly [kən'fə·dənt·lē] *adv.* In a way that shows faith in oneself; with ability to handle a problem.

con·sume [kən·s(y)ōōm'] *v.* To eat; to use up.

con·tem·plate [kon'tem·plāt] *v.* **1** To think deeply about something: *contemplate* the meaning of life. **2** To look at for a long time: *contemplate* the sunset.

con·trap·tion [kən·trap′shən] *n. Informal.* A strange or comical machine.

con·trar·y *adj.* **1** [kən·trâr′ē] Determined to disagree: *Don't be so* contrary. **2** [kon′trer·ē] Totally different: *contrary beliefs.*

cos·set·ed [kos′i·tid] *v.* Pampered; treated like a pet. — **cos·set,** *v.*

coy·ly [koi′lē] *adv.* With pretended shyness.

crave [krāv] *v.* **1** To ask or beg for. **2** To want very much.

crim·son [krim′zən] *n., adj.* Deep red.

cru·sade [krōō·sād′] *v.* To fight for a cause or against an evil.

cru·sad·er [krōō·sā′dər] *n.* One who fights for a cause or against an evil.

cu·bic inch [kyōō′bik inch′] *n.* A unit for measuring volume, equaling one inch wide by one inch high by one inch deep.

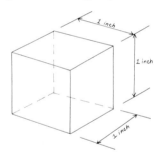

cuffed [kuft] *v.* Hit with the open hand; slapped. — **cuff,** *v.*

cun·ning·ly [kun′ing·lē] *adv.* Cleverly.

cur·few [kûr′fyōō] *n.* A rule or law requiring certain people to stay off the streets after a certain hour in the evening.

cur·ry [kûr′ē] *n.* A sauce or powder made of finely ground spices, used in cooking, especially in India and the Mideast.

D

dab [dab] *v.* To touch or pat a little bit.

de·creed [di·krēd′] *v.* Made a formal order or decision. — **de·cree,** *v.*

de·duce [di·d(y)ōōs′] *v.* To figure out.

de·duc·tion [di·duk′shən] *n.* **1** A conclusion based on reasoning. **2** An amount taken away or subtracted: *a thirty-dollar* deduction.

de·fy [di·fī′] *v.* To refuse to follow (orders); resist openly.

Delft Blue [delft′] *n.* Any of the shades of blue used on the fine china made in the Dutch city of Delft.

de·lib·er·ate·ly [di·lib′ər·it·lē] *adv.* By choice; on purpose.

de·spair [di·spâr′] *n.* A bad or empty feeling that comes when all hope is lost.

des·per·a·tion [des′pə·rā′shən] *n.* Reckless willingness to try anything because there seems to be no hope left.

dig·ni·fied [dig′nə·fīd] *adj.* Proud; having a controlled, formal way of speaking and acting.

di·rect·ed [di·rek′tid *or* dī·rek′tid] *v.* Ordered; told someone to do something or how to do something. — **di·rect,** *v.*

dis·taste [dis·tāst′] *n.* Dislike.

dis·tinct·ly [dis·tingkt′lē] *adv.* Very clearly.

dis·tin·guished [dis·ting′gwisht] *adj.* Set apart from the rest; special; important.

do·i [dō′yē′] *n. Cherokee* Beaver.

draw·ers [drôrz] *n., pl.* Underwear with either long or short legs.

dread [dred] *n.* Great fear, usually of something in the future.

dwin·dle [dwin′dəl] *v.* To get smaller and smaller.

---

add, āce, câre, pälm;   end, ēqual;   it, īce;   odd, ōpen, ôrder;   tŏŏk, pōōl;   up, bûrn;
ə = a in *above,* e in *sicken,* i in *possible,* o in *melon,* u in *circus;*   yōō = u in *fuse;*   oil;   pout;
check;   ring;   thin;   this;   zh in *vision.*

389

e·del·weiss [ā′dəl·vīs′] *n.* A small plant with woolly white leaves and flowers that grows high up in the Alps.

ei·der duck [ī′dər] *n.* A large sea duck found in northern waters.

e·lab·or·ate [*adj.* i·lab′ər·it, *v.* i·lab′ər·āt] **1** *adj.* Fancy; with many parts. **2** *v.* To develop; add more parts or details.

e·lec·tron·ic [i·lek′tron′ik] *adj.* Having to do with electronics. *Electronics* is the branch of engineering that deals with the design of radios, television sets, etc.

em·broi·dered [im·broi′dərd] *v.* Made designs or decorated with stitches. **— em·broi·der,** *v.*

e·merge [i·mûrj′] *v.* To come out and into sight.

en·camp·ment [in·kamp′mənt] *n.* A camping place.

en·chant·er [in·chan′tər] *n.* A magician; sorcerer.

en·core [än(g)′kôr] *interj.* Again! Once more!

en·thu·si·asm [in·thōō′zē·as′əm] *n.* Eager interest or liking.

e·val·u·ate [i·val′yōō·āt] *v.* To judge the value of.

ex·cerpt [*n.* ek′sûrpt, *v.* ik·sûrpt′] **1** *n.* A passage or section taken from a piece of writing. **2** *v.* To pick out and quote (a passage from a piece of writing).

Fa·ree·dah [fə·rē′də] *n.* A Persian female's name.

fash·es [fash′əz] *v.* Worries; distresses; seldom used today.

fazed [fāzd] *v.* Upset; disturbed; confused. **— faze,** *v.*

fe·ro·cious [fə·rō′shəs] *adj.* Extremely fierce or savage.

fetch·ing [fech′ing] *v.* Going to get (something). **— fetch,** *v.*

fid·dle·back chair [fid′(ə)l·bak′] *n.* A straight-back chair with no arms and a center piece down the back that is shaped like a fiddle (a violin).

fifed [fīft] *v.* Played a fife, a small, shrill flute used with drums in military music. **— fife,** *v.*

fin·ick·y [fin′ə·kē] *adj.* Fussy or very particular.

flag·stone [flag′stōn′] *n.* A broad, flat stone used in paving footpaths, terraces, or stone floors.

flax·wo·ven [flaks′wō′vən] *adj.* Made by weaving linen yarn.

fleet [flēt] *adj.* Fast; swift.

flushed [flusht] *v.* Turned red or rosy; blushed. **— flush,** *v.*

flus·tered [flus′tərd] *adj.* Confused; embarrassed; upset.

foo-foo [fōō′fōō] *n.* A popular food in Ghana, made from yams, potatoes, or other vegetables.

for·sook [fôr·sōōk′] *v.* Left behind; abandoned. **— for·sake,** *v.*

Fran·cis·co [frän·sēs′kō] *n.* A Spanish male's name. The equivalent of the English name *Francis* or *Frank*.

fre·quen·cy [frē′kwen·sē] *n.* Station or tuning on a radio receiver.

fu·gi·tive [fyōō′jə·tiv] *n.* A person who is running away from danger or arrest.

G

gaffed [gaft] *v.* Hooked by a gaff, a strong metal hook used to lift large fish out of the water. — **gaff,** *v.*

gaf·fer [gaf′ər] *n.* An old man.

gai·ter [gā′tər] *n.* A covering, as of cloth or leather, for the lower leg or ankle.

gale [gāl] *n.* A very strong wind.

gawk [gôk] *n. Informal* An awkward, stupid person.

gen·tian [jen′shən] *n.* A plant with blue flowers, often seen in the mountains.

girth [gûrth] *n.* A strap or band around a horse's body, used to hold a saddle or pack in place.

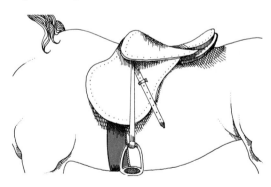

glim·mer [glim′ər] *n.* A faint light.

glow·ered [glou′ərd] *v.* Stared angrily. — **glow·er,** *v.*

Go·li·ath [gə·lī′əth] *n.* In the Bible, a giant killed by David with a stone from a sling.

good even [gŏŏd ē′vən] An old form of *good evening.*

Gra·na·da [grə·nä′də] *n.* A city in southern Spain.

grave·ly [grāv′lē] *adv.* Seriously; solemnly.

gren·a·dier [gren′ə·dir′] *n.* In early times, a soldier trained to throw grenades (small bombs).

griev·ous [grē′vəs] *adj.* Very painful; hard to stand.

gruff [gruf] *adj.* Rough, rude, and unfriendly.

H

hag·gled [ha′gəld] *v.* Bargained for a price. — **hag·gle,** *v.*

Hah·skwa·hot [hä′skwä′hōt′] *n. Cherokee* A big, standing rock.

hale [hāl] *adj.* Strong and healthy.

ha'pen·ny [hā′pə·nē] *n.* A British coin worth half a penny.

haugh·ti·ly [hô′tə·lē] *adv.* Proudly and scornfully.

heart·en·ing [härt′(ə)n·ing] *adj.* Giving courage and cheer.

height·ened [hīt′(ə)nd] *adj.* Increased; deepened.

heil [hīl] *interj. German* Hail or hurrah; used as part of a cheer, greeting, etc.

her·i·tage [her′ə·tij] *n.* A belief, custom, etc., handed down from the past.

her·pe·tol·o·gist [hûr′pə·tol′ə·jist] *n.* An expert on snakes, turtles, lizards, and other reptiles.

---

add, āce, câre, pälm;   end, ēqual;   it, īce;   odd, ōpen, ôrder;   tŏŏk, pōōl;   up, bûrn;
ə = a in *above,* e in *sicken,* i in *possible,* o in *melon,* u in *circus;*   yōō = u in *fuse;*   oil;   pout;
check;   ring;   thin;   this;   zh in *vision.*

Hi·sa·ko [hē′sä·kō′] *n.* A Japanese female's name.

hob·ble [hob′əl] *n.* A strap used to tie together two legs of a horse or other animal to keep it from straying.

Ho·mer [hō′mər] *n.* **1** An ancient Greek poet who lived almost 3,000 years ago. The author of the *Odyssey.* **2** A male's name.

horn [hôrn] *n.* A raised knob on top of a Western saddle.

huck·ster [huk′stər] *n.* A peddler; seller of small articles.

hu·hu [hōō′hōō′] *n. Cherokee* A yellow mockingbird.

hulk [hulk] *n.* **1** An old ship. **2.** A very large and bulky person or object.

Hwei Ming [hwā′ ming] *n.* A Chinese female's name which means "clever." The word *ming* can also mean "light."

I

I·le·sha [ē·lä′shä] *n.* A city in southwest Nigeria.

im·mac·u·late [i·mak′yə·lit] *adj.* Very clean; spotless and neat.

im·pet·u·ous [im·pech′ōō·əs] *adj.* Acting too hastily, often without thinking.

in·can·ta·tion [in′kan·tā′shən] *n.* The speaking of words or syllables supposed to have magical results.

in·con·ven·ience [in′kən·vēn′yəns] *n.* Trouble or bother.

in·cor·por·ate [in·kôr′pə·rāt] *v.* To combine, bring together; to include as part of something else.

in·dig·nant [in·dig′nənt] *adj.* Angry because of something that is not right, fair, or just.

in·di·vid·u·al·ist [in′də·vij′ōō·əl·ist] *n.* A person who believes in living his or her own way, no matter what other people think.

in·sig·ni·fi·cant [in′sig·nif′ə·kənt] *adj.* Not at all important.

in·tel·lec·tu·al·ly [in′tə·lek′chōō·ə·lē] *adv.* Mentally; in a way having to do with intelligence.

in·tent·ly [in·tent′lē] *adv.* With great attention.

i·o·ta [ī·ō′tə] *n.* **1** The ninth letter of the Greek alphabet. **2** A small amount.

J

---

jade [jād] *n.* A type of stone, usually green but sometimes white, used in jewelry or carving.

jounced [jounst] *v.* Shook or bumped. **—jounce,** *v.*

K

Kyo·to [kē·ō′tō] *n.* A large city in central Japan.

Kyu·shu [kyōō′shōō] *n.* An island off southwest Japan.

L

laps·ing [lap′sing] *v.* Slipping back; making a momentary mistake. —**lapse**, *v.*

lar·der [lär′dər] *n.* A place where food is stored; pantry.

li·a·ble [lī′ə·bəl] *adj.* Likely.

lib·er·at·ing [lib′ə·rā′ting] *v.* Setting free; releasing. —**lib·er·ate**, *v.*

lib·er·a·tor [lib′ə·rā′tər] *n.* One who sets free other people or a country.

lieu·ten·ant [lo͞o·ten′ənt] *n.* A military rank below a captain but above a sergeant.

lim·er·ick [lim′rik *or* lim′ər·ik] *n.* A type of humorous five-line poem.

loot [lo͞ot] *v.* To rob by force.

lu·au [lo͞o′ou] *n.* A feast of Hawaiian food.

lu·na·tic [lo͞o′nə·tik] *n.* A person who is mentally ill.

M

ma·hog·a·ny [mə·hog′ə·nē] *n.* Any of various tropical trees yielding reddish brown hardwood, used for furniture.

ma·ma·ci·ta [mä′mä·sē′tə] *n. Spanish* Mom; mommy.

mast [mast] *n.* A long, straight pole that holds up the sails of a sailing ship or boat.

mech·a·nism [mek′ə·niz′əm] *n.* The parts of a machine.

meek·ly [mēk′lē] *adv.* In a modest or obedient way.

mel·low [mel′ō] *adj.* Rich, soft, and pleasant, as certain colors and sounds.

mes·teño [mes·tā′nyō] *n. Spanish* An owner of sheep; a shepherd.

Me·thu·se·lah [mə·th(y)o͞o′zə·lə] *n.* The oldest person mentioned in the Bible, said to have lived 969 years.

Mi·guel [mē·gel′] *n.* A Spanish male's name. The equivalent of the English name *Michael.*

mite [mīt] *n.* **1** A little bit. **2** A tiny bug.

mon·o·cle [mon′ə·kəl] *n.* An eyeglass for one eye.

moor·ing [mo͞or′ing] *n.* The line, cable, anchor, etc., that holds a ship in place.

mor·sel [môr′səl] *n.* A small bite or piece.

mourn·er [môr′nər] *n.* A person grieving for the dead.

mu·ni·tions [myo͞o·nish′ənz] *n., pl.* Materials and supplies used in war, such as guns, cannons, bullets, and shells.

mus·ket [mus′kit] *n.* An old-fashioned gun, now replaced by the rifle.

mus·tang·er [mus′tang·ər] *n.* A person who rounds up and catches mustangs, wild horses of the U.S. plains.

mus·ter·ing [mus′tər·ing] *v.* Assembling; gathering up. —**mus·ter**, *v.*

mus·ter roll [mus′tər rōl′] *n.* A list of the soldiers or sailors in a company or larger military division.

mu·tin·y [myo͞o′tən·ē] *n.* A rebellion against authority, as by a group of soldiers against their commander.

myth [mith] *n.* A very, very old story, usually of goddesses, gods, or heroes, supposed to explain something about how the world got to be the way it is.

---

add, āce, câre, pälm; end, ēqual; it, īce; odd, ōpen, ôrder; to͞ok, po͞ol; up, bûrn;
ə = a in *above*, e in *sicken*, i in *possible*, o in *melon*, u in *circus*; yo͞o = u in *fuse*; oil; pout;
check; ring; thin; this; zh in *vision*.

no·ble [nō′bəl] *adj.* **1** Having a high rank in a society where rank is inherited. **2** Having a fine, honorable, and generous character.

O·ba [ō′bə] *n. Yoruba* Powerful chief. Yoruba is a language of West Africa.

o·blig·ing·ly [ə·blī′jing·lē] *adv.* Helpfully; graciously.

ob·vi·ous [ob′vē·əs] *adj.* Easily seen or noticed; clear; plain.

oc·cu·pied [ok′yə·pīd] *v.* Held, controlled, and policed by enemy soldiers. —**oc·cu·py,** *v.*

O·ke-U·mo [ō′kā·ē′mō] *n.* A mountain in Nigeria.

o·kra [ō′krə] *n.* The sticky pods of a small shrub, used in soups and as a vegetable.

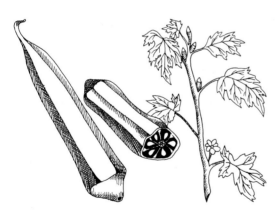

o·me·ga [ō·mē′gə, ō·meg′ə, *or* ō·mä′gə] *n.* **1** The last letter in the Greek alphabet. **2** The end; the last.

or·di·nance [ôr′də·nəns] *n.* An order, or law, made by the government of a city or town.

out·ra·geous [out·rā′jəs] *adj.* Shocking; going beyond all reasonable limits.

Pab·lo [pä′blō] *n.* A Spanish male's name. The equivalent of the English name *Paul.*

pact [pakt] *n.* A binding agreement.

pains·tak·ing·ly [pānz′tā′king·lē] *adv.* Very, very carefully.

pa·le·o·bi·ol·o·gist [pā′lē·ō·bī·ol′ə·jist] *n.* A scientist who studies fossils. Also, *paleontologist.*

pang [pang] *n.* A sudden, sharp pain.

par·chee·si [pär·chē′zē] *n.* A game played on a cross-shaped board. *Parcheesi* is a trademark. The original game, called *pachisi,* is a very old game of India.

pass·port [pas′pôrt′] *n.* A government document stating citizenship and allowing travel in foreign countries.

pa·vil·ion [pə·vil′yən] *n.* A large tent or canopy.

pe·cu·li·ar·i·ty [pi·kyōō′lē·ar′ə·tē *or* pi·kyōōl′yar′ə·tē] *n.* Something odd and unusual.

Pe·king [pē′king′] *n.* The capital of China.

Pe·nob·scot Bay [pe·nob′skot] *n.* A bay in the state of Maine. A *bay* is a body of water partly enclosed by land.

per·il [per′əl] *n.* Danger.

per·plexed [pər·plekst′] *adj.* Puzzled; bewildered.

phan·tom [fan′təm] *adj.* Imaginary; ghostlike; seeming real but not real.

phos·phor·ous [fos′fər·əs] *adj.* Coated with or containing phosphorus, a chemical that glows in the dark.

Pied Piper of Hamelin [pīd′ pī′pər əv ham′lin] *n.* A musician in a German folk story who led the rats out of the city of Hamelin by playing his pipe—a small flute or whistle. In revenge for not being paid he led the children of the city away also. *Pied* means having or wearing two or more colors in patches.

piped up *v. Informal* **1** Spoke up. **2** Said in high-pitched tones.

pix·ied [pik′sēd] *v.* Cast a spell over. — **pix·y** or **pix·ie,** *v.*

plod [plod] *v.* To walk in a slow, heavy way; *plod* through the mud.

plun·dered [plun′dərd] *v.* Robbed of property or goods by force. — **plun·der,** *v.*

poised [poizd] *v.* Balanced. — **poise,** *v.*

pom·mel [pum′əl *or* pom′əl] *n.* A knob that sticks up at the front of the saddle.

port·fo·li·o [pôrt·fō′lē·ō] *n.* A flat case for carrying papers or drawings.

po·tion [pō′shən] *n.* A liquid that is supposed to have medicinal, poisonous, or magical qualities.

pro·ces·sion [prə·sesh′ən] *n.* A formal and serious parade.

pro·claim [prō·klām′] *v.* To make known; announce to the public.

pro·fuse·ly [prə·fyoos′lē] *adv.* In a generous way; abundantly.

pro·nounce [prə·nouns′] *v.* To declare; to announce that something is so.

pros·per·ous [pros′pər·əs] *adj.* Successful; thriving; wealthy and comfortable.

pub·lished [pub′lishd] *v.* Made known to the public. — **pub·lish,** *v.*

puck·er [puk′ər] *v.* To gather or draw up into small folds or wrinkles.

pursed [pûrst] *v.* Drawn into wrinkles; closed by gathering up; puckered, as the lips. — **purse,** *v.*

Q

quak·ing [kwā′king] *v.* Shaking; trembling. — **quake,** *v.*

R

Ra·fa·el [rä·fä·el′] *n.* A Spanish male's name.

raf·ter [raf′tər] *n.* Any of the beams on which the roof of a house is built.

rav·ing [rā′ving] *v.* Talking in a wild way, often because of fever. — **rave,** *v.*

realm [relm] *n.* **1** An area. **2** A kingdom.

rec·ol·lect·ed [rek′ə·lek′tid] *v.* Remembered; recalled. — **rec·ol·lect,** *v.*

re·cruit [ri·kroot′] *n.* A new soldier recently enlisted in, or drafted into, the armed forces.

red·coat [red′kōt′] *n.* A British soldier during the time of the American Revolution.

reg·i·ment [rej′ə·mənt] *n.* An army unit, usually commanded by a colonel.

req·ui·si·tion [rek′wə·zish′ən] *n.* A formal request or demand.

re·serve [ri·zûrv′] **1** *n.* Government land held for a special purpose. **2** *v.* To hold back, keep, or set aside.

re·solved [ri·zolvd′] *v.* Decided firmly; determined. — **re·solve,** *v.*

re·sumed [ri·zoomd′] *v.* Took up again after stopping. — **re·sume,** *v.*

---

add, āce, câre, pälm;   end, ēqual;   it, īce;   odd, ōpen, ôrder;   took, pool;   up, bûrn;
ə = a in *above*, e in *sicken*, i in *possible*, o in *melon*, u in *circus*;   yoo = u in *fuse*;   oil;   pout;
check;   ring;   thin;   this;   zh in *vision*.

395

ridged [rijd] *adj.* Marked by or having narrow, raised strips.

ri·fling [rī′fling] *v.* Searching; turning pages impatiently. — **ri·fle,** *v.*

riled [rīld] *adj. Informal* Angry.

Rip Van Win·kle [rip′ van′ wing′kəl] *n.* In Washington Irving's story, the hero who wakes after sleeping twenty years and finds the world changed.

ro·guish [rō′gish] *adj.* **1** Bad or wicked. **2** Playfully mischievous; liking to cause trouble in a merry way.

S

sa·ho·ni [sa′hō′nē′] *n. Cherokee* Cat.

saun·tered [sôn′tərd] *v.* Strolled; walked in an easy, careless way. — **saun·ter,** *v.*

scamp [skamp] *n.* Someone who gets into mischief or causes trouble; usually, although not always, an affectionate term.

scoffed [skôft] *v.* Showed disbelief; laughed at. — **scoff,** *v.*

scowl·ing [scoul′ing] *v.* Pulling one's eyebrows together and down in an angry frown. — **scowl,** *v.*

scur·ries [skûr′ēz] *v.* Hurries; runs very quickly. — **scur·ry,** *v.*

sen·tries [sen′trēz] *n., pl.* Soldiers stationed to guard a place and to keep certain people from coming in or leaving. — **sen·try,** *n., sing.*

set·tee [se·tē′] *n.* A long bench or sofa with a back and arms, usually for two or three people.

shil·ling [shil′ing] *n.* An old British coin. It had about the same value as a U.S. quarter.

shrilled [shrild] *v.* Yelled in sharp, high-pitched tones. — **shrill,** *v.*

shud·dered [shud′ərd] *v.* Shook and shivered, as from cold or fear. — **shud·der,** *v.*

sieve [siv] *n.* **1** A bowl with holes in it, or one made of mesh (wire net), used to sift out small bits of grain dust, husk, dirt, or straw, leaving the kernels of grain. **2** A strainer.

si·gi·gi [sē′gē′gē′] *n. Cherokee* Grasshopper.

sin·is·ter [sin′is·tər] *adj.* Threatening evil, trouble, or bad luck.

smoke·shed [smōk′shed′] *n.* A building or room filled with smoke for treating or curing meat, fish, or cheese.

snick·er [snik′ər] *v.* To smother a laugh, but not completely, especially when making fun of someone.

sol·emn [sol′əm] *adj.* Serious and impressive. — **sol·emn·ly,** *adv.*

som·ber [som′bər] *adj.* Dark or with only dim light.

spar [spär] *n.* Any of the strong poles used on a ship to hold the sails.

spe·cies [spē′shēz *or* spē′sēz] *n.* A group of living things that are more or less alike.

spec·i·men [spes′ə·mən] *n.* A small amount taken as a sample of a whole group.

spec·tral [spek′trəl] *adj.* Like a ghost; ghostly.

spec·tre [spek′tər] *n. British spelling* A ghost. The American spelling is *specter.*

spec·u·late [spek′yə·lāt] *v.* To form theories; to imagine possible reasons or answers for something.

spi·ral [spī′rəl] *adj.* Winding or curving like a cone-shaped coil.

spite·ful [spīt′fəl] *adj.* Nasty; full of bitter resentment that leads to mean actions.

spurn [spûrn] *v.* To push away with disgust or scorn.

stealth·y [stel′thē] *adj.* Done in a quiet, secret, or sneaky way.

steed [stēd] *n.* An animal for riding, especially a horse.

stee·ple [stē′pəl] *n.* A tall structure that narrows to a point at its top, rising above a church tower.

stock [stok] *n.* The wooden part of a rifle, to which the barrel and other metal parts are fastened.

stu·di·o [st(y)oo′dē·ō] *n.* The place where an artist, musician, etc., works and may also live.

sub·ti·tle [sub′tīt(ə)l] *n.* In foreign or silent films, a printed translation or statement of the words spoken, usually at the bottom of the screen.

suf·fra·gette [suf′rə·jet′] *n.* A woman who fought for women's right to vote. Also, *suffragist. Suffrage* is the right to vote.

surge [sûrj] *n.* A rush; a sudden swelling or flow.

swell [swel] *n.* The long, continuous body of a rolling wave.

syc·a·more [sik′ə·môr] *n.* A tree with broad leaves and bark that peels or flakes off easily.

T

Tam·ba [täm′bä] *n.* A region near the southern end of mainland Japan.

Te·re·sa [te·rā′sə] *n.* A Spanish female's name. The equivalent of the English name *Theresa.*

thick·et [thik′it] *n.* A thick growth of small trees and bushes.

thong [thông] *n.* A narrow strip of leather used for tying or fastening.

thrash·ing [thrash′ing] *n.* **1** Violent movement, turning, and flinging about of the arms and legs. **2** A beating.

thresh [thresh] *v.* To beat or shake grain to separate the seeds (which can be made into flour) from the straw and husks (which cannot be eaten).

Ti·gris [tī′gris] *n.* A river in southwestern Asia, flowing through Iraq into the Euphrates [yoo′frā′tez] River.

tin·ker·ing [tingk′er·ing] *v.* Fooling around with; taking apart and fixing in an experimental way. — **tin·ker,** *v.*

toll·ing [tōl·ing] *v.* Ringing with a deep, solemn sound. — **toll,** *v.*

tongue [tung] *n.* The long pole that extends forward from a wagon or carriage between the animals that pull it.

tor·rent [tôr′ənt] *n.* A rapid flow.

tot·suh·wa [tōt′soo′wä′] *n. Cherokee* Redbird.

tran·quil [trang′kwil] *adj.* Quiet, calm, and peaceful.

---

add, āce, câre, pälm;   end, ēqual;   it, īce;   odd, ōpen, ôrder;   took, pool;   up, bûrn;
ə = a in *above,* e in *sicken,* i in *possible,* o in *melon,* u in *circus;*   yoo = u in *fuse;*   oil;   pout;
check;   ring;   thin;   this;   zh in *vision.*

tread [tred] *v.* To walk on or trample.

trib·ute [trib′yo͞ot] *n.* **1** Money or other payment given by one group of people to another on demand, often as the price of peace and protection. **2** A speech, compliment, gift, etc., given to show admiration, gratitude, or respect.

tri·fling [trī′fling] *adj.* Small or without importance; silly.

tsi·di·li·li [chē′dē′lē′lē′] *n. Cherokee* Chickadee.

U

U·lys·ses [yo͞o·lis′ēz] *n.* The Latin name for *Odysseus,* the Greek hero of Homer's *Odyssey.*

un·cer·e·mo·ni·ous·ly [un′ser·ə·mō′nē·əs·lē] *adv.* In an informal, sometimes rude, way.

un·furl·ing [un·fûrl′ing] *v.* Spreading out or opening; uncurling or unrolling. — **un·furl,** *v.*

un·ground [un·ground′] *adj.* Not crushed into meal or flour; whole.

un·ion [yo͞on′yən] *n.* A combination; the condition of being joined.

un·quench·a·ble [un·kwench′ə·bəl] *adj.* Not able to be put out or satisfied.

V

ven·om [ven′əm] *n.* The poison of certain snakes, spiders, etc.

ves·sel [ves′(ə)l] *n.* **1** A hollow container, such as a bowl, jar, or vat. **2** A ship.

ves·ti·bule [ves′tə·byo͞ol] *n.* An entrance hall.

vict·uals [vit′(ə)lz] *n., pl.* Food.

vig·or·ous·ly [vig′ər·əs·lē] *adv.* In an energetic way.

vir·tue [vûr′cho͞o] *n.* Good quality; moral excellence.

W

wa·la·si [wä′lō′sē′] *n. Cherokee* Frog.

wal·let [wol′it] *n.* A pistol case, usually fastened to a saddle or belt; holster.

wal·low [wol′ō] *v.* To roll or tumble about; to flounder, as in mud or water.

war·rant [wôr′ənt] *v.* To guarantee; to assure the truth or trustworthiness of something.

weath·er·cock [weth′ər·kok′] *n.* A weather vane shaped like a rooster. A weather vane shows which way the wind is blowing.

welled [weld] *v.* Rose up, or flowed, like water in a spring. — **well,** *v.*

wood·cut [wo͞od′kut′] *n.* A print or picture made with a carved block of wood.

Y

yam [yam] *n.* A kind of sweet potato.

ye [yē] *pron.* You; seldom used today.

yer [yər] *pron. Dialect* Your.

Yo·ru·ba [yō·ro͞o′bə] *n.* A West African tribe from the area of what is now Nigeria.

young′un [yung′ən] *n. Dialect* Young one; a child or young animal.

Z

zo·ol·o·gy [zō·ol′ə·gē] *n.* The science that has to do with animals, their classification, structure, development, etc.

Index to Authors and Titles